Samn Stockwell • Denslow Brown • Sabrina Bunks

Sarah Ives • Jo Brooks • Jill Harker • Diane Remy

Beth Reasoner • Randy Parker • Charlene LaVoie

Marcia Cameron • Alicia Woodson

Sandy Anderson • Barbara Beckelman • Libby Smith

Amy Allison • Anne Frye • Ellen Richard

Francesca (Ariel) Jenkins • Tina Yoxheimer • Ellen McCarthy

Laura Manby • Chloe Wheatley • Chanda O'Donnell

Julie Haddon • Esther Brienes • Sarah Giordano • Filis Rose

Anne Szost • Rachel Portnoy • Denise Hackney

Anne Arkin • Liz Seaborn • Cel Noll • Mev Miller

Fran Reed • Dora Odarenko • Ellen Mayer • Lynn Stenberg

Lys Guillion • Dawn Shewchuk • Robin Baena

Sarah Campbell • Judy Campbell • June Dunn • Kaia James

Karen Bernstein • Sharon Leslie • Dawn McDaniel

Jill Bornsec • Sandy Martin • Caroline Forbes

Judy Mortner • Susan Smith • Robin Baslow

Georgia Merola • Betsy Gooch • Marie Gall • Meg Profetto

Elaine Ward • Star Petrizzi • Nanette Raimond • Susan Grillo

Lindsay Nagy • Sarah Brown • Barbara Rodgers

Caroline Cowles • Carolyne Libby • Karen Cazary

Michelle Jarrett • Maryam Jubera • Beth McEntee

Lori Ensign • Siobhan Williams • Erin Kelly

Lauren Blanchard • Robin Whiting • Shirley Anderson

Sherilyn Pearce • Kristina Calvello • Teri Keiser

Heather Lyons • Kris Sabatelli • Jessica Glenn

Nancy Morgan • Amy Cheek • Nancy Judson

Carmen Russo • Erica Tetro • Maddie Sobel • Jodi Harlow

Robin Fukuyama • Donna Risolo • Sharon Berger

Nancy Berrero • Rosemary Redi • Zoe Cruz • Taylor Ross

Ildiko Makos Conley • Melissa Lardiere • Polly Molden

Emily Habansky • Maria dos Santos • Gail Cristiano

Jessica Pressley • Susan Hennessey • Debbie Gomes

Susan Myers • Yvette Nieves • Carolyn Schwartz • DJ Zupaniac

Alice Sun Tooley • Erin Strawn • Barbara McFerran

Madeline Martino • Vinda Daniels • Amy Weber

Jennifer Sisca • Angelita Pine • Caroline Griswald

Evelyn Turro • Purnima Ayarwal • Heather Stanko

Debbie Naples • Gail Ostrow • Daisy Quinones • Anita Senes

Courtney Carey • Jess Carey • Noelle Angers

Maggie Dunford • Karen Brown • Emma Middlebrook

Ana Velasquez • NykoleBlake • Elizabeth Bullis Weisse

Zoe Gardner • Sarah Koskoff • Lisa Strachan

Sheddi London • Amy O'Rourke • Shiobhan Dacres

Roxanne Delfino • Erma Elliot • Jovanna Garcia

Aminah Ashby • Cadence Carrol • Meredith Bell • Polly Walden

Rhiannan Alterio • Sarah Almodovar • Leanne Irwin

Alison Dunn • Connie Busch • Cindy Davis • Laura Diehl

Rose Lauture • Jennifer Leslie • Tori Mitchell • Heather Neil

Angelique Vanterpool • Melissa Wells • Lagusta Yearwood

Stephanie Zinowski • Victoria Forester • Lucilla Alton

Laura Cerato • Jennifer Laferlita • Jennifer Krawitz

Jessica Basista • Jennifer Doree • Nicole Deveau Jalbert

Dayna Mankowski • Kaitlen Austin • Christine Ferrer

Alison Fichera • Becky Gomes • Maya Kuznetsov

Jamie Records • Katie Ryckelynel • Nicole Strayer

Kate Traub • Nancy Clark • Gayle Colcone • Melanie Hardy

Autumn Leonard • Yuka Yazaki • Kate Habansky

# The Best of
# BLOODROOT
## VOLUME ONE
### Vegetarian Recipes

# Selma Miriam & Noel Furie
## with Lagusta Yearwood

Photography by Noel Furie

Anomaly Press
85 Ferris Street • Bridgeport, Connecticut 06605
203 576 9168 • www.bloodroot.com

We encourage the reproduction of up to five recipes and any of the introductory material, properly credited, for feminist and vegetarian purposes. Please write to us for more information and/ or recipe exchange.

Bloodroot drawing by Laura Louise Foster

©2007 Anomaly Press
*a division of* Mermaids and Crones Enterprises
85 Ferris Street
Bridgeport, Connecticut 06605

ISBN 0-9778549-0-6

Library of Congress Control Number: 2006934673

This book is printed on 100% post-consumer recycled paper.
Printed in Canada

Anomaly: *deviation from the rule. Something out of keeping, especially with accepted notions of fitness or order. Exceptional, unusual, nonconforming, surprising, something that refuses to submit to classification or explanation.*

# dedication

Feminism is the politics which informed the creation and maintenance of Bloodroot and our lives. Some time in the late 1990's, feminism as we knew it began to be disparaged. In particular, Catharine MacKinnon and Andrea Dworkin were maligned. Because we admired their work, we somewhat capriciously decided to name our two newly adopted rescued cats for them. We let Andrea know about our naming, and she was very pleased. She later relayed the information about their namesakes to Catharine.

Andrea spoke at Bloodroot several times, always to a packed audience. She was generous and brilliant, and what she wrote and cared about spoke to many women's experiences.

We dedicate these two books to her, in gratitude for her amazing courage.

# acknowledgements

There are many people who deserve our recognition and appreciation for what they have given to make these two books possible and many also who through the years have contributed time and energy to Bloodroot herself.

Most important are our workers. Please note the two pages listing the names of women who have worked at Bloodroot in the past thirty years and who have enriched our lives in various ways.

Alison Dunn was our manager for over five years. She was a leavening agent, making manageable work schedules and cooking plans that were practical. She is an intuitive cook and passionate vegetarian and, though she moved to Illinois, we know our connection to her will be long lasting.

We love working with Rose Lauture. She has taken over the scheduling of staff and presides over the stove with skill and authority. She is a natural cook who, when she learns a new recipe says, "But this is so easy!"

Stephanie Zinowski, who runs a vegan café at Wesleyan University, works with us Saturdays and in summer. Her speed and efficiency cooking here, as well as her stocking and organizing are legendary. We're grateful for her warmth and generosity.

Suzanne Beck is a careful and focused cook. We're appreciative of her precision, her attention to detail and exceptional sense of responsibility. Carmen Russo has presided over the Tuesday-night stove for ten years. Angelita Pine worked here a decade ago and is back. It's a treat to have her particular warmth and intelligence. Angelique Vanterpool is also back and we are pleased she is. Kate Habansky brings graciousness and a sense of order to our kitchen. Lauren Mallon is warm, generous, and enthusiastic in her work. Dayna Mankowski, the crafty scientist, comes from Middletown on occasion to help out. We are fortunate for new workers: Jennifer Koenig, Julia Lundy, Sarah Verbil, and old friend Valerie Wilkie.

Charlene LaVoie has been with us a very long time. She worked here when we first opened in 1977. When she left to go to law school she promised to be back. We were skeptical, but indeed she came to work again. When she moved to Winsted,

Connecticut to work for the Nader Foundation we thought we wouldn't see much of her. However, we were again wrong. She comes here twice a month to rule over the counter in the kitchen. She is also our major source of legal help.

We've known Krystyna Colburn almost as long as Charlene. She lives in Massachusetts and comes here every month to do our payroll. What we treasure is her loyalty and her fierce feminist intelligence. She, Charlene, and Carolanne Curry are the advisors and stabilizers of our lives.

Carolanne has been here since 1988. She solves difficult and tricky problems for us with aplomb. We've entered the electronic age kicking and screaming; however Carolanne has organized a website for us as well as generally taken on myriad business problems as they have arisen.

Nancy Morgan, who used to work here but then moved to Pennsylvania, runs a little advertising service for us by sending out postcards to our mailing list every other month, listing menu selections and favorite new books. As can be imagined, it is a large and repetitive effort, greatly appreciated. This idea originated with Sabrina Bunks (Selma's daughter) who has consistently given us good business advice.

Bloodroot enjoys support from animal rights advocates. In particular, a Friday night group including Jack and Sheila Faxon (who come from Stockbridge, Massachusetts, each week), Pedro Hecht, Esther Meckler, Stephanie Underhill and many others. These people care intensely, as we do, about the creatures of this earth.

Our friend and customer Donna Andrade has liked our food and our feminism so much that she bought a house on our street so that she can visit often. We feel she understands our purpose particularly well.

We love discussing feminist and political issues with Ludger Viefhues and Kevin Bailey, who come weekly from New Haven.

For many years we had a women's night here—the G. Knapp Historical Society. It commemorated the only Fairfield County woman who was killed for being a "witch." Lucia Kimber was its membership chair and secretary, coming almost every week for Wednesday dinner.

Many others come weekly. Indeed they are our community. When our dining room ceiling was raised Anne Demchuk and Maelyn Bellemore brought ladders to paint it. A year later, they refreshed our outdoor trim, highlighting the mermaid over our door which was designed by Edie Platt and built by Kathy Thomas.

Over the years, we have been fortunate to become friends with several men in related businesses. John Moretti of Fountain of Youth Health Foods in Westport, Connecticut, helps us by adding items we need to his orders. We appreciate that he and his store remain determinedly vegetarian.

Some six years ago, we discoved Mike and Tony's organic farm, Urban Oaks in New Britain, Connecticut. Their beautiful, locally grown produce is delivered to us each week by Brian. It's a pleasure to have a business relationship with them.

And recently, The Fat Cat Pie Company has been selling our oatmeal sunflower bread at their restaurant and coffee shop. We appreciate the respect they have shown us as peers in this business and are delighted to be friends with them.

We are the recipients of many gifts that we treasure. Folks bring us pictures of mothers and sisters and grandmothers to decorate our wall. Michelle and Terry Cappellieri brought us Terry's grandmother's dining table (so that he could still dine at it) and a quality collection of soup pots. We are lucky to experience this generosity.

George Roberts (Pipe Dreams Plumbing) has been a friend for more than twenty years. Besides being a largish elf and lots of fun, he has kept our plumbing functional all this time.

We are fortunate and grateful that attorney Renn Gordon, a frequent customer at Bloodroot, has been willing to help with our business legal concerns.

Shane Taylor, our electrician, lights up our days in more ways than one. Our kitchen is especially bright because of him!

These books have had help as well in their assembling. Corrine Groark typed early drafts. Karen McInerney created the two cover designs. We're pleased for her enthusiasm for our food and for this project. The books are as beautiful as they are in part because of her efforts.

Thank you, thank you to all.

# in appreciation

Neither of these two Best of Bloodroot books would exist if it were not for the efforts of Lagusta Yearwood. First and most important, she is a passionate "foodie," who is also a vegan and has been for 14 years. She operates a vegetarian meal delivery service between New Paltz and New York City as well as working with us one day every other week. Lagusta is regularly searching for and developing vegan dishes, as well as studying the history of food and cooking. And as a intelligent and unusually political person, she constantly mulls over how to lead a responsible life. Since we are trying to do something similar at Bloodroot, we do inspire each other! Secondly, Lagusta wanted these books to exist so much that she typed all the recipes in them, debating with us about ingredients and procedures since she was determined to make both as nearly perfect as possible. We are grateful—though our gratitude does not begin to express all we feel.

# Table of Contents

## Welcome

Welcome to Bloodroot! If you have been here before, you will remember that our menu is written on two blackboards, with a wine and beer list next to the desk, where you will place your order with the woman sitting there. She'll remind you to bring your order slip to the kitchen counter after paying her and giving your name, so that you can be called when your meal is ready. You will recall that there is no waitressing or tipping, and so we ask you to clear your own table.

The menu has always been "seasonal," and so the selections of soups and salads, entrees and desserts change to reflect the time of year. The window wall facing Long Island Sound looks out on the herb-edged terrace. On the opposite wall is a unique collection of many, many old pictures of women.

This is how it has been for thirty years. We've been cooking; people come to eat. Some come often, others less frequently. Maybe because we know their names, maybe because there is no waitressing, maybe because we're vegetarian and therefore attract a certain kind of customer, but for whatever reason, these customers are our friends, and this is our community.

When we started Bloodroot, it was because we wanted and needed a community. As feminists, we needed a place for women to go to be treated with respect and not be hassled. From the beginning, there have been men who have understood the context we wished to create, some of whom have become good friends.

This community is very fluid. There are times customers have several meals a week here; then they stop, sometimes to return later. Many of the women who have worked with us over the years keep in contact with us; some do not. We know we are richer for all the connections, and we hope those who have been here as workers, customers and friends are also.

i

Community makes a pattern more complex than couple-ness can.[1] A feminist community encourages each woman to figure out who she can be. Obviously such a community presupposes feminist values, so there is an assumed agreement on some political issues: you can't be anti-choice, anti-affirmative action, racist, pro-pornography or homophobic and be a feminist. There are ways to explore our needs for affection and intercourse (of all sorts), and the means of self-expression and recognition of our work which is more satisfying and less lonely in the context of community.

We began Bloodroot in order to form a community where we could live our values as feminists. We chose appropriate books for the bookstore and we chose to be vegetarians because animal rights were a necessary part of a feminist agenda.[2] Gradually, the food became more and more important to us. We don't serve either the outsize portion all-you-can-eat stir fried whatever, nor do we want to make our food into architectural contortions topped with obscure sauces. We are devoted "foodies." We want our food to be both delicious and relatively easy to prepare. We want ingredients to be from local farms (when possible) and grown without pesticides and herbicides. We want to enjoy it ourselves.

---

[1] This is a recognition of the limitations of coupleness rather than criticism.

[2] Carol Adams discusses this at length in her books, e.g. *The Sexual Politics of Meat: A feminist-vegetarian critical theory* (first published in 1990), *Neither Man Nor Beast*, and *The Pornography of Meat*, all published by Continuum, New York, NY.

# Economics and Success

Often people say how remarkable it is that a venture like ours, especially in Bridgeport, is a success. Well, much of that depends on how one measures success. In our capitalist society, it is how much money one earns which designates success. At Bloodroot we have a different measure. We have work we love, customers we truly like, and a rhythm to our lives which makes us feel fortunate. Not to mention that we eat very well indeed. As for cash, sometimes we do just fine, and sometimes, when there are a lot of snowstorms and few diners, we worry about how the staff will be paid. But we do have long term financial stability because Selma's mother believed that the only safe way her daughter should start her risky restaurant venture thirty years ago would be if she owned, not rented, the waterfront property. Selma's mother Fay convinced Selma's father to finance the down payment toward that end. Also, Selma had money earned doing landscape design that she kept in a separate account, despite the disapproval of her husband and some friends. Without this "nest egg" Selma could not have imagined that she had the right to make real her dreams.

Better cash flow is grand, but we've adjusted our expectations and are grateful that we are able to manage as well as we do. Realistically some financial resources are required to begin a business like ours. We're fortunate that we had those resources, and therefore in the long run, we have had sustainability. That is our "measure" of success.

# Our Collective

We started Bloodroot as a collective. In the heady days of the 1970's, there existed a widespread counter-culture belief that businesses could be better structured without a hierarchy—so the structure of a business collective called for shared decision-making and responsibilities. Luckily, we began with Samn Stockwell, who had had a lot of feminist collective experience. Learning from her experience, we decided that collective membership would require full time work in the restaurant, and additionally the member would make a long term commitment to our organization versus merely a casual association. We also agreed that a stock purchase in the business of Bloodroot would not appreciate, so any woman leaving would not be able to adversely affect the financial stability of the business. Collective members have come and gone. Time with us has ranged between two years and twenty four. Right now there are two of us. Are we a collective? Well yes, we remain structured without a hierarchy and find it still works for us. These days the idea itself is mocked and most collectives have disappeared. Even the kibbutzim in Israel are gone. We were recently interviewed by journalist Deborah Emin, writing for *Gay City News*, who said she had been in a kibbutz years ago in Israel, and how could we imagine this structure could be successful? How did we still do it? It made us think. Our "collective" has evolved since the late seventies. Can two be a collective? Why not? And we do have major input from three other women who have been a mainstay of our lives at Bloodroot for many years. Any critical issue is sorted out with them—Charlene LaVoie (associated with us for 27 years), Krystyna Colburn (for 22 years) and Carolanne Curry (for 18 years). They have lent intelligence, moral support, physical work and sometimes money to keep our collective intention and spirit alive.

And certain collective concepts still inform our ways of working. We don't have a chef but we do have several cooks. While not everyone "does the stove" (that is, prepares and serves the hot food), several members of our workforce do. Everyone does dishes. The woman presiding over the counter (i.e. directing the "stove" person, the salad maker, and the wine and beer server) has perhaps the most demanding job in the kitchen. Much like that of a concert conductor, she coordinates everyone so that the food goes out to our customers in a timely and well-presented manner.

We've discovered that it's best to make use of the particular skills individual women have. One is fast and efficient making our soups and well organized at restocking and reordering what is needed. One is great at scheduling workers and manages to keep everybody happy in the process. She has unusual intuitive abilities regarding other people's needs. Some are particularly skilled at being "bossy" at the counter (a very good thing!). We appreciate a salad maker whose salads are appropriately-sized and beautiful, and we are grateful to have a "runner" who not only makes sure the tables are clean, but is able to keep up with the dishes as well. When we are working on a new recipe, everyone present tastes to determine seasoning. At one time or another, most of the women who have worked with us have contributed to this taste-testing. It is only after all have agreed that the dish is the best it can be that we record our conclusions in a recipe. We want our food to be easily replicable, whether by one of our staff or by you at home—so of course, we willingly share our recipes, and in return we benefit from customers sharing their own recipes with us.

# History

In 1976, Selma made the decision to both get a divorce and start a business which would be a center for feminists and their friends. While her parents were not happy about the divorce, her mother Fay nevertheless decided to lend family money to make the business possible. Selma asked Samn Stockwell and Betsey Beaven to work with her, and so the Bloodroot Collective was born. Pat Shea and Noel Furie joined soon afterward. Samn left after about a year, Pat after six years. In the mid 1980's, Liz Seaborn became a collective member and left after several years. Betsey left at the end of 2001.

Most of the women left because they wanted to pursue other ways to make a living or for other personal reasons. Of course people's needs and lifestyles can change and sometimes values once shared are no longer held in common. We are sad when a worker or collective member leaves, and disappointed when her values diverge substantively. If someone has stayed too long after such a shift, everyone is negatively affected. And when, in one case, such changes were expressed in actions— the potential consequence of which could damage our business financially—our response went beyond disappointment to anger. The absence of that person's negativity in the workplace, however, was and is a relief to everyone here. It has left us conscious of how much we treasure what we have: this way of life. We feel fortunate to have been able to create it, maintain it and defend it as well as to share it with so many workers, customers and friends.

Selma's mother Fay died in 1980. She had been a first wave feminist, and she was both worried for, and proud of Bloodroot. Shortly after she died, Selma's father Alex told us he did not want to go into a nursing home, though some thought he needed that kind of care. Instead he came to live at Bloodroot, in a room overlooking the tidal inlet off Long Island Sound. This is our Mermaid Room, and once was the living room of the family who owned the machine shop (now restaurant) attached to their house. Alex had done so much for Bloodroot that caring for him was little to ask. We feel lucky there were many hands to help, and we're proud that he was able to die with dignity in that room.

Selma named this business "Bloodroot" for a native New England wildflower. It's usually a flower of the woods, yet here it is thriving in the sandy soil near the water. It has a branching root, each piece of which throws up a vertically furled leaf. The white flower is *square*, and emerges through the funnel of the protective leaf. This flower is quite fragile and lasts only a few days. There is a sterile double form, also square, which lasts longer. The leaf, stem and root all bleed red juice when broken. Why, people ask, should a vegetarian restaurant call itself Bloodroot? And why not? Why is "blood" assumed to be about violence instead of being our lifeblood? We like the way the plant grows—joined, but each part separate, never invasive, but long lived. We secured permission to use a particular drawing of the Bloodroot flower made by Laura Louise "Timmy" Foster, who with H. Lincoln Foster (both now deceased) were passionate rock gardeners and great friends.

# Our History with Feminism

It seems presumptuous to try to summarize second wave feminism, so we will simply say that this is how *we* experienced it. The 1960's were a time of great change. There was the shameful Vietnam War debacle, but there was also the Civil Rights movement. Black and white activism predated feminism and made us as women optimistic about change and the possibility that ordinary folk could make a difference in the world. One of the tools we used was consciousness raising, a technique developed by Paolo Freire, a liberation theologist in South America.[3]

At the time we were angry, but we had great hope. Much feminist work was being written. Hundreds of woman's bookstores sprouted in the late seventies. Ours was unusual in that we combined a bookstore and a restaurant. What did we expect? At least more women in all walks of life previously reserved for men, but much more. We wanted more women doctors, but we wanted a different health care system—more women lawyers and legislators, but also a legal system which took into account women's child care needs and recognized rape and abuse. Ecology was a new word and a new movement. Of course it was feminist to embrace it. Traditional religions teach the inferiority of women and so there was a need for "women's spirituality." We required a recognition that the "patriarchy" was harmful to women (and other living things). We didn't want a piece of the pie; we wanted a new recipe altogether.

There are many writers whose work spoke to us: Robin Morgan, Gloria Steinem, Susan Brownmiller, Germaine Greer, Jill Johnston, Phyllis Chesler and Janice Raymond. Mary Daly seemed to have a particular clarity of vision. She wrote of the sado-society, the structure of which is determined by male religions. While *Beyond God the Father*[4] and *Gyn/Ecology*[5] described her analysis well, our favorite of her books is *Pure*

---

[3]This is of particular interest now that the papacy has made this kind of political priest unwelcome.

[4]Daly, Mary, *Beyond God the Father*, Boston, MA, Beacon Press, 1973.

[5]*Gyn/Ecology: The Metaethics of Radical Feminism*, Boston, MA, Beacon Press, 1978.

*Lust.*[6] We were fortunate to be able to study with her each week at the time she was writing it and then to share dinner with her afterward. She is an important mentor in our lives.

Andrea Dworkin and Catharine MacKinnon also affected us greatly. Andrea's *Women Hating*[7] starts with fairy tales and goes on from there. Our favorite of her books is *Right Wing Women.*[8] Written in the 1980's, she showed that conservative men (and a right wing lifestyle) seemed to promise safety and stability to women. She wrote that women had a choice of either the farm or brothel system. In the former, you got married, had lots of babies, and obeyed your husband. Abortions were out of the question. Family values came first, and you were protected and taken care of except when he found a younger woman for whom he threw you over. The brothel system was supported by left wing men. They were for abortions, opposed commitment, and figured sex should be "free." They agonized over class and minority rights (any and all minorities), but not women's rights. They were against the war in Vietnam, and considered their girlfriends to be the cause of all their troubles.

Our country still wants to separate women into the political left or right. Dworkin's analysis confused and upset the lefties (right wingers never noticed), and so Dworkin and MacKinnon's criticism of pornography was seen as an alliance with the right wing. In both cases (farm and brothel) woman was (is) the quintessential "other." Man is the norm. This continues today—women call other women "guys." It's supposed to be a compliment.

In *Pure Lust*, her most challenging book, Mary Daly reasoned that to be a true feminist, a woman must *cherish* this sense of otherness, while remaining aware of the punishment society exacts from those who choose not to fit the appropriate roles for women. Mary also wanted us to bond with women across ethnic, race and class lines—to see all politics and behavior from the vantage point of how an individual event or

---

[6] *Pure Lust*, Boston, MA, Beacon Press, 1984.

[7] Dworkin, Andrea, *Woman Hating*, New York, NY, EP Dutton, 1974.

[8] Dworkin, Andrea, *Right Wing Women*, New York, NY, Putnam Perigee, 1983.

process can hurt or help women. This bonding, this *Passion for Friends*,[9] as the title to Janice Raymond's book puts it, is essential for feminism to exist. Mary also made clear that a feminist is a woman who persists in her vision and politics, especially when feminism is no longer in fashion. Like right now.[10]

Catharine MacKinnon is a lawyer who actually changed our national law to recognize sexual harassment in the workplace. In *Pornography and Civil Rights*,[11] she and Andrea Dworkin pointed out the abuse that pornography inspires. MacKinnon writes brilliantly on the intersection of feminism and the law in *Feminism Unmodified*,[12] and more recently in *Women's Lives, Men's Laws*.[13] We were fortunate that she arranged for us to audit a class she taught at Yale Law School in the late 1980s.

Audre Lorde, "warrior poet," always wanted to include our little band of cooks in the feminist literary parties in NYC. When she lived on Staten Island, she visited Bloodroot often. She demanded that we recognize our differences and celebrate them. She was black, a mother, a lesbian, and a fighter against the cancer industry. Before she died, we attended a conference celebrating all the aspects of her life, all of which she demanded be respected. ("I Am Your Sister" in Boston, 1990).

Sheila Jeffreys, once of England and now in Australia, is an historian. Her first book was *The Spinster and Her Enemies*.[14] Within its pages she showed that the nineteenth and twentieth century derogation of spinsters was about hatred of independent (not male associated) women. In *Anticlimax*[15] and *Lesbian*

[9] Raymond, Janice, *A Passion for Friends*. Boston, MA, Beacon Press, 1986.

[10] Daly, Mary, *Pure Lust*. Boston, MA, Beacon Press, 1984. pp 397-398.

[11] Dworkin, Andrea and MacKinnon, Catharine, *Pornography and Civil Rights*, 1988. (612) 822-1476.

[12] MacKinnon, Catharine, *Feminism Unmodified*. Cambridge, MA, Harvard University Press, 1987.

[13] MacKinnon, Catharine, *Women's Lives, Mens Laws*, Cambridge, MA, Harvard University Press, 2005.

[14] Jeffreys, Sheila, *The Spinster and Her Enemies*, London, England, Pandora, 1985.

[15] Jeffreys, Sheila, *Anticlimax*, London, England, The Women's Press, 1990.

*Heresy*,[16] she went further to say that after the Stonewall Riots and the gay rights movement began, some gay men wanted to prove their masculinity by embracing sadomasochism. The presumptions of the LBGT movement (a political association of lesbian, bisexual, gay and transgendered people) are the acceptance of all sexual lifestyles, without a feminist analysis. These days postmodern theory has been enlisted to support sexual libertarianism as well as the practice of sadomasochism. A thorough analysis of the antifeminism of postmodern theory is discussed in *Lesbian Heresy*, (p. 79-97) Sheila Jeffreys (Spinifex 1993).

Although primarily a poet, Judy Grahn also wrote *Another Mother Tongue*[17] in order to explore how gay men and lesbians have always stretched the definitions of maleness and femaleness in various societies and ethnic groups. She explores how thinking of difference in these broader terms breaks down stereotypes; in fact, it is antithetical to them. Janice Raymond's *Transexual Empire*[18] is a criticism of the medical industry for reinforcing these stereotypes with drugs and knives.

---

[16] Jeffreys, Sheila, *Lesbian Heresy*, Australia, Spinifex, 1993.

[17] Grahn, Judy, *Another Mother Tongue*, Boston, MA, Beacon Press, 1984.

[18] Raymond, Janice, *The Transexual Empire—The Making of the She-Male*, New York, NY, Columbia University Press, 1994. "My main point is to show how so-called health values of therapy, hormonal treatment and surgery have replaced ethical values of choice, freedom and autonomy; how these same "health" values have diffused critical awareness about the social context in which the problem of transsexualism arises; how more and more moral problems have been reclassified as technical problems; and indeed how the very notion of health itself, as generated by this medical model, has made genuine transcendence of the transsexual problems almost impossible."

# Art

In all these years at Bloodroot some wonderful artists and artisans have exhibited their work and much of it continues to enrich our daily lives. Myriam Fougére from Quebec made beautiful porcelain and rakú images of women and of shells. Sudie Rakusin is a classic oil painter whose images of women are fierce and compelling. Suzanne Bellamy from Australia made extraordinary egg-shaped pottery pieces, and a population of whimsical women. One of her sculptures which we own is called "Ship of Fools." Caroly Van Duyn created powerful hooded figures and Anne-Marie de Bartolet made paper collages of iconic women's images. These are only a few...

# Music

In the seventies and eighties many musicians stirred our emotions. Even before Bloodroot began, Alix Dobkin sang "The Woman in Your Life is You." We never tire of hearing it. Kay Gardner sang "Wise Woman." Other songs and/or singers we love include Cris Williamson's "Waterfall," Linda Shear's "Family of Women," Naomi Littlebear's (of Izquierda) "Sisters Take Care of Sisters" and "Fists of Fire." Roberta Kosse and Jenny Malmquist's oratorio "Return of the Great Mother," Margie Adams "I've Got a Fury," Ferron's "Testimony," Monika Jaeckel's "Witch is Witch," Willie Tyson, Laura Wetzler, Mary Watkins, Berkeley Women's Music Collective, OVA, and Malvina Reynolds. Ntosake Shange's play and music *for colored girls who have considered suicide / when the rainbow is enuf.* And many, many more. Musicians come here to play even though we had no sound system. Alix and Kay came many times. So many moving and powerful memories!

# Literature

And books. There was Adrienne Rich's *Of Woman Born*[19] and *Dream of a Common Language*.[20] Olga Broumas' *Beginning with O*,[21] Monique Wittig's *Les Guerilleres*,[22] and *The Straight Mind*,[23] many of Marge Piercy's books, Susan Griffin, Susan Brownmiller, Jill Johnston's *Lesbian Nation*,[24] and Judy Grahn's *The Work of a Common Woman*.[25] Virginia Woolf's *Three Guineas*,[26] Joanna Russ, Barbara Smith, Julia Penelope, and Judy Chicago. Elizabeth Gould Davis' *The First Sex*,[27] Anne Cameron's *Daughters of Copper Woman*,[28] Audre Lorde's *Zami*,[29] *The Uses of the Erotic*,[30] and *Burst of Light*.[31] Patricia Monaghan, June Arnold, and June Brindel's *Ariadne*,[32] Marilyn French, Barbara Kingsolver, Amoja Three River's *Cultural Etiquette*,[33] Paula Gunn Allen, Chrystos, Marilyn Frye, and Irena Klepfisz. Elena Dykewoman, James Tiptree Jr. (Alice Sheldon), Elizabeth Fisher's *Woman's Creation*,[34] Alice Walker's *The Color Purple*,[35] Lilian Faderman's

[19] Rich, Adrienne, *Of Woman Born*, New York, NY, Bantam, 1976.

[20] Rich, Adrienne, *Dream of a Common Language*, New York, NY, Norton, 1978.

[21] Broumas, Olga, *Beginning with O*, New Haven, CT, Yale University Press, 1977.

[22] Wittig, Monique, *Les Guerilleres*, New York, NY, Avon Books, 1969.

[23] Wittig, Monique, *The Straight Mind*, Boston, MA, Beacon Press, 1992.

[24] Johnston, Jill, *Lesbian Nation*, New York, NY, Simon and Schuster, 1973.

[25] Grahn, Judy, *The Work of a Common Woman*, New York, NY, St. Martins Press, 1978.

[26] Woolf, Virginia, *Three Guineas*, New York, NY, Harcourt Brace, 1938.

[27] Davis, Elizabeth Gould, *The First Sex*, New York, NY, Penguin, 1971.

[28] Cameron, Anne, *Daughters of Copper Woman*, Vancouver, Canada, Press Gung (?) 1981. Revised edition, Madeira Park, BC Canada, Harbour Publishing, 2002.

[29] Lorde, Audre, *Zami*, Freedom, CA, Crossing Press, 1984.

[30] Lorde, Audre, *The Uses of the Erotic*, Brooklyn, NY, Out and Out Books, 1978.

[31] Lorde, Audre, *Burst of Light*, Ithaca, NY, Firebrand, 1988.

[32] Brindel, June, *Ariadne*, New York, NY, St. Martins Press, 1980.

[33] Three Rivers, Amoja, *Cultural Etiquette*, Box 28, Indian Valley, VA, 24105, 1990.

[34] Fisher, Elizabeth, *Woman's Creation*, New York, NY, McGraw Hill, 1979.

[35] Walker, Alice, *The Color Purple*, New York, NY, Washington Square Press, 1982.

*Surpassing the Love of Men*,[36] Toni Morrison's *Sula*,[37] *Beloved*,[38] and *Paradise*.[39] John Stoltenberg's *Refusing to be a Man*,[40] Suzy Charnas, Z. Budapest, Jim Mason's *An Unnatural Order*,[41] Allen Johnson's *The Gender Knot*,[42] Jeffrey Masson and Amy Lansky's *The Impossible Cure*.[40] Michael Pollan's *Botany of Desire*,[11] Lynn Margulies' *What is Life*,[45] Emma Donaghue's *Kissing the Witch*,[46] Anne Marie MacDonald, Sarah Strong's *Burning the Sea*[47] Barbara Walker's *Women's Encyclopedias* and *Treasures*[48] and *The Crone*,[49] and all her knitting books! We do love to read.

[36] Faderman, Lilian, *Surpassing the Love of Men*, New York, NY, William Morrow, 1981.

[37] Morrison, Toni, *Sula*, New York, NY, Bantam Books, 1973.

[38] Morrison, Toni, *Beloved*, New York, NY, Signet Books, 1988.

[39] Morrison, Toni, *Paradise*, New York, NY, Alfred A. Knopf, 1998.

[40] Stoltenberg, John, *Refusing to be a Man*, Portland, OR, Breitenbush Books, 1989.

[41] Mason, Jim, *An Unnatural Order*, New York, NY, Simon and Schuster, 1993.

[42] Johnson, Allen, *The Gender Knot*, Philadelphia, PA, Temple University Press, 1997.

[43] Lansky, Amy, *The Impossible Cure*, Portola Valley, CA, R.L. Ranch Press, 2003.

[44] Pollan, Michael, *Botany of Desire*, New York, NY, Random House, 2003.

[45] Margulies, Lynn and Sagan, Dorion, *What is Life*, Berkeley, CA, University of California Press, 1995.

[46] Donaghue, Emma, *Kissing the Witch*, New York, NY, Harper Collins, 1997.

[47] Strong, Sarah, *Burning the Sea*, Los Angeles, CA, Alys Publishing, 2002.

[48] Walker, Barbara, *Women's Encyclopedia of Myths and Secrets*, San Francisco, CA, Harper and Row, 1983.

[49] Walker, Barbara, *The Crone*, San Francisco, CA, Harper and Row, 1985.

# Health and Disease

Being a feminist in the seventies meant being on the cutting edge politically. Being vegetarian was an alternative lifestyle choice. At Bloodroot we put the two concepts together because at the time two members of our N.O.W. chapter were fierce animal rights supporters. In our discussions with them it became clear that the exploitation of animals had much in common with the exploitation of women and people of color.[50] The question became: what right do we have to raise other sentient creatures in order to eat them? So it wasn't from a health perspective that we started as vegetarian, but rather because our *feminist* perspective expanded to include consciousness of animal exploitation.

Also, because of our feminism, we felt it important to seriously explore the foods of diverse peoples around the world. This decision inevitably led to questions such as: How was scarcity made palatable? What do you do if you don't have much besides rice or corn to eat? Historically, most people ate very little meat. Even in the near past, meat and poultry were treats, not daily food. (Imagine a presidential candidate today promising as Herbert Hoover did, "...a chicken in every pot.")

Because of scarcity of meat in our ancestors' diets, they relied upon and became creative in the cooking of grains and other complex carbohydrates: rice, potatoes, corn, barley, wheat. These foods, which provided a diverse and healthful diet were (and still are) cooked with skill and ingenuity by poor people around the world.[51] Following in this long tradition, we have

---

[50] *An Unnatural Order* by Jim Mason, discusses this at length, as does Carol Adams in the above mentioned books.

[51] In *Why Some Like It Hot*, Gary Paul Nabham, (Island Press, 2004) discusses food, genes, and cultural diversity and concludes that in various geographic niches, people and certain plants have evolved together, the local plants conferring particular health benefits. The agricultural Europeans became used to fewer beneficial grains and more empty calories after the industrial revolution, and have adjusted to a less than optimal diet over a longer period of time compared to indigenous hunter-gatherer populations. As a result, these peoples are more vulnerable to diabetes, obesity and alcoholism once they lose the protection of traditional herbs and food stuffs due to adopting an empty, high calorie, fast food diet.

scoured ethnic cookbooks for our own cuisine. After thirty years of cooking and eating meals high in complex carbohydrates, we know this food is not only delicious but has always been healthy.

Humans are omnivores. This means we can survive on a multiplicity of foods. We are able to eat meat, but we don't have the short gut or canine teeth of true carnivores. (A dog or cat cannot control desire for raw meat left on the counter. Raw meat doesn't usually tempt most human appetites, but, even after a heavy meal, a bowl of fruit will do just that.) Wealthy Victorians who ate a lot of meat as a sign of status suffered from gout. Today, most Americans assume they need meat of some variety three times a day. The high incidence of colon cancer, heart disease, and other degenerative diseases is a direct result of this high consumption of animal protein.

We know that potentially fatal diseases can be divided into two categories: the first are plagues and epidemics caused by microbes: either bacteria or viruses carried by rats, mosquitoes, or other animals or encouraged by overcrowding and poor sanitation. Included here are syphilis, malaria, T.B., and today, AIDS and Ebola. They kill those with weak immune systems first (especially children), which explains the short average life span during the plagues. Historically, if you didn't die from the plague, you probably lived a long life.[52]

The second group of potentially fatal diseases includes cancer, diabetes, obesity and heart disease as well as asthma and other systemic immune system diseases. The causes of these degenerative diseases are directly attributable to our lifestyle, the side effects of society's high consumption of goods: autos, air conditioners, computers, plastics, etc. as well as to our diets. Individually we have little influence over the pollution of our environment resulting from the manufacture or use of goods. Yet we are all subject to, and many of us made sick with systemic disease by the poisons these products put into our environment. We must be aware of these negative forces and act politically to oppose them wherever we can.

---

[52] *The Fourth Horseman: A Short History of Plagues, Scourges and Emerging Viruses*, by Andrew Nikiforuk, Penguin, Canada, 1991 (out of print, but well worth tracking down).

However, we do have greater control over the food we consume. Studies such as those documented in *The China Study*[53] provide proof of the damage done by a diet heavy in meat and dairy. Clearly, the consumption of food processed and loaded with additives or sprayed with chemicals cannot be good for the human body either. Nor are animal products dosed with antibiotics or bovine growth hormones.[54] The intake of adulterated foods, genetically altered crops, junk food and animal proteins, as well as the fact that we live in a polluted environment and spend much of our time inactive in front of a computer or television screen, makes us fertile ground for this second group of diseases. And these diseases are killing us today—more slowly and painfully than any plague. The answers modern medicine has to these illnesses are: slash, burn and poison. Also modern medicine extends "life" at any cost.

So what can we do? Check ingredients on labels, join Community Supported Agriculture,[55] and buy organic food as much as possible. It is not genetically engineered or sprayed with poisons. Eat a minimal amount of dairy and animal protein, or none at all. Be vegan! And move your body. Humans were not meant to sit all day—get up and get out to the garden. Rake leaves. Shovel the snow. Take a walk.

Currently we (Noel and Selma) use very little of this country's available and expensive health care. Neither of us has health insurance. When needed, we take homeopathic remedies or naturopathic medicines and herbs. Sometimes acupuncture is appropriate. Yoga has been helpful for relaxing and keeping limber. We are fiercely political in all aspects of our lives. We oppose the powerful corporations/industries responsible for polluting the air and water as best we can and we try to make the best possible life choices at work and in our homes. We stay

---

[53] T. Colin Campbell, *The China Study*, Dallas, TX, Benbella Books, 2005.

[54] See *Cancer-Gate: How to Win the Losing Cancer War* by Samuel Epstein MD, Baywood Publishing, 2005 for documentation on how it is easy and cheap for industries to pollute with carcinogenic substances. Their leaders then serve on boards of The National Cancer Institute and The American Cancer Society.

[55] In which consumers buy shares of the expected crops a farmer will grow.

healthier when we eat organic, locally grown foods, when we move our bodies in work and play, when we use our intellectual energy in political causes important to us, and particularly when we create gardens, good food, photographs, weavings and other fiber arts. Such work keeps us alive in the deepest sense of that word.

# Cooking Class

## "First Choose your Carbohydrate"

At the time of the Atkins Diet craze a number of people asked about our views on carbohydrates and to teach a cooking class addressing the subject, which we agreed to do. We called the class, "How to Think and Cook Like A Vegetarian," We said it was an opportunity to deconstruct the popular misconception of meat as the only possible center of a "real" meal.

To begin, everyone was asked to describe what they considered "comfort" food. Most responses were foods high in carbohydrates: mashed potatoes, pasta, bread, etc., as well as foods high in fats: gravies and sauces. We were not surprised at the positive recall by everyone. So we decided that we would celebrate the carbohydrates by creating delicious and satisfying meals with one or another of them as the center or entrée. Sauces and gravies would be added to demonstrate a wide range of possible tasty food combinations. In the first class, we cooked pasta, rice, cornmeal polenta, potatoes, quinoa, millet, barley and buckwheat groats. Using these as the base of the meal, we topped them with sauces and gravies made earlier, then frozen. In this way, with a well stocked freezer, our students learned how quickly satisfying meals can be cooked. Some combinations we suggested: shiitake or miso gravy to go over baked or mashed potatoes, tomato sauce for pasta and polenta, or peanut sauce for wheat or rice noodles. There are many possibilities, especially when we begin to think ethnic. This is exactly what we asked our students to do for the second class.

At that one we talked about the culinary vegetarian riches to be found in the food of peoples all over the world. As the base of their diets for hundreds of years, people have relied upon variations of rice and beans, or, in the Mid-East, lentils and rice.* And they still do. Since the European discovery of Andean potatoes, they have been a dietary staple around the world: In Ireland, Irish mashed potatoes with cabbage and kale. In

---

*See recipes for: Feijoada, Mid-east Lentils and Rice, and Black-eyed Peas and Rice (served with collards) for examples.

Ecuador, llapingachos: potato cakes with peanut sauce. And of course, latkes: Jewish potato pancakes from Eastern Europe and now popular here in the United States.*

In Mexico, tortillas and dumplings are made with cornmeal slaked in lime (masa harina). There are many uses for these foods, from stews to enchiladas. From Italy we have polenta, cornmeal cooked soft like a pudding, or stiff to be fried and then topped with sauce.** We are inspired by the ingenuity of cooks around the world who have been making art out from what some would consider to be limitations. We hope the reader will be inspired as well.

Finally, for our third class, we discussed meat analogs. Chinese Buddhists have been making faux meat, poultry and fish dishes for centuries. In the vegetarian health food movement, seitan, tempeh and tofu are used in place of meat, or on their own as a source of protein.*** They are particularly desirable when a person new to vegetarianism still craves the texture of animal protein/meat. We have found all these foods satisfying and have created many recipes using them.

This chapter contains three sections; first, a collection of recipes for sauces and gravies, and second, vegetable accompaniments we make at home, or at Bloodroot. They are easy to prepare and good enough to share, and third, sample dinners.

Here are brief notes on cooking a variety of carbohydrates:

**Rice:** Long grain white rice such as Basmati and Jasmine benefit from being washed in a strainer a few hours before dinner, turned into a small frying pan, and covered with about a ½ inch of water. Twenty minutes before dinner, turn the heat on to very low and cover the pan. Check after ten minutes. If rice seems almost done, turn off heat and put cover back on. If it seems dry, add a splash of water. One cup of rice will serve four people amply.

---

*See recipe for Kartofchin for another example.

**See recipes for Enchiladas with Beans and Potatoes, Polenta with Fancy Mushroom Ragout, Tamales, and Estofado with Dumplings for examples.

***See recipes for Sweet and Sour Tempeh or Tempeh-stuffed Baked Potato, Greens-stuffed Tofu Pockets, Seitan Skirt Steak and Soy Meatloaf for examples.

2

Alternatively, whether the rice has been soaked or not, turn the heat on high and boil vigorously in the frying pan until holes appear. Turn heat to very low and cover. Don't stir! We particularly like a packaged blend of rice which contains split baby garbanzo beans and daikon radish seeds. It is called "Jasmine Blend" and comes from Indian Harvest: 1-800-346-7032.

To make a pilaf, first sauté chopped onion and garlic in olive oil until softened. Add rice and continue frying until it becomes translucent. Dissolve 2 tablespoons tamari in 1½ cups water (for 1 cup rice) and add to pan. Cover and lower heat to simmer. Cook until done. Don't stir. This technique is particularly appropriate for the plump grains of Arborio rice, which benefit from the addition of oil (or butter) and broth. However, *do* stir and scrape often, adding the broth just a little at a time, waiting for each addition to be absorbed before adding the next. The result should be creamy and rather sticky. You may want to add Parmesan cheese to it as well.

**Sticky rice**, used for sushi and for Asian desserts, should be soaked, often overnight, and then steamed. Use 1½ cups rice to 2 cups water. Nishiki is a preferred Japanese brand.

**Wild rice** needs a lot of water: 1 cup rice to 4 cups water. Cook at a low boil 35 to 50 minutes. Taste to determine whether it is done.

**Brown rice** with the best, nutty flavor is the short grain. Use 1½ cups water to 1 cup rice and simmer at a low boil 45 minutes.

### Other Grains

**Quinoa** is a delicious nutty grain from the Andes with more protein than is in any other grain. It must be rinsed before cooking. We use it in soups and bread, but it will stand on its own as a tiny grain, similar in looks to millet.

**Millet** may be steamed with a little cinnamon to use with cous-cous a dish usually made with wheat formed into little "cous-cous" balls.

**Barley** is chewy. Boil it in lots of water, then drain.

**Buckwheat Groats.** Traditionally Eastern European Jews pan-roasted or baked groats (kasha) with an egg stirred into the mix to accentuate the nutty flavor. We prefer to boil the groats in lots of water until just popped and then drain. Don't overcook. They make an interesting alternative to brown rice.

**Potatoes** come in so many varieties. "Waxy" ones make good salads and soup ingredients since they don't fall apart, and mealy ones are good for baking and mashing. We do like Yukon Gold. If you live near local farms where heirloom varieties are grown, you will find them to be a special treat.

**Pasta**. DeCecco is a good brand and Rustichella is even better. A pot with a light weight fitted strainer is a good tool. Lift the strainer to test how done the pasta is. Many Italian cooks add some of the pasta cooking water to thin out sauces served with the meal. Farro pasta, made of an ancient wheat variety, is reported to be healthy for 90 percent of folks who can not tolerate wheat.

**Cornmeal**. Polenta is corn meal porridge. You can make a stiff one this way: Stir together 1½ cups organic cornmeal with 1⅓ cups cold water. Bring 2 cups water to a boil with 1 teaspoon salt. Pour boiling water into cornmeal mix, stirring well. Return to pot, add 2 tablespoons olive oil, stir, and cover. Simmer 10 minutes. Uncover, raise heat to moderate and stir off and on with wooden spoon until the polenta is stiff enough to hold spoon upright. Turn out onto large round dinner plates to form thin cakes. Let cool, wrap in plastic and chill. Later, this stiff polenta may be cut into wedges, dipped in flour and fried crisp in oil.

Soft polenta is made by boiling 3 cups water with 1½ teaspoons salt. Stir together 1 cup cornmeal and 1 cup cold water. Combine as above. Cook uncovered over low heat 15 to 20 minutes, stirring occasionally. Cover to keep warm and reheat in a steamer. Replacing ¼ cup cornmeal with ¼ cup buckwheat groats ground in a small coffee mill will add a nutty flavor to the polenta.

**Masa** is cornmeal slaked in lime. You can buy "masa harina" dry, or already made up wherever there are Mexican markets. It has a wonderful flavor, used for tortillas, tamales, or as dumplings in stews and soups. Cooking it well requires more learned skills than the other carbohydrates listed here—however, see recipes for more information.

4

## GRAVIES

# miso gravy

1. Finely chop **2 tablespoons onion** and sauté in saucepan in ½ **cup grapeseed oil** together with **2 cloves** crushed **garlic** and **6** minced **mushrooms**. While sautéing, add ½ **teaspoon dried thyme** and ½ **teaspoon dried basil**. Cook over medium heat, stirring frequently, until well browned.

2. Add ½ **cup unbleached white flour**. Cook several minutes, stirring. Add **6 oz. brown ale** such as Newcastle, and enough **water** to make gravy (vegetable cooking water is best if you have it). Add **3 tablespoons red** *or* **brown miso, 1 tablespoon tomato paste, 2 tablespoons dry sherry**, and **1 tablespoon tamari**.

3. Simmer slowly ½ hour and correct seasoning.

*makes about 1 quart of gravy*

# shiitake-soy paste gravy

Our favorite gravy. Kimlan Soy Paste should be available in Asian markets.

1. Place **6 dried shiitake mushrooms, 1 seeded dried ancho\* chile pepper,** and **2 sundried tomatoes** in a bowl. Cover with boiling water and set aside.

2. Mince **1 small onion** and slice **1 to 2 cloves garlic.** When shiitakes have softened, squeeze liquid back into bowl and slice the mushrooms thinly. Sauté shiitakes, onion, and garlic in ⅓ **cup grapeseed oil.** When onions just begin to caramelize, add ⅓ **cup flour** and ¼ **cup nutritional yeast\*\*** (optional).

3. Use a blender to purée ancho chile, sundried tomatoes, and reserved liquid. Add to pot together with **1½ cups water, 1 bottle of a honey brown ale,** ½ **teaspoon dried thyme,** ½ **teaspoon dried basil, 2 bay leaves, 2 tablespoons tamari,** ¼ **cup soy paste,** and **2 to 3 tablespoons tomato paste.** Bring to a simmer and correct seasoning. Add **water** as needed.

*1 to 2 quarts gravy*

---

\*Available in Latina markets.
\*\*Available in health food stores.

# dijon mustard-french lentil gravy

From Lagusta Yearwood, adapted from a recipe in *The Millennium Cookbook* by Eric Tucker and John Westerdahl.

1. Pick over ½ cup French lentils to be sure there are no small stones. Cover with water and cook, covered, over low heat, until very tender. This will take 1 to 2 hours, or more.

2. Meanwhile, coarsely chop 2 large onions. Sauté onions in 2 to 3 tablespoons olive oil over moderate to low heat. Stir occasionally. It will take 15 to 20 minutes for onions to begin to caramelize. Add ½ tablespoon dry thyme leaves, crumbled, and ½ tablespoon dry tarragon leaves while onions cook.

3. Add 12 oz. of a Belgian-style beer and 2 tablespoons Dijon mustard. Bring to a simmer and cook until liquid reduces to approximately ½ cup. Add 3 tablespoons dry sherry, fresh ground pepper and 2 teaspoons salt. Combine with drained cooked lentils. Adjust seasoning. Add 1 to 2 tablespoons tomato paste and 2 tablespoons grapeseed oil.

4. Turn mixture into a food processor to purée. Add water if gravy is too thick. Serve over mashed potatoes or rice, or with **cauliflower fritters** (see index).

*makes about 3 cups*

# slow-roasted tomato sauce

1. Preheat oven to 350°F.

2. In a shallow baking pan, place **8 to 12** quartered **garden tomatoes**—any variety. Peel cloves of a whole **head of garlic**. Add to pan. Add **2** whole **hot garden chilies**. Coat with **quality olive oil**.

3. Roast at 300°F for 3 hours, stirring occasionally. Add the leaves of **one bunch basil** after about 2½ hours.

4. Sauce is done when it begins to caramelize at the edges of the pan. The garlic will dissolve. Scrape sauce into a pot and add **salt** to taste. If there is an excess of oil, pour it off and save it, it's delicious: garlic-, tomato-, and hot pepper-scented.

5. Add **water** to sauce to make a good consistency, and cut up a few **fresh tomatoes** to deepen flavor and texture. Bring to a boil and serve or freeze for a midwinter's taste of August.

# spicy tomato sauce

This goes well with stuffed vegetable dishes, especially stuffed eggplants.

1. Chop **1 small onion** finely. Sauté in **2 tablespoons olive oil** with **2** crushed **cloves garlic, 2 teaspoons oregano**, and **1 teaspoon basil**. When golden brown, add **15 oz. canned** plain **tomato sauce**. Rinse out can with ¼ **cup red wine** and add to sauce. Finally, mince **1 tablespoon jalapeño peppers** and add to the simmering sauce. Cook about 10 minutes and taste, particularly for salt.

*2½ cups sauce*

# marinara sauce

1. In a three-quart pot, fry **2 medium onions**, coarsely chopped, **3 cloves garlic**, coarsely chopped, **1 teaspoon dried oregano**, and 1 teaspoon dried basil in ¼ cup olive oil. Let onions sauté about 10 minutes, then add a **6 oz. can tomato paste**. Cook the sauce a few minutes then add **6 oz.** of **water**, using the tomato paste can. A **splash** of **red wine** may also be added.

2. Cook the sauce until it thickens. Add a **28 oz. can** of **tomatoes in purée**. Bring the sauce to a boil adding **1 tablespoon salt, 1 teaspoon pepper**, and **3 tablespoons pesto**, if you have it. Turn down to a simmer, and cook a good 2 hours to develop full flavor.

*makes over a quart of sauce*

# putanesca sauce

Named for Italian streetwalkers, this sauce is always made with olives; other ingredients are intended to make a savory, well-flavored sauce. We usually serve this with fresh cavatelli pasta, steamed broccoli, and a grating of Parmesan cheese over the pasta and sauce.

1. Use a small knife, preferably with a curved blade, to cut ⅔ cup green cured olives and 3 tablespoons black cured olives away from their pits. You will find olives like these at Italian groceries. Set aside. Thinly slice 1 large onion, 2 seeded Italian green peppers, and 1 head fennel. Chop and save the feathery leaves of the fennel, but discard the hard upper green part of the stalks.

2. In a large saucepan heat 3 tablespoons olive oil. Add onions, pepper, and fennel with a pinch of hot pepper flakes and 1 to 2 cloves chopped garlic. Sauté gently for about 5 minutes or until vegetables have wilted and are turning golden. Add 3 tablespoons tomato paste and cook, stirring, another 5 to 10 minutes. Now add ⅔ cup red wine and 1 28 oz. can plum tomatoes. Use a wooden spoon to coarsely break up tomatoes. Simmer, covered, 45 minutes.

3. If available, add dried porcini, soak ½ cup of them in hot water first. Then add both mushrooms and their soaking liquid to the sauce. Also, slice and fry ⅔ cup button mushrooms in 2 tablespoons olive oil in frying pan and add to sauce. Finely chop ½ bunch straight leaf parsley and add. Taste for salt. Depending on the saltiness of the olives, you may need to add 1 to 2 teaspoons salt.

# mushroom ragoût

This is good with polenta and kale.

1. Finely dice **1 large onion**. Mince **2 cloves garlic**. Sliver **1 hot jalapeño pepper**. Sauté all in **adequate olive oil**, stirring until vegetables wilt and begin to caramelize. Turn into a saucepan.

2. While onion cooks, prepare mushrooms: soak **¼ cup dried porcini mushrooms** in ½ **cup hot tap water**. Discard stems and slice **4 cups fresh shiitake mushrooms, 3 cups cremini mushrooms** and **3 cups portobello mushrooms**. Retain and use the stems of the latter two.

3. Fry sliced mushrooms in small batches in a large frying pan over very high heat adding **olive oil as needed**, turning often until well browned. As each batch is cooked, turn into saucepan.

4. Drain porcini, squeeze out soaking water and slice thinly. Fry them as well. Deglaze frying pan with porcini soaking liquid. Also add **2 cups** plain (canned) **tomato sauce, 1 cup water**, and **1 cup red wine**. Scrape up all burnt bits and when all is simmering, add to sauce pot.

5. Add **2 teaspoons fresh tarragon leaves**, minced (*or* 1 teaspoon dried crumbled leaves) and add ⅓ **cup tamari**. Finally, chop enough straight leaf **Italian parsley** to make ½ cup and add, together with fresh ground **pepper** to taste. Cover and simmer 30 minutes.

*8 servings*

# sun-dried tomato gravy

1. Dice **1 medium onion, 2 small green peppers, 1 red pepper, and 1 fresh jalapeño pepper,** removing seeds first. Peel and chop **2 cloves garlic.**

2. Heat **2 tablespoons olive oil** in a large frying pan and sauté vegetables over high heat, adding **1 teaspoon dried oregano, ½ teaspoon ground cumin,** and **1 teaspoon dried basil** to the pan. Fry until peppers are well browned. Turn off heat and set pan aside.

3. Place ⅔ **cup sun-dried tomatoes** in a small pot. Add ¾ **cup water,** cover pot and simmer 5 minutes. Remove tomatoes, reserving liquid. Chop and add to vegetables in the frying pan along with **2½ tablespoons tamari** and the reserved tomato soaking liquid. Dice ¾ **cup seitan** (wheat gluten) and coarsely chop **1 tomato,** fresh or canned. Add these to the frying pan also, together with **1 cup water.** Cover and simmer 15 minutes. Correct seasoning.

*makes approximately 1 quart of sauce*

# sun-dried tomato, shiitake, and artichoke heart sauce

1. Soak **1 cup dried shiitake mushrooms** in **2 cups hot** tap **water**. When soft, slice thinly. Reserve soaking liquid.

2. Measure **2 cups sun-dried tomatoes**. Place in a pot with **2 cups water**. Bring to a simmer. Remove from pot and chop coarsely.

3. Meanwhile mince **4 cloves garlic** and **3 shallots**. Set aside.

4. Slice the contents of a **package of frozen artichoke hearts** (about **2 cups**) in half-inch pieces. Heat **¼ cup olive oil** in a frying pan and sauté the artichoke hearts and the shiitake mushrooms over high heat until they begin to brown a little. Add **½ teaspoon hot pepper flakes** and reduce heat. Add garlic and shallots and sauté until wilted. Add **2 tablespoons fresh basil**, chopped, or **1 teaspoon dried basil**. Turn into a saucepot.

5. Add mushroom soaking liquid, the sun-dried tomatoes with their liquid, if any, **3 tablespoons tomato paste**, **2 teaspoons salt**, and **4 cups canned plum tomatoes**, cut up. Bring sauce to a simmer and cook 10 minutes. Taste and correct seasoning. This is nice served on a tubular pasta such as penne or with shell shapes. Be sure to garnish with fresh chopped **parsley**.

*makes about 2 quarts sauce*

# MEXICAN CHILE-BASED SAUCES

# molé rojo

A good sauce for enchiladas.

1. Remove seeds and stems from **2 dried pasilla chilies** and **2 dried guajillo chilies**. Pour **1½ cups** boiling **water** over them and let sit 20 minutes.

2. Coarsely chop **2 cups onion**. Slice **3 garlic cloves**. Sauté the onion over low heat in **2 tablespoons olive oil** until onion wilts. Add garlic and cook 2 more minutes. Turn off heat and let cool a few minutes.

3. Quarter **1 pound (about 6) fresh Roma tomatoes**. Turn into a food processor. Add the contents of the frying pan and the softened chilies (save the soaking liquid). Also add **1 teaspoon dried oregano**, **1 tablespoon red wine vinegar**, and **1½ teaspoons Kosher salt**. Process. Now add the soaking liquid and blend.

4. Heat a cast iron skillet over medium heat and simmer the contents of the processor for 15 to 20 minutes.

5. Use the sauce to dip softened tortillas in, then fill them and add more sauce on top before baking enchiladas. Bring some to the table to serve, as well.

*about 1½ quarts sauce*

# ancho-guajillo chile sauce

1. Tear **9 dried ancho chilies*** into pieces, discarding the seeds. Similarly treat **6 guajillo chilies.*** Toast, stirring, in a dry skillet. When they smell "roasted," turn into a bowl. Add **5 cups hot tap water** and let soak 10 minutes.

2. Peel **4 cloves garlic.** Turn garlic into a blender with chilies and the soaking water, **2 cups tomatoes (canned),** and the following herbs and spices: **½ teaspoon oregano;*** **1 teaspoon** *each* **whole cumin, whole peppercorns,** and **whole coriander; 8 whole cloves, 3 bay leaves,** and **2 teaspoons salt.** Pulverize.

3. Heat **2 tablespoons grapeseed oil** in a large skillet and sauté **½ teaspoon achiote seeds.*** When the oil turns orange-red, strain out the seeds and discard. Add sauce from blender to the oil together with a handful of fresh **epazote leaves.*** Cook until color changes. If gravy seems too thin, add some **masa harina*** and stir to thicken.

*makes about 1 quart sauce*

---

*Available in Latina markets.

**Preferably Mexican, rather than Mediterranean oregano.

# PEANUT SAUCES

## szechuan peanut sauce

1. Combine ½ of a **7 oz. jar sesame paste** (Lan Chi brand is preferred, it is available in Asian markets) and ½ **cup organic peanut butter** in a large bowl (Or put into a food processor. Add liquids and process until smooth.) Boil ½ **cup water** and brew a **tea bag** in it for 4 to 5 minutes. Discard tea bag and add tea slowly to the peanut butter mix, whisking as you do. Add ¼ **cup soy sauce** and **2 teaspoons rice wine vinegar.**

2. Add **1 rounded tablespoon chile-paste-with-garlic** (a Chinese condiment) to ⅔ cup of the peanut butter mix. Mix well and chill.

3. Serve peanut sauce with **1¼ lbs.** cooked **fresh very thin Chinese egg noodles.** Garnish with chopped **scallions** with remaining sesame peanut sauce on the side.

*makes about 2 cups*

# salsa de mani
## (peanut sauce)

An Ecuadorian sauce served over fried potato cakes
(**Llapingachos**, see index).

1. Toast ½ **pound unsalted peanuts** in a 400°F oven
   until lightly browned, stirring every few minutes for
   10 to 15 minutes. Set aside.

2. Chop **3 scallions** and crush **2 cloves of garlic.** Sauté
   in frying pan with **1 tablespoon grapeseed oil** with
   ⅓ **teaspoon red pepper flakes,** ½ **teaspoon dried
   rosemary,** ½ **teaspoon dried oregano,** and ¾ **teaspoon
   ground cumin.**

3. Use a blender or food processor to pulverize the
   peanuts with the sautéed vegetables and seasonings,
   adding ¼ **pound tofu** and **2 to 3 cups water** as
   needed. Try to get the sauce as smooth and creamy
   as possible. Flavor with **2 to 3 tablespoons tamari**
   and ½ **tablespoon miso.** Mix again and correct
   seasonings. Add **Tabasco sauce** if not spicy enough
   for your taste. Turn sauce into a pot and bring to a
   simmer. Cook to blend flavors, then turn off heat and
   reheat gently when ready to use.

*makes about 1 quart*

# spicy peanut sauce I
## for salad or pasta

This makes a large quantity of sauce, so if you are not serving a crowd, divide the recipe in half. In a pinch, lemon juice could be substituted for the tamarind juice, but it is widely available in Indian markets, Asian markets, and well-stocked supermarkets.

1. Weigh ½ oz. peeled garlic cloves. Put into food processor. Add 2½ oz. peeled, coarsely chopped ginger. Add 1½ teaspoons red pepper flakes, ½ cup tamarind juice, and ½ cup rice wine vinegar. Process.

2. Add 2½ cups peanut butter, 1½ cups coconut milk, 2 cups grapeseed oil, ½ cup tamari, and 3 tablespoons sugar. Process until smooth.

3. Taste and correct seasonings. Top salad or pasta with sauce and chopped peanuts. Sliced sunchokes (Jerusalem artichokes) and thinly sliced radishes are good garnishes.

*makes about 2 quarts*

# spicy peanut sauce II
## for dipping

1. Chop **1 teaspoon lemongrass** very fine. Combine
   **1 tablespoon tamarind juice** *or* **1 tablespoon
   lime juice** with **1 teaspoon chili-paste-with-garlic**
   (available in jars in Chinese markets), **2 tablespoons
   minced garlic, 1½ cups creamy peanut butter**
   (preferably unsweetened, from a health food store),
   **2 cups coconut milk, 1 tablespoon maple syrup** *or*
   **agave nectar, 2 teaspoons salt**, and **½ cup shallots**,
   minced. Refrigerate.

*makes 3½ cups*

# INDIAN GRAVIES AND SAUCES

# dahl

Dahl is a gravy made of lentils or beans. Masur is made from red lentils; moong from split mung beans, both of which are generally available. We also like chana and urad dahl, available at Indian markets. Even supermarket split peas can be used.

1. Soak **1 cup lentils** (dahl) in **water** to cover for about 1 hour. Drain, checking carefully to make sure there are no stones. Turn into a pot, cover again with fresh **water** and add **1 teaspoon fresh turmeric**. Bring to a boil, cover, and simmer for 1 hour or more, until the dahl is tender. Add **water** as necessary, checking every 10 minutes.

2. To season dahl, chop ½ **onion** and mince **1 clove garlic**. In a small frying pan, melt **4 tablespoons butter** *or* **grapeseed oil** and begin cooking ½ **teaspoon whole black mustard seeds** until seeds begin to pop. Add onion and garlic and turn heat off. Finely dice enough **ginger** to yield **1 teaspoon**; add to pan. Chop ¼ **of a hot chile pepper** and add to pan. Add ¼ **teaspoon ground cumin**, ½ **teaspoon ground coriander**, and the crushed seed of **1 cardamom pod**, if available. A mortar and pestle or a rolling pin work well. Simmer all together about 5 minutes.

3. Add above sauce, called a "tadka," to the dahl with **1½ teaspoons salt**. Simmer another 30 minutes and taste. You may need more salt. Dahl should be a thin gravy to serve over rice, so add **water** as necessary.

*makes 3 to 4 cups*

# masoor dahl

1. Rinse **1½ cups masoor dahl (red lentils)** and turn into a saucepan. Add **1 teaspoon finely chopped ginger, 2 minced cloves garlic, 1 teaspoon chili powder,** and **½ teaspoon turmeric.** Add **1¼ cups water** and bring to a boil. Simmer until dahl is tender.

2. Use a potato masher to crush. Add **1 teaspoon salt, 2 cups water, 2 chopped fresh chiles** (or to taste) and **3 tablespoons lemon juice,** or, even better, **tamarind juice** (available in Indian and Asian markets).

3. Serve with **chopped cilantro,** over **rice.**

*makes about 1 quart*

# rasam

A thin spicy gravy served with South Indian food. From Abhilasha Sandeep.

1. Wash **2 cups oily toor dahl\*** very thoroughly in hot water. Bring **6 cups water** to a boil with **4 teaspoons salt** and add dahl and cook covered 20 minutes until very soft. Add **4 cups more water** and cook covered 15 minutes. Whisk to make a thin sauce.

2. Add **½ teaspoon turmeric, ¼ cup dried coconut, 2 teaspoons tamarind paste\*\*** and **4** diced **plum tomatoes**. Stir well over low heat. Set aside.

3. Heat **1 tablespoon oil** in a small frying pan. Add **2 teaspoons black mustard seed, 1 tablespoon hot pepper flakes,** and **4** fresh **jalapeño chiles**, seeded and minced. Sauté until mustard seeds begin to pop and chiles have softened. Add **3 tablespoons rasam powder\*** and stir well.

4. Pour contents of frying pan into rasam.

*makes approximately 2½ quarts*

---

\*Available in Indian markets.

\*\*Lemon juice may be substituted for tamarind.

# sambhar

This sauce freezes well, though potatoes don't. So, add them to the sauce when you heat it up. Then cook the sauce until potatoes are tender. A trip to an Indian grocery store is essential.

1. Rinse **2 cups toor dahl** and cover with water. Add **1 teaspoon turmeric.** Cook until soft.

2. Soak **tamarind** to yield **2 tablespoons.** When soft discard seeds. Set aside.

3. In a dry pan roast **1 teaspoon coriander seed,** **¼ teaspoon fenugreek seed** and **½ teaspoon cumin seed.** Crush in mortar and pestle. Mix **½ cup dried coconut cream,** with the above spice mixture, called a masala. Add **2 tablespoons sambhar powder.** Set aside.

4. In a small pan, warm a bit of **grapeseed oil** and sauté **2 teaspoons minced garlic, 1 sliced onion, 2 teaspoons black mustard seeds, 1 tablespoon grated ginger,** and **½ teaspoon asafetida.** Add **2 tablespoons minced chiles.** When soft, add **1 cup chopped tomato, 1 cup diced potato,** and **1 bunch curry leaves.** Add this mixture to dahl, along with tamarind, **1 tablespoon salt,** and crushed seeds and coconut cream.

5. Serve with (or cook with) **okra, eggplant,** and chopped cilantro.

*makes about 1 quart*

# MISCELLANEOUS SAUCES

## barbecue sauce

1. Sauté **2 to 3 cloves** chopped **garlic, 1 tablespoon diced ginger,** and **½ teaspoon red pepper flakes** in a little **grapeseed oil.** Add **1 cup catsup, 2 tablespoons molasses, ⅓ cup red wine, 1 tablespoon soy sauce, 1 tablespoon mustard, ½ tablespoon horseradish,** and **1½ tablespoons chili powder.** Dilute with **brewed coffee** to make a thick sauce.

## dairy-free "cheese" sauce

To serve with polenta and sautéed vegetables such as mushrooms, eggplant, peppers, broccoli, and swiss chard.

1. In a pot, whisk together **1 cup nutritional yeast** (available in health food stores), **⅓ cup whole wheat flour, 3 tablespoons arrowroot,** and **1 teaspoon salt.** Measure out **3 cups water** and add some of it to the dry mix, using a whisk to stir. Turn heat on, and add water gradually, whisking all the while. Add as much water as seems necessary to get a good creamy consistency. Finish by adding **⅓ cup grapeseed oil.** Use a fork or potato masher to coarsely break up **1 pound tofu.** Stir into sauce. Cover to keep warm until serving time.

*6 servings*

# Favorite Vegetables

## roasted gingered beets

1. Cut tops and root off a **dozen medium-sized beets.** Rinse briefly. Place close together in a shallow pan. Drizzle with **oil**. Cover with foil. Roast at 400°F for one hour or until a knife-pierced beet indicates tenderness.

2. Use a paper towel to push skins off beets while they are still hot. Slice into a pot and add pan juices, if any. Add ½ **cup water** and 2½ **tablespoons dried candied ginger** (the kind which comes in syrup). Also add ½ **teaspoon dried thyme, 1 teaspoon salt,** and ½ **teaspoon fresh ground pepper.** Simmer all together to blend flavors. Add **1 to 2 tablespoons lemon juice** and taste to adjust seasoning.

3. Top with ¼ **cup** chopped **fresh dill**. Serve at room temperature.

## broccoli

Homegrown small heads of broccoli are best if cut into flowerets, placed in a shallow pan with a little **olive oil** and **gomahsio** (sesame salt in a ratio of 8 to 1, see glossary) and broiled. When brown and crispy, sprinkle with a little **tamari**. Even broccoli haters (like Selma) love this one.

# alison's brussels sprouts

Cut **2 cups sprouts** in half lengthwise. Place in a medium-sized pan with a split **clove of garlic**. Add ¼ **cup of water**. Cover and cook over moderate heat 5 minutes. Add a splash of **olive oil**. Cover again and continue cooking, turning every now and then, to brown sprouts. **Salt** and serve immediately.

# cannelini beans

Soak **2 cups** picked-over **beans** several hours or overnight. Cook in fresh water with **fresh sage, 3 to 4 cloves of garlic**, and 1 quartered **onion** and ¼ **cup olive oil**. When done, **salt and pepper** to taste. Add more olive oil and a chiffonade (thin strips) of **fresh sage**.

# tequila carrots

Cut **carrots** in long ovals. Use a large frying pan (preferably cast iron) to sauté carrots over medium heat in **butter (2 tablespoons to ½ pound carrots)** *or* **grapeseed oil**. Cook 10 minutes uncovered, or until carrots are tender. Add **1 tablespoon** chopped **fresh dill** and **salt** and **pepper**. Mix well. Turn heat to high and add **2 tablespoons tequila**. Tilt pan to flame. When flame settles down, serve immediately.

## cauliflower latkes

Steam **1 small head of cauliflower** divided into flowerets in the least amount of water possible. Mash drained cauliflower with potato masher or fork. Add **3 beaten eggs**, nutmeg, salt, and pepper to taste, and ½ to ¾ **cup unbleached white flour**. This mixture will be used to make small pancakes ("latkes") and must rest ½ hour minimum in the refrigerator before cooking. Be cautious with the flour, a little more can be added later. Sauté small cakes (3″ to 4″ in diameter) in **butter** *or* **oil**. Turn. When brown, serve with sour cream.

## corn

If you live where corn is grown locally, you are indeed fortunate. Our favorite method is to steam husked corn in a large covered frying pan in a very small amount of **water**—½ **cup or so**. It's done in 5 minutes. Serve with **butter** or **coconut oil** and **smoked sea salt**.

## baby Japanese eggplant

Split lengthwise and score diagonal lines with a knife. Drizzle with **olive oil**. Sprinkle with **gomahsio** (see glossary) and broil. Eggplant will puff up a little when done. Sprinkle with **tamari** and serve immediately, or cool and use as finger food appetizers.

# fried eggplant

This eggplant is good hot or cold and makes a great open-faced sandwich on toasted **Italian bread**.

Cut **one medium** *or* **2 small eggplants** into slices. (No need to peel.) Heat **enough** good quality **olive oil** to thinly cover the bottom of a frying pan. Place eggplant slices in single layer in the hot oil and fry over high heat, turning occasionally, until the eggplant is well browned. Remove to a platter and repeat the process until all slices are done. Season with **tamari** and **balsamic vinegar** to taste.

If eggplant feels soft, sprinkle slices with **sea salt** and let drain ½ hour in a colander. Pat dry with absorbent paper and proceed with recipe.

## roasted eggplant

1. Preheat oven to 450°F.

2. Cut **eggplant** into 2″ pieces (no need to peel).

3. Cover the bottom of a shallow pan with **olive oil**, add the eggplant, and bake until starting to brown. At this point, if desired, peel **garlic cloves** and add to the pan. Continue baking until the eggplant is well browned and the garlic is soft.

4. Remove from oven. Add **salt** to taste. Good hot or cold.

# fried kale

1. Bring **3 quarts of water** to a boil in a large pot. Meanwhile, remove stems from **2 pounds kale**. Shred kale into thin strips and then wash it thoroughly in cold running water.

2. When the water has boiled, add the shredded greens to the pot, stir once or twice, and then immediately drain in colander, pressing out excess liquid.

3. In a large frying pan preheat **3 tablespoons olive oil** over medium-high heat. Add the greens and fry, stirring constantly, until it begins to wilt. Add **1 large clove** minced **garlic**. Fry 1 or 2 minutes more to cook the garlic, and then add **1 tablespoon tamari**. Continue frying until the liquid has evaporated. Taste for seasoning and add a little **salt** if necessary.

## onions

Whether you saw the movie *Like Water for Chocolate* or not, the trick of putting a slice on your head *before* you chop them really does keep the tears away. We don't know why, but it works!

If you love raw onions, but they don't love you, try this: slice onions for salad and squeeze **lime** *or* **lemon juice** over the slices. Marinate for 30 minutes. When you make your salad vinaigrette, cut back on the vinegar or lemon juice in accordance with the amount used for the onions. Toss all together. You should find that the onions are easier on the palate and in the stomach.

WATER VIEW

# sourdough spiced deep-fried onion rings

1. Stir together: **1 cup sourdough** (see glossary; if thick, dilute with water), 1½ teaspoons cayenne, 1½ teaspoons salt, ½ teaspoon fresh ground black pepper, ¼ teaspoon dried crumbled oregano, pinch thyme, and ⅛ teaspoon ground cumin seed.

2. Slice and separate into rings **1 large sweet onion.** Turn into the sourdough mix and let soak ½ hour.

3. Remove rings one at a time. Dredge in **flour** *or,* if you like, a **flour-coarse cornmeal mix.** Set rings onto a cookie sheet and refrigerate.

4. Deep fry in **grapeseed oil** at 350°F to 375°F. A large cast iron skillet or a wok works well.

5. If you like, make a **mayonnaise dip.** See recipe for **curried mayonnaise** made of almonds (or purchase vegan mayonnaise). Season mayonnaise with **catsup** and **horseradish.**

*4 appetizer servings*

# fresh shiitake mushrooms

Cut stems off mushrooms. Place them upside down on a baking sheet. Drizzle with olive oil and sprinkle with Kosher salt. Broil until brown and a little crispy. Sprinkle with tamari.

# potatoes gremolata

1. Chop herbs: 2 tablespoons Italian parsley, ½ teaspoon fresh thyme, and 1 teaspoon fresh rosemary. Grate 2 teaspoons lemon zest. Combine with ½ cup olive oil and 2 minced garlic cloves. Set aside.

2. Cut 4 large well-washed Yukon Gold potatoes into wedges (no need to peel them). Pat dry with paper towels.

3. Heat 2 tablespoons grapeseed oil into a large cast iron skillet. Heat oven to 400°F. When oil is hot, add potato wedges and sauté in the oil. Turn heat down to medium and season potatoes with fresh ground pepper and salt. Turn occasionally.

4. When browned on all sides (about 10 minutes), add gremolata seasonings and place in oven for 5 minutes more cooking.

## sake-steamed yukon gold potatoes

Adapted from *The Breakaway Japanese Kitchen*, by Eric Gower.

Peel **3 Yukon gold potatoes** and cut into thick wedges. Cook in boiling **water** until not quite done. Drain in a colander. Heat **grapeseed oil** in a large frying pan and sauté the potato pieces over high heat for 5 minutes or until they brown a little. Add **1½ cups sake** and continue cooking until sake almost disappears (it will spatter and be messy). Add **2 tablespoons tamari** and mix well. The potatoes should be coated with a delicious brown gravy. Serve immediately.

## oven-roasted potatoes

From Alison Dunn.

1. Preheat oven to 500°F. Wash and cut up **potatoes**. You will need **12 small russets**, *or* **fingerlings**, *or* **2 to 3 medium-sized potatoes**. They need not be peeled, just washed. Cut into eighths, or if big potatoes, narrow wedges.

2. Combine in a bowl: **3 tablespoons olive oil, 1½ tablespoons chili powder, 2 teaspoons ground cumin,** and **2 cloves** crushed **garlic**. Turn potatoes into bowl. Add **Kosher salt** and **fresh ground pepper** to taste. Stir all together.

3. Roast on an appropriately-sized cookie sheet, spreading potatoes into one layer. Turn after 15 minutes. Roast until crisp.

## pesto mashed potatoes

1. Peel **6 russet potatoes** and cut into 2″ pieces. Peel **6 large cloves of garlic**. Turn potatoes and garlic into a pot and barely cover with water. Add **2 teaspoons salt** and cook about 15 minutes or until just done.

2. Meanwhile chop enough fresh **basil leaves** to measure **2 cups**. Grate **½ cup Parmesan**. Turn basil and Parmesan into a food processor and add **1 teaspoon Kosher salt** and **½ teaspoon crushed red pepper flakes**. Turn machine on and add **⅓ cup olive oil**. Turn off when blended and set aside.

3. Drain water from cooked potatoes and garlic. Return pot to stove and shake over medium heat to dry. Use potato masher to coarsely crush potatoes. Now add the contents of the processor together with **½ cup cream**. Turn off heat and cover pot to keep warm until serving.

## summer squash

If you have a garden, grow the yellow squash with green ends called *Zephyr*. It has the best flavor. Slice **2 squash** into long ovals. Put into a medium-sized frying pan with **2 tablespoons butter** *or* oil and **3 tablespoons water**. Cover. Cook over medium heat until water is mostly gone. Uncover and continue frying to brown, turning slices so both sides will color. Season with **salt** and **pepper**. Serve immediately.

## zucchini strips

Cut **zucchini** into sticks about ½″ x ½″ x 4″. Roll in a little **flour** seasoned with **salt** and **pepper**. Fry in a little **grapeseed oil** over high heat, turning as each side browns. Turn out onto plate and sprinkle lightly with **tamari** and **gomahsio** (see glossary).

# GARDEN RECOMMENDATIONS

Here in the Northeast, certain varieties have superior flavor. We find that "Fortex" pole beans are the most delicious, and "Zephyr" yellow summer squash has the best flavor. "Antohi" yellow Romanian peppers are early, dependable, and good-flavored. Seed of the above are available from Johnny´s Seed in Maine.

We love tomatoes, especially heirloom Brandywines. However, it´s a long summer waiting for them. So we grow "Fourth of July" from Burpee seed, a hybrid which bears the earliest good-tasting fruit, usually starting the last week in June and continuing until the end of September. It is a most generous plant.

The following are five satisfying dinner recipes inspired by various ethnicities and geographies. They are all relatively easy to prepare, and should demonstrate how diverse vegetarian meals can be.

# a thai dinner

With a small can of Maesri Thai chili paste and a couple cans of coconut milk on hand, you can produce an extremely easy dinner. We use frozen "chicken" strips from Taiwan, a soy protein. This is the one entrée we don't take off our menu without customer complaint. Here it is with vegetables and tofu.

1. Dice a **red** *or* **green sweet pepper** and **2 tablespoons lemongrass** (*optional*). Choose whatever vegetables you want: **green beans, eggplant, broccoli.** Beans should be cut in half, eggplant in 2" cubes, and broccoli into flowerets.

2. Sauté all in **2 to 3 tablespoons grapeseed oil** until they soften and begin to brown. Add half the contents of a small can of **Maesri Thai chili paste** and cook a few more minutes. The amount of chili paste used determines how hot this dish will be. Add **2 or more cans organic Thai coconut milk.** Bring to a boil and simmer until vegetables are done. **Tofu** cut into 2″ cubes may be added at this point.

3. Season to your taste with **tamari** and **lime juice.** Serve over **jasmine rice** and garnish with chopped **peanuts** and slices of cut **golden pineapple.**

# ratatouille

A Mediterranean summer vegetable stew.

1. Peel and slice **3 onions**. Use a large frying pan and good **olive oil** (start with **2 to 3 tablespoons** and plan to use more) to sauté the onions while you cut up the other vegetables. Add **1 teaspoon dried oregano** to the pan, and cook until onion just begins to brown.

2. Peel **2 medium eggplants** and cut into 2″ cubes. Slice **4 to 6 Italian frying peppers** and **4 small zucchini**.

3. Add eggplant to frying pan with more olive oil. Fry over higher heat until eggplant becomes tender and begins to brown. Now turn these vegetables into a pot.

4. Add a **few tablespoons more olive oil** and cook the zucchini and peppers in the same manner, over moderate heat, until they glaze and brown. Meanwhile, dip **5 to 6 small tomatoes** in **boiling water**, then **cold water**, and slip off their skins. Chop coarsely and set aside.

5. Add zucchini and peppers to pot with eggplant. Cover and simmer 15 minutes, or until flavors blend. Season to your taste with **salt** and **pepper**. Fold in the chopped, uncooked tomatoes. Turn the ratatouille into an ovenproof casserole. Just before dinner, heat oven to 400°F and bake ratatouille for about 15 minutes, or until tomatoes begin to glaze. Serve with **brown rice**.

*4 to 6 servings*

# mexican beans
# with ancho chile peppers

The ancho chiles (the main ingredient in chili powder) give this dish its special flavor.

1. Beans soaked in water overnight are best. However, you can cover dry beans with water, bring to a boil and turn off heat. Keep covered 1 hour.

2. Choose **red kidney beans, pinto beans,** *or* **black beans.** Soak **1½ cups** as above. Drain, add fresh **water to cover** and simmer until tender. A sprig of **epazote,**\* if available, adds flavor and digestibility to the beans.

3. Chop **1 large onion, 1 large green pepper,** a **stalk** or two of **celery,** and **2 cloves of garlic.** Sauté in a soup pot in **2 tablespoons grapeseed oil** over high heat. Add **½ teaspoon ground cumin, 1 tablespoon dried oregano,** crumbled, and **1 tablespoon chili powder.** Turn heat down and sauté until vegetables are golden.

4. Remove stems and seeds from **2 dried ancho chiles.** Cover with **2 cups boiling water.** Let sit 5 minutes. Turn into a blender to purée. Turn this liquid into the pot together with the contents of a **28 oz. can** of **organic tomatoes.** Season all with **1 tablespoon salt** and **tamari** to taste. Add cooked beans and bring mixture to a boil to blend flavors. Taste and correct seasoning. If stew is too moist, stir together **⅓ cup cornmeal** and **¼ cup water.**

---

\*Available in Mexican markets.

Turn into pot and simmer until cornmeal is cooked and has thickened the mixture.

5. Serve with cooked **rice**, **avocado slices**, chopped **onions**, and chopped **cilantro**.

*4 to 6 servings*

ORGANIC WINES AND BEERS

# an indian dinner

This is but one version of many possible Indian dishes. The combination of spices is what makes it taste so good.

1. First choose your vegetables.* Peel and slice **2 to 3 potatoes**, cut up **1 small cauliflower** into flowerets and slice (don't peel) **3 to 4 baby eggplants**. Par boil the cauliflower. Slice **1 large onion**. Set aside.

2. Use a large frying pan and **2 to 3 tablespoons grapeseed oil** to sauté first the potatoes and then the eggplant until browned. Turn each out into a bowl as they brown. Add **2 tablespoons oil** to pan and sauté onions, then garlic. Add spices (all available in Indian grocery stores): **1 teaspoon black mustard seed, 1 teaspoon whole cumin seed, 1 teaspoon whole coriander seed, 2 teaspoons ground cumin,** and **1 teaspoon turmeric**. Cook over moderate heat, stirring often. Peel and chop **6 cloves of garlic**.

3. In a separate pan, cover **1 cup basmati rice** (available in Indian markets) with water to 1″ above the rice. Boil uncovered until holes appear in the rice. Turn heat very low and cover pan. Check after 10 minutes. Rice should be done. Leave covered off heat.

---

\* Othervegetables could include summer squash and/or tomatoes, or green beans.

4. Add garlic to other vegetables and sauté a few minutes more. Add cauliflower and other vegetables and **2 to 3 curry leaves**, if available (find them in Indian markets) and stew until all are done. Chop **1 bunch cilantro** and add with **salt** and **pepper** to taste. This recipe makes a dry stew. **Water** *or* **coconut milk** may be added to give it a gravy. Drained canned **chickpeas** may be added if you like.

5. Serve with cooked rice and **lime pickle** (also available in Indian markets) and **yogurt** if you like.

*6 servings*

# lentils and rice

This Syrian recipe is but one of a myriad in which grains and pulses (beans, lentils) are combined. These ancient combinations are the original comfort food, supplying us with the right amino acids. This one was the "mess of pottage" for which Esau reputedly sold his birthright. The large amount of quality of olive oil is essential for the good flavor.

1. Pick over **2 cups French lentils** to remove stones and debris. Turn into a soup kettle with **3½ cups water** and bring to a boil. Turn heat down and simmer 15 minutes.

2. Add **1 cup long grain white rice** and **1 cup water** and simmer 15 minutes more.

3. Meanwhile, thinly slice **2 large Spanish onions**. In a frying pan, sauté the onions in **1 cup** of best-quality **olive oil** over moderate heat, stirring on occasion. This will take 15 to 20 minutes.

4. When onions begin to glaze and brown, turn them with oil into pot of lentils and rice. Add **1½ teaspoons salt, 1 teaspoon paprika**, and **½ teaspoon cayenne**. Continue cooking until lentils and rice are well-cooked. Correct seasoning. Serve with **pita bread**, and, if you like, **yogurt** and **feta cheese**.

*6 servings*

# Autumn

## DESSERTS

# tomato, cabbage, and rice soup

A good way to use up the last of the garden tomatoes.

1. Finely dice **1 carrot, 1 leek**, well washed, and ½ **small bunch of celery**, including **leaves**. Sauté in a soup pot in **1 tablespoon grapeseed oil** with ½ **tablespoons whole fennel seeds.** When golden brown, add **2 cups water** and **1 tablespoon pesto,** if you have it, otherwise add **1 teaspoon dried basil.** Cover and simmer for 1 hour.

2. Coarsely chop **5 cups fresh tomatoes.** You need not skin them. Add to soup pot with ¼ **cup canned tomato paste.** Alternatively, add **1 quart canned tomatoes with purée,** breaking up the tomatoes somewhat in the soup pot. Cut up ¼ **small cabbage** into 1½″ squares and add to simmering soup. Cook another 30 minutes. When cabbage and tomatoes seem done, add ⅓ **cup white rice** and cook 10 minutes more.

3. Season soup with **2 tablespoons brown sugar, 2 teaspoons salt,** and **1 tablespoon lemon juice.** Taste and correct seasonings if necessary. Garnish each serving with **sour cream.**

*6 servings*

# lima bean squash soup

1.  Soak **2 cups dried baby lima beans** overnight in water to cover.

2.  In the morning, cook beans in their liquid, adding more if necessary, with **1 large onion**, peeled and cut up, and **3 carrots**, scraped and cut into 1″ pieces. When quite soft, purée in food processor or blender.

3.  Meanwhile, cut up **1 Hubbard squash**. Scrape out seeds and stringy fiber with a spoon. (Seeds can be washed, dried, and roasted with coarse salt and a little oil for a snack.) Steam or bake until soft. Scrape out and purée enough squash to measure **2½ cups**.

4.  Combine lima and squash purée. Season with ¼ **cup tamari**. Add water until you like the consistency of the soup. Chop **1 tablespoon fresh sage**, ½ **tablespoon fresh rosemary**, and add **salt**, freshly ground **black pepper**, and **1 to 2 tablespoons lemon juice** until seasoning is just right. Taste and judge.

5.  Serve with **sour cream** and slivered **fresh sage leaves**.

*6 to 8 servings*

# beet and cabbage soup

1. Finely chop **1 large onion** and shred or grate **5 to 6 beets** and **1 large parsnip**.

2. Sauté the onion and **2 crushed garlic cloves** in **¼ cup grapeseed oil**. Add the beets and parsnips, **¼ cup wine vinegar** and **1½ cups water**. Add **2 cups canned tomatoes**, **½ teaspoon sugar**, **1 tablespoon caraway seeds**, **2 tablespoons tamari**. Simmer, covered, 45 minutes.

3. Peel and dice **3 medium Idaho potatoes**. Coarsely slice **½ large cabbage** and boil in **1½ quarts water** until potatoes and cabbage are just done.

4. Combine both mixtures in one pot and taste for seasoning. Despite the tamari, some **salt** may be necessary. A Russian soup like this one should be sweet, sour, and salty.

5. Serve with **sour cream** and **chopped dill**.

*8 to 10 servings*

# curried apple
# and potato soup

1. In a small pan over high heat roast **1 teaspoon cumin seeds** by shaking the pan until seeds are browned. Cool and crush with mortar and pestle.

2. Peel and dice **3 medium potatoes**. Put the potato cubes in a small bowl, cover with **2 cups water**, set aside.

3. Peel and chop **2 medium onions**. Dice **1 carrot, 1½ large green peppers** and **1 stalk celery with leaves**. Chop all vegetables uniformly in size.

4. In a large soup kettle over high heat, sauté all vegetables except the potatoes in **2 tablespoons grapeseed oil**. As the vegetables are cooking, add **2 cloves minced garlic** and the following spices: **1 teaspoon ground roasted cumin seed, 1½ teaspoons whole mustard seed, ¼ teaspoon turmeric, ¼ teaspoon ground cloves, ¼ teaspoon coriander, ½ to 1 tablespoon good quality curry powder** and **1 bay leaf**. Continue to sauté vegetables and spices until they are well browned. Scrape bottom of pot often. Add **2 tablespoons tawny port** and scrape browned bits at bottom of pot.

5. Add the potatoes and their water, **1 tablespoon tamari, 1 teaspoon salt, ½ teaspoon pepper, 1 cup heavy cream, 2 cups milk,** and **½ cup raisins**. Cook until the potatoes are done.

6. While the potatoes are cooking, peel and dice **1½ cups tart apples**, such as Mutsu or Fortune. Add the diced apple to the soup and heat through. Taste for salt, pepper, and tamari. You may wish to make the soup spicier; if so, add more curry. Once the apples have been added, do not boil the soup or their texture and flavor will be lost. Reheat gently.

7. Garnish each serving of soup with **yogurt, sunflower seeds**, and **pomegranate seeds**. The seeds are an especially interesting finish to this soup.

*8 to 10 servings*

SABRINA AND SELMA

# cream of cauliflower soup

1. Cut out the core of **2 large heads of cauliflower.**
   Slice off hardest part of core and leaves and discard.
   Cut up remainder of core, barely cover with **water** in
   a pot. Peel **6 cloves garlic** and add to pot. Simmer
   until core is very tender. Purée or put through sieve.

2. Meanwhile, thinly slice flowerets of the cauliflower.
   You will be using about ½ to ¾ of them, the rest may
   be saved for salads.

3. In soup pot, melt **2 tablespoons butter.** Add
   **2 tablespoons flour** and cook together a minute
   or two. Add ⅔ **cup heavy cream** and gently bring
   to a boil.

4. Add the puréed cauliflower core. Also add
   **1½ tablespoons tamari, dash Tabasco, freshly
   ground nutmeg,** and **freshly ground pepper.** Dice
   **3 oz. Swiss cheese** and add to simmering soup. Add
   **2 cups water, 1½ cups milk,** and **2 teaspoons lemon
   juice.** Taste for seasoning. Add **salt** if necessary
   (despite the tamari, it will probably be necessary).
   When seasoning is right and a little too salty, add
   sliced cauliflowerets. Cook till barely done. Don't
   overcook. Serve with chopped **parsley.**

*6 servings*

# broccoli mornay soup

1. Remove the flowerets from **4 bunches broccoli** and set aside. Use a small sharp knife to peel the stems, discarding the hardest bottom part. (The peeling takes time but the outside of the stem is too stringy and tough to use and the inside provides the substance and flavor of the soup.) Cut the peeled stems into 1 inch pieces, barely cover with water and cook until soft. When done, purée the stems in their liquid.

2. Meanwhile, melt ¾ **stick sweet butter.** Add ¾ **cup flour** and stir for several minutes. Add **2 cups heavy cream** and the puréed broccoli stems and liquid. Add ½ **cup tamari,** a dash of **Tabasco,** and **4 oz. Swiss cheese.** Also add some grated **nutmeg,** the **juice** of ½ to 1 **lemon** and **milk** *or* **cream** if soup is too thick. When seasoning is right, thinly slice about half the flowerets lengthwise and add them to the soup. (The rest may be used for omelets or with salads.) Continue cooking until flowerets are barely done and still crisp. Do not overcook. Reheat leftover soup with care so that flowerets retain their freshness.

*about 8 servings*

# czech mushroom soup

This is a rich, hearty soup. From *Mushroom Cookery* by Rosetta Reitz, Gramercy Publishing Co., and used with her permission. An excellent cookbook, unfortunately now out of print.

1. In a large soup kettle bring to a boil **1 quart water** with **1 teaspoon caraway seed, 2 teaspoons salt,** and ½ **teaspoon pepper.**

2. Meanwhile, peel and dice **4 medium to large potatoes** and add to the pot. Turn down the flame to slowly cook the potatoes. Cook 15 minutes or until potatoes are soft.

3. Meanwhile, stir **4 tablespoons unbleached white flour** into **2 pints sour cream** in a bowl and mix thoroughly. Stir this mixture into the soup pot and don't worry about curdling—it will smooth itself out later. Turn off flame.

4. Slice ½ **pound mushrooms** and add them to the soup. Cover, turn the flame on low, and simmer 10 minutes or until mushrooms are soft.

5. Garnish with fresh **chopped dill.**

*8 servings*

# cream of chestnut soup

1. Using a small sharp knife, cut an "X" in the flat side of **2½ pounds chestnuts**. Heat ½ inch **grapeseed oil** in a small frying pan and add the chestnuts in batches of 10. Fry, stirring for 10 minutes. Remove chestnuts to a paper towel. When they cool, pull off the shell and brown skin. This is tedious, but less difficult than boiling or baking the nuts.

2. Coarsely chop **5 carrots, 5 leeks**, split and well washed, **2½ small bunches celery**, including leaves, and **2½ onions**. Sauté in **4 tablespoons butter** in a pot. Chop **1 bunch straight leaf parsley** and add to pot. When vegetables begin to brown a little, add **10 cups water** and **1 tablespoon salt**. Simmer 1 hour.

3. Pour cooked vegetables and their broth through a strainer into another pot or bowl, pressing down on the vegetables. Use about half the vegetable broth to simmer about ⅔ of the peeled chestnuts until they are quite tender. Purée in a food processor or blender or use a potato masher to coarsely crush chestnuts. Return to soup pot.

4. To finish the soup, add **1½ cups half-and-half** (or light cream) and **1 tablespoon lemon juice**. Slice the remaining chestnuts into the puréed soup and heat gently, adding as much of the remaining vegetable broth as you like to thin the soup. Taste for salt.

5. Serve hot, and garnish soup with salted whipped cream: whip **1 cup heavy cream** with **½ teaspoon salt** until stiff.

*8 to 10 servings*

# butternut squash soup
## with chestnut cheese dumplings

A delicious four-ingredient soup. Dumplings make it even better.

1. Weigh **butternut squash.** You will need about
   **4 pounds—2 large squashes.** Peel, scrape out,
   and discard seeds. Cut into large chunks. Place in
   a pot with **7 to 8 cups water** and **1 split vanilla
   bean.** Cook until squash is tender.

2. Cut an "x" on the flat side of **8 chestnuts** using a
   sharp knife. Sauté in **2 tablespoons grapeseed oil**
   in a small frying pan for 5 to 10 minutes, shaking the
   pan every now and then. Let cool. Peel. This is the
   easiest and most flavorful way to prepare chestnuts.
   Set them aside.

3. Scoop out **1 cup of softened squash** and reserve for
   dumplings. Remove vanilla bean* and purée squash
   and liquid in a food processor. Return to pot, add
   **1 tablespoon salt** (or to taste).

4. **Chestnut cheese dumplings:** place reserved squash
   in unwashed processor. Add **1 cup ricotta cheese,**
   **¼ cup Parmesan, 2 eggs,** and **1 teaspoon salt.** Turn
   machine on. When well blended, add **6 to 7 chestnuts.**
   Process until they are chopped, not puréed. Now add
   **1 cup flour.** Process. Mixture should hold its shape. It
   if doesn't, add another tablespoon of flour. Turn into a
   bowl and refrigerate.

---

*Don't discard it—rinse, dry, and place in sugar container. It will still yield
flavor. A vanilla bean is an expensive ingredient but it makes this soup
special in a way extract will not do.

5. Bring a pot of **salted water** to a simmer. Dip a spoon into the boiling water, into the batter to form a dumpling, and dip into boiling water. Repeat. Cover pot and let simmer 5 minutes. Use a slotted spoon to lift dumplings out. Drain on absorbent paper.

6. When ready to serve, heat soup with 2 dumplings per diner. Garnish bowl with a chiffonade of **fresh sage leaves** and chopped remaining **chestnuts**.

*6 to 8 servings*

ROSE AND CHARLENE

# waldorf salad

1. Prepare **alfalfa sprouts**\* three to four days in advance, or buy sprouts.

2. **Prepare mayonnaise**: have ready in a small pitcher **1 cup grapeseed oil**. In a food processor or with an electric mixer beat thoroughly **2 egg yolks**. Keeping the machine on, add **1 tablespoon lemon juice**, **½ teaspoon salt**, a grating of **nutmeg**, a pinch of **pepper**, and **¼ teaspoon good quality prepared mustard**. Then add the oil (machine still on) in a slow dribble at first and then more quickly at the end. Turn machine off. Add **½ cup sour cream**, turn machine on and mix thoroughly into the mayonnaise. Set aside.

3. Core (do not peel) **3 large firm apples**, such as Honey Crisp or Fortune, and dice into ½″ pieces to make **4 cups chopped apples**. Toss with **2 tablespoons lemon juice**. Dice celery to yield 1½ cups and add to apples together with **2 cups chopped walnuts**.

4. Fold mayonnaise into apple-walnut-celery mix. Taste for salt, pepper, and lemon. Chill until ready to serve.

5. Arrange the waldorf salad on a bed of **Boston or Bibb lettuce**, garnish with **avocado slices, alfalfa sprouts**.

*8 servings*

---

\*Alfalfa sprouts: put 2 tablespoons alfalfa seeds in a jar with a screen or cheesecloth lid. Soak them in water for a minimum of 1 hour and not longer than overnight. Drain the water off and set the jar in a dark spot. Rinse the seeds at least once every day. When the sprouts are grown to about 1″ they may be refrigerated until ready for use.

# fennel salad with salt ricotta

1. Slice **2 "bulbs"** of **fennel** in half lengthwise, discarding any discolored outer stalks and the feathery leaves. Crisp several hours in **water** in refrigerator.

2. Slice the fennel thinly. On beds of mixed **escarole** and **romaine lettuce**, arrange slices of the fennel, thin slices of **salt or "table" ricotta cheese**, and a few **Italian olives**. Both olives and cheese are available in Italian delicatessens. About ½ lb. of cheese and ¼ lb. of olives should be adequate.

3. Drizzle with **vinaigrette** (see glossary).

*8 servings*

# brussels sprouts and grape salad
### with sour cream dressing

1. For each diner, trim **6 brussels sprouts** and slice in half lengthwise. Steam until barely tender. Slice about **8 red or purple grapes** in half lengthwise and remove seeds. Scatter sprouts and grapes on a bed of **Boston lettuce**. Drizzle a little **vinaigrette** (see glossary) over lettuce and top sprouts and grapes with a spoonful of **Sour Cream Dressing**.

2. **Sour cream dressing:** mix together **1 cup sour cream**, **1 tablespoon tamari**, **½ teaspoon lemon juice**, **1 tablespoon finely chopped fresh herbs** (such as scallions, dill, burnet, or parsley), fresh ground **pepper**, and **1 tablespoon gomahsio** (see glossary). Taste sauce and adjust it. This sauce is good with broccoli or also as a dip for raw vegetables.

*dressing makes enough for 6 to 8 servings*

# roasted pepper and sun-dried tomato salad
## with water buffalo mozzarella

1. To roast **peppers**, choose large, heavy ones. A mix of red and green will look nicest. Preheat broiler very hot. Place rack so that peppers don't touch the flame and roast, turning peppers as they blacken. As each pepper is fully roasted, place it in a paper bag and fold it closed. Remove one pepper at a time and use a knife to pull the skin off. Carefully cut around the stem so that it and the core and seeds come out together, letting the pepper drop into a bowl or jar. Barely cover the peppers with the best **extra virgin olive oil** you can afford, and add a splash of **balsamic vinegar**. Store refrigerated.

2. Place a handful of **sun-dried tomatoes** in a pot with ½″ of water and stew until softened, adding more water if necessary. Remove and chop coarsely. Pour a little **olive oil** and **balsamic vinegar** over them. If available, **fresh basil** or **oregano leaves** may be sprinkled over the tomatoes.

3. **Water buffalo mozzarella** is a very soft, creamy cheese. It is expensive and perishable. Domestic mozzarella, if fresh and locally made, can substitute. Lay leaves of **Boston lettuce** on a plate and top with strips of peppers. Arrange two or three slices of mozzarella and a spoonful of sun-dried tomatoes on top. Slices of **onion**, a few wrinkled **Italian olives**, and **vinaigrette** complete the salad.

# roasted bosc pears
## with walnuts, blue cheese, and raspberry vinaigrette

1. Preheat oven to 400°F. Peel and core **6 barely ripe Bosc pears**. Cut lengthwise into eighths. Place on a shallow baking sheet and sprinkle lightly with **Sucanat** (or organic sugar). Roast for 10 minutes. Remove from oven and cool. Turn roasted pears into a shallow container and refrigerate.

2. Bake ⅔ **cup walnuts** in a 300°F toaster oven for 10 to 15 minutes. Cool and chop coarsely. Set aside.

3. Blend **3 tablespoons raspberry vinegar** (Boyajian makes a very good one) with **1 tablespoon balsamic vinegar** and ⅔ **cup olive oil**. Set this dressing aside.

4. To compose the salad, arrange **mesclun** or **baby greens** on plates. Make a pinwheel of pear slices. Cut thin slivers of **blue cheese** (we prefer Valdeon) to place as you will. Sprinkle with walnuts. Use dressing judiciously. A whole **nasturtium flower** is a pretty garnish.

*8 servings*

# creamed
# "chicken of the woods"

1. Be sure you have correctly identified your
   mushrooms. While most large, tree-trunk-growing
   mushrooms are not poisonous, most also remain
   woody and inedible after cooking. When either
   *Polyporus sulfurous* (Chicken of the Woods) or
   *Polyporus frondosus* (Hen of the Woods) is fresh, soft,
   and juicy, you will have excellent eating. Sometimes
   you will find one that is tough at its center, but
   tender at the edges. Trim off edges or use the whole
   mushroom, depending on its condition. Cut into
   1″ pieces.

2. Heat **sweet butter** in a frying pan and add cut-up
   mushrooms. Cook over high heat. Mushrooms will
   quickly absorb any amount of butter you add to the pan,
   so be careful not to add too much, just enough to fry
   mushrooms to light brown. Pour in **cream**, light or
   heavy to your taste, and cover pan. Stew mushrooms
   about 5 minutes. Add more cream if needed or reduce
   liquid in pan if too much sauce remains. Add **salt, pepper,**
   and **lemon juice.** Now chop **straight leaf parsley**
   and add. Serve over **rice, noodles,** or on **toast.**

# moussaka

1. **Make filling:** melt **2 tablespoons butter** in a frying pan and sauté **¼ cup pignoli nuts** and **1 large Spanish onion**, finely chopped. When onions are soft and light brown, add **8 oz. canned tomato sauce**, **⅓ cup red wine**, and **2 tablespoons tomato paste**. Simmer ingredients together a few minutes. Add **8 oz.** (the tomato sauce can) **water**, **¼ cup** chopped **straight leaf parsley** and **1 teaspoon salt**. Simmer another 5 minutes. Add another **¼ cup red wine** and **¾ teaspoon cinnamon**. Let cool. Beat **2 small eggs** in a bowl and slowly stir cinnamon-tomato sauce into the eggs.

2. Prepare cheese by grating **¼ pound kefalotiri** and **½ pound kasseri**. Both are available at Greek markets and are necessary to the flavor of this meatless moussaka.

3. **Prepare eggplant:** peel and slice lengthwise (½″ thick) **2 large eggplants**. Fry the slices in a very hot frying pan or on a very hot griddle in as little **olive oil** as possible to keep eggplant from sticking. Using a large, deep ovenproof casserole dish, line the bottom with half the fried eggplant slices and sprinkle with about ¼ of both cheeses. Spoon the tomato-cinnamon-pignoli sauce over and top with remaining eggplant slices. Add most of the remaining cheese.

4. **Make béchamel sauce:** in a pot, melt ½ **stick butter.** Add ¼ **cup flour** and cook together, stirring, a few minutes. Add **2½ cups milk** and whisk together until sauce comes to a boil. Season to taste with **salt**, **pepper**, and **nutmeg.** Beat **3 egg yolks** in a medium bowl and add hot sauce gradually to the yolks, stirring well so that they do not curdle. Spread sauce over eggplant casserole. Top with the last of the grated cheeses and bake at 350°F until browned and bubbling, about 1 hour.

*6 to 8 servings*

# baked swiss chard
## with mushrooms and ricotta

1. Thoroughly wash **3 pounds Swiss chard** *or* **beet greens**. Parboil in liquid that clings to leaves. Drain well, reserving broth for **mornay sauce** (see following recipe). Chop finely and turn into a bowl.

2. Thinly slice **1½ pounds mushrooms**. Finely chop **3 cloves garlic** and **1½ medium onions**. Sauté all 3 vegetables in a frying pan with **4 tablespoons sweet butter** and **2 tablespoons grapeseed oil** until mushrooms begin to brown. Add to chard with **1½ cups ricotta cheese**, **½ cup grated Parmesan cheese**, and **salt** to taste. Cool.

3. Oil a 9″ x 13″ pan and sprinkle with **breadcrumbs**. Add **4 eggs** and **4 yolks** to cooled vegetables. Stir well and taste for seasoning. Turn mixture into pan, smoothing the surface with a spoon or spatula. Top with **breadcrumbs** and **Parmesan cheese**, then drizzle lightly with **olive oil**. Bake at 375°F until puffed and crisp on top.

4. Meanwhile, prepare **mornay sauce**, **rice pilaf** (see following recipes), and **grilled tomatoes**: slice **4 medium tomatoes** in half crosswise and **salt** lightly. Sprinkle cut halves with **breadcrumbs, Parmesan cheese**, a little dried **oregano**, finely chopped **garlic**, and **fresh basil** (*or* **pesto**, if available). Dot with **butter**. Just before serving the Swiss chard, broil tomatoes briefly until toasted and sizzling brown.

5. Serve the baked Swiss chard with rice pilaf. Spoon Mornay Sauce over each serving, and place a broiled tomato half on each plate.

*8 servings*

# mornay sauce

1. In a saucepot, melt **4 tablespoons sweet butter** and add ¼ **cup flour.** Cook together a few minutes, stirring constantly. Add **1 cup half-and-half** and bring to a simmer.

2. Add up to **2 cups** reserved **broth** from the Swiss chard. Dice ¾ **cup cheese** (we use **Havarti**) and add to sauce. Simmer until thickened and smooth, stirring with a whisk.

3. Season with **1 to 2 teaspoons lemon juice,** a few drops Tabasco, ¼ **teaspoon salt,** and a **dash** of **tamari.**

*makes about 1 quart*

# rice pilaf

1. Finely chop **1 small onion** and fry in **3 tablespoons olive oil,** along with ½ **cup very fine noodles,** crumbled (we use thin Greek noodles called **fides,** available in Middle Eastern markets). After a few minutes, add ½ **cup pignoli nuts.** Continue frying a few more minutes, then add **2 cups white rice** and fry until rice is opaque and noodles are brown.

2. Add ¼ **cup currants, 1½ tablespoons tamari, 3½ cups water** and ½ **teaspoon salt.** Cover and cook over low heat until rice is tender. Add more water if necessary, and taste for salt before serving.

*6 to 8 servings*

# szekely gulyas
## with potato dumplings

See recipes for Cabbage Strudel and Cucumber Salad.

1. Drain **1 pound seitan** (wheat gluten, available in health food stores) and set aside liquid. Cut seitan into 1″ cubes and set aside.

2. Dice **1 large Spanish onion** and sauté slowly in **2 tablespoons grapeseed oil**. Dice a small **green pepper** and add to pan with **½ teaspoon hot Hungarian paprika** and **3½ teaspoons sweet Hungarian paprika**. Sauté slowly, stirring, for 10 to 15 minutes. Add **1 clove garlic**, crushed, and sauté until garlic softens. Add **2½ tablespoons flour** and cook, stirring, 5 minutes more.

3. Dice **1 fresh tomato** and add to pan with **1 cup** of the reserved **seitan liquid** *or* **water** flavored with **1 tablespoon tamari**. Cover and simmer over lowest heat ½ hour.

4. Add seitan, **¼ cup dry white wine** (*or* **water**), **1 teaspoon dried marjoram**, and fresh ground **pepper**. Simmer another 10 minutes.

5. Drain and chop **1 cup sauerkraut**. Add to stew and simmer 15 minutes more. Finally, add **¾ cup sour cream** and stir in.

6. **Make potato dumplings:** wash and peel **1 Idaho potato** and grate into bowl. Fork-beat **1 egg** and add to potatoes together with **pinch salt** and **⅓ cup flour**. Stir together. Chop enough **onion** finely to measure **¼ cup** and add.

70

7. Bring a pot of water to a boil, add **2 teaspoons salt** and use a fork to twirl walnut-sized dumplings. It may be necessary to use your fingers to help form them. Slip into pot and cover. Simmer 10 minutes.

8. If you like, prepare **cucumber salad** and **cabbage strudel** (see following recipes) to serve with Gulyas. When ready to serve, reheat Gulyas with dumplings. Serve in shallow bowls, liberally sprinkled with freshly chopped **straight leaf parsley**.

*6 to 8 servings*

# cucumber salad
## for gulyas

1. Peel and slice **2 large cucumbers**. Sprinkle with **salt** and let stand 1 hour. Drain and squeeze dry.

2. Mix together: **2 tablespoons vinegar**, pinch **paprika**, grating of **pepper**, **1 small clove garlic**, minced, **2 teaspoons grated onion**, and ½ **cup sour cream**. Mix together and add cucumbers. Taste for **salt** and add if needed.

3. Garnish salad with chopped **dill**.

*5 to 6 servings*

# cabbage strudel

1. You will need ½ **pound phyllo sheets** brought to room temperature. (See glossary for info on phyllo).

2. Use a heavy knife to thinly slice a **small cabbage**, discarding core. Cabbage should measure **1 quart**. Turn into bowl and sprinkle with **2 teaspoons salt**. Toss and let stand 1 hour. Toss cabbage every now and then.

3. Drain cabbage and squeeze as dry as possible. Melt **4 tablespoons sweet butter** in a frying pan and fry cabbage over high heat until wilted and beginning to brown. Remove from heat. Grate **pepper** over cabbage and stir in ⅔ **cup sour cream**. Taste to be sure enough pepper was added. Let cool. Preheat oven to 400°F.

4. Melt **4 tablespoons sweet butter** in a small pan.

5. Layer 10 sheets of phyllo on top of each other, first brushing each one with butter before placing the next one on top. Generously sprinkle every third sheet and the last one with **breadcrumbs** (homemade are best). Spread cabbage over most of phyllo and roll up, tucking in ends. Use spatulas to transfer roll to **buttered** cookie sheet, and use a French chef's knife to cut partly through, forming slices about 1½ inches wide. Don't cut through to the bottom of the roll until after baking. Butter tops of strudel.

6. Bake until browned, about 20 minutes. Strudel slices can be reheated.

*8 servings*

# halushkin

1. Drain **2 pounds** homemade *or* purchased **sauerkraut**. Squeeze dry. Sauté until well browned in ¾ **stick sweet butter** (unsalted). Turn into a large casserole dish.

2. Finely shred ¼ **of a medium-sized cabbage** and sauté in the same frying pan in ½ **stick sweet butter**. Add cabbage to sauerkraut.

3. Cook **6 to 7 cups egg noodles** in boiling water until done. Drain and add to sauerkraut and cabbage. Add **1 tablespoon poppy seeds** and about **1 teaspoon salt** (taste to see how much is needed) and another **3 tablespoons butter**. Cover with foil and reheat in oven before serving.

4. Serve with **cucumber salad** (see following recipe) and **applesauce**: peel, core, and slice **8 apples**. Stew in ⅓ **cup apple juice** *or* **cider** with **2 tablespoons brown sugar** and ¼ **teaspoon cinnamon**.

*6 to 8 servings*

# cucumber salad
## for halushkin

1. Peel and slice **5 thin cucumbers**. Sprinkle with coarse **salt** and let stand 1 hour.

2. Rinse cucumbers thoroughly in cold water. Turn into a clean dishtowel, roll up, and squeeze until cucumber slices are very dry. Turn into bowl and add **3 tablespoons** chopped **fresh dill**, **½ cup sour cream**, **2 tablespoons vinegar**, and fresh ground **pepper**. Taste to see if **salt** is needed.

*6 to 8 side dish servings*

ANGELIQUE

# oyster mushroom-taleggio tart

A savory Autumn supper dish, to serve with salad and beer.

1.  Make **pie crust** (see recipe) to fit in a 9″ pan. Use foil and dry beans to weight down the foil, and bake at 400°F for 10 minutes. Remove foil and beans and bake 10 minutes more. Remove from oven.

2.  Meanwhile, slice **8 oz. oyster mushrooms**\* and **1 tablespoon shallots**. Set aside. Heat **1 tablespoon olive oil** in a medium frying pan. Toast **1 teaspoon whole cumin seed** in the oil. Once seeds sputter and pop, add mushrooms and shallots. Cook over high heat until mushrooms begin to brown. Turn off heat. Season with **salt** and **pepper** to taste. Set aside.

3.  Thinly slice **6 oz. taleggio cheese** (discard rind). Set aside.

4.  Spread bottom of pie crust with **2 to 4 tablespoons sour cream**. Top with mushroom mixture. Arrange cheese slices on top of mushrooms. Bake at 375°F for 20 minutes, or until cheese melts.

*4 to 5 servings for a light supper*

---

\*Or fresh shiitakes, or a combination of both.

# pasta putanesca

Named for Italian streetwalkers, this sauce is always made with olives; other ingredients are intended to make a savory, well-flavored sauce.

1. Use a small knife, preferably with a curved blade, to cut **⅔ cup green cured olives** and **3 tablespoons black cured olives** away from their pits. You will find olives like these at Italian groceries. Set aside. Thinly slice **1 large onion, 2 seeded Italian green peppers**, and **1 head fennel**. Chop and save the feathery leaves of the fennel, but discard the hard upper green part of the stalks.

2. In a large saucepan heat **3 tablespoons olive oil**. Add onions, pepper, and fennel with a pinch of **hot pepper flakes** and **1 to 2 cloves chopped garlic**. Sauté gently for about 5 minutes or until vegetables have wilted and are turning golden. Add **3 tablespoons tomato paste** and cook, stirring, another 5 to 10 minutes. Now add **⅔ cup red wine** and **1 28 oz. can plum tomatoes**. Use a wooden spoon to coarsely break up tomatoes. Simmer, covered, 45 minutes.

3. If available, add **dried porcini**: soak **½ cup** of them in hot **water** first. Then add both mushrooms and their soaking liquid to the sauce. Also, slice and fry **⅔ cup button mushrooms** in **2 tablespoons olive oil** in frying pan and add to sauce. Finely chop **½ bunch straight leaf parsley** and add. Taste for salt. Depending on the saltiness of the olives, you may need to add **1 to 2 teaspoons salt**.

4. For best flavor and mindful of the putanesca theme, **fresh cavatelli** is the best pasta to use. In a large amount of boiling salted **water**, cook **1½ pounds cavatelli** or other pasta until just done. Taste to be sure. Drain well.

5. As a final garnish, steam **1 bunch broccoli**, tops only, divided into rosettes, until barely done and still bright green. Spoon sauce over pasta and top platter or individual plates with broccoli rosettes. Serve with freshly grated **Parmesan cheese**.

KATE

# solianka

This Russian dish was adapted from Rosetta Reitz' *Mushroom Cookery.* Solianka gets better upon reheating

1. Core and slice **1 cabbage**. Slice **3 medium onions**. Using ¼ **cup grapeseed oil**, first fry the cabbage slices until lightly browned. Remove to a large bowl, then fry onions, adding more oil if needed. Sauté until light brown.

2. Soak **1 oz. dried porcini mushrooms** (*Boletus edulis*) in hot water to cover.

3. Using a large shallow pan, layer half the cooked cabbage on the bottom. Place the onions on top. Now peel and slice **2 small cucumbers** and add them. Slice ½ **pound fresh mushrooms** on top of the cucumbers. Peel and slice **2 apples** and arrange on top. Drain and chop dried mushrooms, saving the liquid, and add them to the casserole. Top pan with remaining cabbage.

4. **Make sauce:** heat **3 tablespoons grapeseed oil** in a pot and sauté **1** crushed **clove garlic**. Add **1½ tablespoons flour** and cook together a minute. Add **15 oz. canned tomato sauce**. Add ¼ **cup brown sugar, 1½ tablespoons tamari**, fresh ground **pepper**, juice of ½ **lemon** and dried mushroom liquid, being careful not to add grit or sand that may be at the bottom. Add ½ **cup water** to the sauce and taste for seasoning. Sauce must be very overseasoned, sweet, sour and salty to compensate for no seasoning at all in the solianka.

5. Carefully pour as much sauce as you can over casserole, cover with foil, and bake at 375°F for 1 hour. Uncover and bake 10 minutes to brown.

6. Cook **2 cups whole buckwheat groats** in boiling **salted water** until barely tender. Drain in a colander.

7. Cut solianka into squares and serve with buckwheat groats. Spoon remaining sauce over both. Serve with **sour cream**.

*8 to 10 servings*

TWENTY-NINTH ANNIVERSARY PARTY

# black bean chili

1. Pick over ½ **pound black beans**; cover with water and let soak 4 hours or overnight. Drain, turn into a pot; add fresh water and a sprig of **fresh epazote.*** Cover and cook over lowest heat several hours or until beans are very tender.

2. Chop **1 onion, 1 red pepper, 1 green pepper** and **¼ cup jalapeños**. Sauté vegetables in **2 tablespoons olive oil**. Slice **4 large garlic cloves** and add to pan. Use a small pot to toast **1 tablespoon cumin seed**, then crush with a mortar and pestle. Add to vegetables together with **1 tablespoon good quality chili powder** and **1 teaspoon salt**.

3. When vegetables are beginning to brown and caramelize a bit, add **14 oz. crushed canned tomatoes, 14 oz. tomato juice** and **1 oz. bittersweet chocolate**.

4. Combine vegetables and beans and cook both together for at least 30 minutes. Season to taste with tamari. Discard the epazote.

5. Serve over rice, or with **corn dumplings** (see following recipe). Garnish with **cilantro**. **Guacamole** (see index) goes well with this dish.

*6 to 8 servings*

---

*Available in Mexican markets.

# corn dumplings

1. Soften **3 tablespoons butter**. Place in mixer bowl with flat beater attachment. Turn machine on and add **3 eggs, 1 teaspoon salt, ½ cup drained canned corn kernels, 1½ tablespoons minced jalapeño chile** and **⅓ cup shredded cheddar cheese**. Now add **masa harina**. Start with **½ cup** and mix until barely thickened. You may need another ¼ to ½ **cup** of **masa harina**.

2. Heat **water** in a wide shallow pot. Dip spoon in boiling water, and scoop out dumplings. Simmer 5 minutes, or until they float. Serve with **black bean chili** (see previous recipe).

*makes about 1 dozen dumplings*

# tamale pie

From *Wings of Life*, Julie Jordan, Crossing Press, and used with permission.

1. Soak **1 cup dried kidney beans** overnight.* When ready to use, bring the beans to a boil in a pot with **3 cups water** and turn down to a simmer. Add a **sprig of fresh epazote**, if available. Cook the beans until done (about 45 minutes) and set aside.

2. **Prepare the filling:** chop **4 medium onions** and start to fry on high heat in a soup pot with **4 tablespoons grapeseed oil**. Add **2 green peppers**, coarsely chopped, **2 stalks celery**, finely chopped, **3 or more cloves garlic**, crushed, **1 bay leaf**, **1 teaspoon dried basil, 1 teaspoon oregano**, **1 teaspoon ground cumin**, and **2 tablespoons chili powder**. Stir the bottom of the soup pot frequently, making sure the vegetables don't burn but brown evenly.

3. When vegetables are browned, add the cooked beans to the soup pot, adding as much liquid as necessary for the chili to be thick but not dry.

4. Turn the heat on high and add **1 quart canned tomatoes**, ¼ **cup red wine vinegar**, ½ **cup cashews**, ¼ **cup raisins, 1 teaspoon salt**, and some freshly ground **black pepper**. Bring to a boil and let chili cook ½ hour to develop flavor. Add more bean liquid if necessary.

---

*If beans cannot be soaked overnight, they can be brought to a boil in water, removed from heat for 1 hour and then returned to stove and cooked until tender.

5. **Meanwhile, prepare cornbread topping:** mix **1 cup cornmeal, 3 cups water,** and **1 teaspoon salt** in a pot. Bring the mixture slowly to a boil, stirring constantly with a spoon or whisk so it doesn't lump. Cook the mixture until it is thick, forming a cornmeal mush. Remove from the heat.

6. Beat **2 large** *or* **3 small eggs** in a bowl with a fork. Spoon some of the hot mush into the eggs, stirring constantly until eggs and mush are combined.

7. Pour chili into a lightly oiled baking pan. Spread the cornmeal mush evenly over the chili. (Optional: you can top the tamale pie with **½ cup of grated Monterey Jack cheese** if you like.) Bake the pie at 350°F for about 40 minutes or until the crust is brown and firm.

8. Take the pie out of the oven and let rest at least 10 minutes or more to allow the pie to set. Tamale pie is even better reheated the second day, when the layers have firmed up.

9. Serve with **guacamole** (see following recipe).

*8 servings*

# guacamole

1. Cut **2 large ripe avocados** in half lengthwise.
   Remove pit and any brown fibers clinging to flesh.
   Peel off skin. Mash avocadoes with fork until some
   avocado is puréed but some is still chunky.

2. Add **1 tablespoon onion**, finely chopped,
   **1 tablespoon** canned **hot chile peppers**, chopped
   (we use **jalapeño** peppers), and **1 tablespoon**
   **fresh cilantro**, chopped. Add **salt** and **pepper** and
   mix well.

3. Finely dice **1 medium tomato** and fold in.

*makes 2 to 3 cups*

# green tomato pie

A savory dish that appears to be Pennsylvania Dutch in origin. Proportions are hard to be specific about since it depends on how big your pan is and how many green tomatoes you have. From Roberta (Sage) of A Woman's Place, Athol, NY.

1. Make **pie crust**: combine **5 cups all-purpose flour** and **2 teaspoons salt** in a mixer. Dice ¾ **pound butter**. Add to mixer and use flat beater to blend into oat-sized flakes. Fork beat **2 egg yolks** (discard whites or save for another purpose) and combine with ½ **cup ice water**. Add to mixer. Blend briefly; add more ice water only if necessary. Gather dough into a ball, wrap in plastic wrap and refrigerate.

2. Using a large pan, for example, one 11″ x 17″, roll out enough pie crust to fit and line pan.

3. Thickly slice **8 to 10** very hard **green tomatoes**, removing stem end.

4. Slice **2** very **large onions** and sauté in fry pan in ½ **stick sweet butter**.

5. Slice **1 pound Swiss cheese** and **1 pound Muenster cheese**.

6. Sprinkle pie crust-lined pan with **breadcrumbs**. Layer tomato slices, cheeses, and sautéed onions in pan. Sprinkle with **coarse salt, lots of fresh ground pepper**, and about **2 tablespoons brown sugar**. Repeat layers until ingredients are used up. Top with more **breadcrumbs** and a **drizzle** of **wine vinegar**.

7. Roll out crust to top pie. Crimp edges and slash. Bake at 375°F until brown. Leftover portions can be reheated in an oven or toaster oven.

*10 to 12 servings*

# processor piecrust

Very easy pie crust.

1. In food processor combine **1¼ cups flour** and **½ teaspoon salt**. Pulse to combine.

2. Dice **6 tablespoons butter**. Turn into processor. Separate **1 egg**, discarding white (or save for other purposes). Combine **yolk** with **2 tablespoons ice water**.

3. Turn processor on. When mix is pebbly, add yolk and water mixture. Pulse 10 to 12 times. If mix is dry, sprinkle on a little more ice water. Gather dough into a ball and roll out, or else chill in refrigerator.

*makes enough for one 9″ pie shell*

# coconut oil/butter piecrust

Best flaky pie crust.

1. Place **6 cups pastry** (*or* all-purpose) **flour** and **1 teaspoon salt** in mixer. Blend with flat beater. Turn off.

2. Dice **¾ pound unsalted butter**. Add to mixer. Turn on and blend to oatmeal-flake stage. Turn off.

3. In a 2-cup measure, combine **1 cup water** and **¼ cup coconut oil.**\* Add to mixer and blend. If mixture is dry, add **1 to 2 tablespoons** more **water**. Don't over beat. Chill before using.

*6 to 8 crusts*

---

\*If coconut oil is solid, heat it until just melted, not hot.

# apple pie

Here's how we do this old favorite.

1. Choose tart apples, and for the best pie, choose
   several varieties such as Cortland, Mutsu, Gala, or
   Fuji. If you can choose only 1 type of apple, choose
   Mutsu. It is an excellent all-around apple. You will
   need **4 to 6 apples** per pie.

2. In a bowl combine **⅓ cup flour**, **⅓ cup sugar**,
   **¼ teaspoon salt**, **¼ teaspoon cinnamon**, and a dash
   of either **nutmeg** *or* **cardamom**. Grate **rind of ½ lemon**
   and set aside. Use a dry whisk to stir dry ingredients.
   Peel, core, and slice apples. Turn into a bowl and toss
   with flour-sugar mix and with lemon rind.

3. Preheat oven to 400°F. Roll out **pie crust** (see recipe)
   and line Pyrex pie plate with crust. Heap apples in
   crust. Dot top with **butter** (use 1 to 2 tablespoons).
   Roll out top crust; place over apples and crimp crust
   edges. Slash top of pie for steam to escape. Brush
   crust top with **1 egg** which has been fork beaten with
   **1 tablespoon water**. Bake until browned, about half
   hour to 45 minutes.

*one pie*

# apple custard tart

1. Preheat oven to 400°F. Roll out **pie crust** (see index) for 1 pie pan. Prick around bottom of crust with fork tines. Use foil and dried beans or lentils to weight down the crust while it bakes 5 to 10 minutes.

2. Meanwhile, peel, core, and slice enough crisp **apples** like Mutsu or Fortune to yield **3 cups** sliced.

3. Remove partially baked crust from oven, remove foil and beans and arrange apple slices in shell. Sprinkle lightly with **cinnamon**, lower heat to 375°F and bake 20 minutes.

4. Beat **1 large** *or* **2 small eggs** with ¼ **cup honey**. When well mixed, add ¼ **cup flour** and ½ **cup heavy cream**. Mix well to be sure honey is dissolved. Flavor with **2½ tablespoons cognac** or ¾ **teaspoon vanilla extract**, as you prefer.

5. Sprinkle **1½ tablespoons currants** over apples in pie crust and pour custard over the apples. Bake another 25 to 20 minutes. Sift **powdered sugar** generously over pie. This pie is best served warm and can be reheated. Offer **crème fraîche** on the side.

*one tart*

# tarte tatin

For best results, two frying pans of different diameters are needed.

1. **Make pastry:** combine **2 cups unbleached white flour** and **1 teaspoon salt**. Mix with flat beater. Add **1 cup unsalted butter**, first cut into bits. Fork-beat **1 egg yolk** with **3 to 4 tablespoons water**. Add. Mix briefly. Press dough together with hands, wrap in plastic film, and refrigerate.

2. Peel, core, and slice **8 large Mutsu** *or* **Cortland apples**. Grate **rind** of **1 lemon** over apples, then squeeze the **juice** and add to bowl. Sprinkle lightly with **ground cardamom**. Toss apple slices to mix.

3. In a 12″ frying pan, melt ⅔ **cup sugar** over moderate heat. When melted but not brown (just a little golden), remove from heat. Arrange approximately ¾ of the apples neatly in pan. Dot top with **4 tablespoons unsalted butter**. Place pan over moderate heat for 15 minutes or until juices thicken and caramelize. If heat is too high, sauce will burn. Remove from heat.

4. Preheat oven to 375°F. Roll out half the pastry into a rather thick 10″ circle, reserving remainder for another baking session, stored in the refrigerator. Lift cooked apples into a deep 10″ diameter skillet, moving one section at a time. Arrange remaining apple slices on top. Top with crust, tucking under wedges which exceed the perimeter.

5. Bake until lightly browned. Remove from oven and cool 10 minutes. Use a knife or spatula to run around the edge of the pan. Upend the pan so that the tarte slides out upside down onto a platter.

6. Serve with **whipped cream**. Tarte Tatin is best served warm.

*one 10" pie*

STEPHANIE AND YUKA

# maple apple cobbler

Very rich, very delicious.

1. Preheat oven to 400°F. In a mixer combine **3 cups flour, ¾ teaspoon baking powder,** and **¾ teaspoon salt.** While mixing add **½ pound sweet butter** cut into small pieces. Do not worry about overbeating. Remove from mixer and press about ⅔ of this "pastry" into a 9″ x 12″ baking dish.

2. Finely chop **½ cup walnuts** and mix into remaining pastry with **1 tablespoon date sugar.*** Set this "streusel" aside.

3. Peel, core, and slice **4 to 5 apples.** Press apple slices into pastry in pan. Pour **¾ cup maple syrup** over slices and sprinkle lightly with **cinnamon.** Bake for 10 minutes.

4. Meanwhile whisk together in a large mixing bowl: **3 cups sour cream, 3 egg yolks,** and **½ cup maple syrup.** If too thick for pouring, add up to **⅓ cup apple juice** *or* **cider.** Pour over apples in oven and top with reserved streusel. Sprinkle again with **cinnamon** and bake 30 minutes longer. Cobbler is done when streusel is lightly browned and there is a minimum of movement with pan is jiggled.

5. Serve with warm **heavy cream.**

*12 servings*

---

*Available at health food stores.

92

# cinnamon apple cake

1. Preheat oven to 350°F. You will need an 8″ springform pan, ungreased.

2. Place **6 oz. cream cheese** in a mixer. Add **¼ pound unsalted butter** and **1 teaspoon vanilla extract**. Set aside.

3. Peel and dice **3 cups tart crisp apples**, such as Mutsu. Stir together **2 tablespoons sugar, 1 teaspoon cinnamon** and **¼ teaspoon cardamom**. Toss apples with half of the sugar and spices; reserve the rest.

4. Add a scant cup **sugar** to mixer with **1 teaspoon grated lemon rind**. Use a flat beater to mix for about 4 minutes. Add **2 eggs**, one at a time, beating well after each. Add **3 egg yolks** (reserve whites for other purposes) and beat again. Turn off machine.

5. Use a dry whisk to stir together **1½ cups flour, 1¾ teaspoons baking soda, 1½ teaspoons baking powder**, and **¼ teaspoon salt**. Add flour blend to mixer and stir briefly. Add apples and turn into pan. Sprinkle top with remaining spiced sugar.

6. Bake 1 hour and 15 minutes. Invert on rack until completely cool. Use a knife to loosen sides of pan. Serve with whipped cream.

*one 8″ cake*

# molasses apple gingerbread

1. Butter an 8″ square pan. Preheat oven to 325°F.

2. Peel, core, and slice **3 to 4 tart apples**. Stew 1 apple in a little **cider** and mash to yield ⅓ cup applesauce. Set aside. Line buttered pan with remaining raw apple slices.

3. In a pot melt together ⅔ **stick sweet butter** and ⅔ **cup molasses**. When melted, let cool.

4. In a bowl, use a whisk to stir together **1⅓ cups white unbleached flour, 1 teaspoon baking soda, 1 teaspoon ginger, ⅓ teaspoon salt, ½ teaspoon nutmeg, and ½ teaspoon cinnamon.**

5. In a separate bowl, beat **1 egg**. Add ⅓ **cup buttermilk** and the cooled butter and molasses. Stir together with flour mix and the reserved ⅓ **cup applesauce**. Do not stir too much. Turn into pan over apple slices and bake until cake pulls away from sides of pan.

6. Serve this cake warm with whipped cream melting over it. Beat together until stiff **1 cup heavy cream, 1 teaspoon honey, and ½ teaspoon vanilla.**

*one 8″ square cake*

# apple poppy seed strudel

This recipe is adapted from an heirloom one which appeared in the newspaper *The Forward* many years ago.

1. Prepare **puff paste** (see following recipe). You will need a double recipe for the filling below.

2. Heat **½ cup sugar** in **½ cup water** until dissolved. Add **¾ cup poppy seeds** and simmer over low heat 10 minutes. Grate **rind of 1 lemon** and squeeze its **juice**. Add both to poppy seeds together with **½ cup breadcrumbs** and **⅓ cup raisins**, chopped. Set aside.

3. Peel and core **6 Mutsu apples**. Cut into thick slices. Heat **1 cup sugar** in **¾ cup water** and cook until syrupy. Grate **rind of 1 lemon** over syrup and stir in. Turn apple slices in syrup until partly cooked. Remove onto a plate or tray and let cool.

4. Roll out strudel dough into a 12″ x 16″ rectangle. Spread thinly with half the poppy seed filling. Layer half the strudel with the apple slices and sprinkle lightly with **cinnamon**. Fold other half over and press edges together. Transfer to baking sheet. Prick dough with fork. Beat **1 egg yolk** with **1 tablespoon water** and brush on strudel. Bake at 375°F until puffed and browned.

*makes 3 flattened rolls approximately 8″ x 12″*

AUTUMN

# puff paste

1. Place **2½ cups flour** in a mixer. Add **2 tablespoons grapeseed oil, 1 teaspoon salt,** and **2 teaspoons sugar.** Use flat beater to mix. Meanwhile, add up to **¾ cup water.** Dough should not be sticky. Knead well in mixer. Shape into a ball, place in a plastic bag, and refrigerate.

2. Cut **½ pound sweet butter** into pieces and add to same mixer bowl (no need to wash it). Add **1 cup flour** and mix until blended. Shape into a rectangle about 4″ x 6″.

3. Remove dough from refrigerator and pat/roll it out into a shape about 10″ x 16″. Place butter mix in center and fold sides over. Use rolling pin to gently press dough back to 10″ x 16″. Butter should not break through. Fold in thirds, wrap in plastic, and refrigerate. Let chill 1½ hours.

4. Roll out and fold, roll out and fold, and refrigerate 1 hour. Repeat rolling and folding two times again. Let rest 1 hour or until needed.

# lekach

Jewish honey cake served at Rosh Hashonah and after Yom Kippur.

1. In a small pot, heat ⅔ cup brewed coffee,
   1 tablespoon instant coffee (or coffee substitute),
   1 tablespoon unsweetened cocoa, ½ teaspoon
   cinnamon, ¼ teaspoon ground cloves, ¼ teaspoon
   allspice, ¼ teaspoon nutmeg. When all is blended,
   remove from heat and let cool. Preheat oven to 350°F.

2. Separate 6 eggs, placing whites in a mixer and yolks
   in a bowl or food processor. Beat yolks with ½ cup
   grapeseed oil and 1¼ cups honey. When yolks
   seem light in texture, add cooled coffee and spices.

3. In a bowl, use a whisk to stir together 2½ cups flour,
   1½ teaspoons baking powder, and 1½ teaspoons
   baking soda.

4. Beat egg whites until stiff. Meanwhile, fold together
   flour mix and egg yolk mix, adding ⅔ cup chopped
   walnuts and ½ cup raisins as you fold. Now fold in
   the stiff beaten egg whites gently but thoroughly.

5. Turn batter into one greased and floured tube pan or
   two loaf pans. Bake at 350°F until cake has browned
   and pulled away slightly from the sides of the pan.
   Turn out onto a rack and cool.

6. Honey cake is traditionally served with afternoon tea
   or coffee or as a dessert with brandy. However, you
   may serve it with **honey-sweetened whipped cream**:
   beat until stiff 2 cups heavy cream, 1½ tablespoons
   honey, 1½ teaspoons vanilla extract.

# louisiana pear pecan cake

1. Preheat oven to 350°F. Choose firm **Bosc pears** and peel, core, and dice enough to measure **2 cups.** Set aside. Chop ¾ **cup pecans** and set aside.

2. Butter a 9″ cake can and line with waxed paper.

3. In mixer, cream ½ **cup** (1 stick) **sweet butter** with ⅔ **cup sugar** and **1 teaspoon vanilla extract.**

4. Meanwhile, stir together: **1½ cups flour, ¼ teaspoon salt, 1 teaspoon baking soda** and **½ teaspoon cinnamon.**

5. Add **2 eggs** to butter mix. Beat well, scrape down and mix again.

6. Add ¾ **cup buttermilk** to egg mixture and use a rubber spatula to fold flour mix, pears and pecans into cake. Don't overmix. Turn into prepared pan and put into oven. Bake until cake pulls away from sides of pan—½ hour to 45 minutes. Cool 5 minutes on a rack and then turn out.

7. When cake is cool, serve with **whipped cream.**

*8 servings*

# pear custard pie

1. Prepare **4 to 5 Bosc pears** as follows: Peel, core, and slice the pears. Place in a shallow pan with ¾ **cup apple juice**, ½ **teaspoon dried ginger, pinch each cloves** and **cinnamon, 1 teaspoon lemon juice** and a **strip** of **lemon peel**. Cover and simmer 5 to 10 minutes. Cool.

2. Roll out a **pie crust** (see index) and bake at 400°F about 8 minutes, using foil and beans to hold crust flat while baking. Remove crust from oven and remove foil and beans.

3. Make a custard by beating **2 eggs** in a bowl with a whisk. Add ¼ **cup flour** and continue beating. Add **2 tablespoons maple syrup**, ¼ **cup** of the **pear cooking liquid**, and ¼ **cup heavy cream**. Beat well. Finally, flavor with one of the following: 2½ **tablespoons plum wine, 2 tablespoons cognac**, or ¾ **teaspoon vanilla extract**, as you prefer.

4. Arrange sliced pears in pie crust. Pour custard over. Sprinkle with 1½ **tablespoons currants** and bake at 375°F until puffed and browned, about 20 minutes. This pie is best served warm.

*makes one pie*

# pears isabel

Named for Isabel Brach who inspired this adaptation of zabaglione. Any fruit is appropriate: oranges, mangoes, strawberries, or raspberries.

1. In the top of a double boiler (or in a stainless steel bowl that will fit on the rim of a pot as a double boiler does) place **5 egg yolks** and ¼ **cup honey**. The bowl or double boiler top must be stainless steel or enamel or the sauce will discolor. Put enough **water** in bottom pan to last 10 to 15 minutes without touching upper bowl.

2. Beat and/or stir constantly with whisk over low-medium heat until sauce becomes quite thick and sticks to sides of bowl (about 10 to 15 minutes).

3. Remove from heat and add a **scant ½ cup Grand Marnier liqueur**, whisking until sauce is smooth.

4. Place in refrigerator until sauce is very cold.

5. Whip **1 cup heavy cream** until stiff and fold into sauce until mixture is smooth and even. Fold, do not stir.

6. Fill a glass serving bowl with **5 to 6** sliced **comice pears**. Top with the sauce.

*6 to 8 servings*

# "indian" pudding

A Massachusetts specialty.

1. Preheat oven to 275°F.

2. Bring **1 quart milk** to a boil and gradually whisk in **1 scant cup ground cornmeal.** * Cook, stirring, about 5 minutes or until cornmeal is slightly thickened. Set aside.

3. In a Pyrex loaf pan or other baking dish, combine **1 cup milk, ½ cup molasses, ¾ teaspoon cinnamon, ½ teaspoon ginger,** and **½ teaspoon nutmeg.** Add cornmeal and stir together well.

4. Bake 1 hour, then pour **1 cup milk** over the top. Don't mix in. Bake 4 hours more.

5. Serve warm with **ice cream** *or* **heavy cream.**

*6 to 8 servings*

---

*If you can get fresh ground cornmeal from a health food store, your pudding will taste much better.

# sour cream pumpkin pie

You can use pumpkin if you like, but we use Hubbard squash.

1. Cut up **1 Hubbard squash**. Scrape out seeds and stringy fiber with spoon. Steam or bake until soft.

2. Measure out **1½ cups cooked squash**. In a food processor, mix squash together with scant **⅓ cup sugar**, **1 teaspoon cinnamon**, **½ teaspoon ginger**, **¼ teaspoon nutmeg**, **⅛ teaspoon cloves**, and **¼ teaspoon salt**. When well mixed, add **1 cup sour cream** and **3 egg yolks**, reserving whites in a mixer bowl. Preheat oven to 375°F.

3. Roll out **pie crust** to fit pie (see index).

4. Beat **egg whites** until rounded peaks form. Gradually add **3 tablespoons sugar** and beat until stiff but not dry. Fold egg whites into squash mixture; turn into unbaked pie shell. Bake 40 to 45 minutes or till puffed and brown. Let cool.

5. Serve topped with whipped cream; Beat together until stiff **1½ cups heavy cream**, **1½ tablespoons sugar** and **½ teaspoon vanilla**.

*one pie*

# cranberry almond tart

1. Make **processor pie crust** (see recipe). Roll out and fit into a 10″ quiche pan with removable bottom. Weight with foil and beans and bake in a 350°F oven until just set but not brown. Remove foil and beans (save for future pie baking) and set prebaked crust aside.

2. Soften **2½ tablespoons unsalted butter**. Put **¾ cup almonds** into a food processor and pulverize with **3 tablespoons sugar**. Add butter, **½ teaspoon vanilla**, **¼ teaspoon almond extract**, and **3 egg yolks**. Process.

3. Spread almond butter mix over pie crust. Top with **12 oz. cranberries**, sprinkle with **⅓ cup sugar** and bake at 350°F until berries pop, about 30 minutes. Cool.

4. Serve with **crème fraîche** *or* **whipped cream**.

*one 10″ fruit tart*

# cranberry kissl

The New England name for fruit pudding is flummery; the Russian name is kissl.

1. Simmer **1 package (4 cups) cranberries** in **2 cups** good **organic fruit juice**. Perhaps local fresh apple cider will do.

2. Put cranberries and juice through a food mill (such as a foley food mill) or a similar sieve. Return to pot. Add scant **1 cup water**, **¾ cup maple syrup**, **pinch** of **salt** and bring back to a simmer.

3. Stir **¼ cup potato starch** into **½ cup cold water**. Combine thoroughly, then add to simmering pot while stirring or whisking well. Kissl should thicken immediately. If it doesn't, stir together another **1½ tablespoons potato starch** with a few tablespoons cold water, and add.

4. Cool in pot about 10 minutes. Stir again and turn into glass dessert dishes. Chill until kissl "sets up." Serve with **heavy cream** and **slivered almonds**.

*6 to 8 servings*

# persimmon, walnut, and buttermilk pudding

1. Toast **1 cup walnuts** in oven or toaster oven at 375°F until light brown. Turn into food processor and chop coarsely. Turn out and set aside.

2. Choose very soft, even overripe **persimmons**. Remove calyx at stem end (do not peel) and purée in processor until there are 2 cups persimmon pulp.

3. Melt **5 tablespoons** butter in a small pot. Set aside. Preheat oven to 400°F.

4. In a bowl, use a whisk to stir together 1½ **cups flour, 2 teaspoons baking powder, 2 teaspoons baking soda,** ⅓ **teaspoon salt,** ⅓ **teaspoon cinnamon,** and ⅓ **teaspoon nutmeg.**

5. In mixer, beat **5 eggs** until foamy. Add ⅔ **cup honey** and beat until mixed well. Add **3 cups buttermilk** and the cooled melted butter. Mix again. Turn off machine.

6. Butter a 9″ x 12″ baking pan, either enameled or Pyrex. Combine flour mix, persimmon purée and egg mix and quickly turn into prepared pan.

7. Bake until puffed and slightly withdrawn from pan sides, about 1 hour.

8. This pudding is best served warm, with **whipped cream**. It can also be chilled and served cold. **Persimmon slices** are a nice garnish.

*10 to 12 servings*

# WINTER

## SOURCES

## DESSERTS

# onion soup

1. Thinly slice enough **onions** to yield **6 cups**. Simmer, covered, in a soup kettle with ½ **stick unsalted butter** and **1 tablespoon grapeseed oil** for 20 minutes. Uncover pot, add ½ **teaspoon** crushed **dried thyme, 1½teaspoons salt**, and ¼ **teaspoon sugar**. Raise heat slightly and cook onions, stirring occasionally with wooden spoon, until they are a rich medium brown color. It will take at least 45 minutes, and is the secret to the good flavor of this soup.

2. Stir in ¼ **cup unbleached white flour** and cook a few minutes more, stirring. Add **2½ quarts water** and bring to a boil, stirring up browned particles. Add ⅓ **cup tamari** and ½ **cup dry white wine**. Simmer another half hour and taste. Add **salt** and **pepper** as you need it.

3. Dry out stale pieces of **French bread** in a 300°F oven and rub the crisped surfaces with a peeled clove of **garlic**.

4. When ready to serve, put **1 tablespoon** each **grated Swiss cheese** and **grated Parmesan** in each bowl—you will need ½ **cup** of each cheese total. A **splash** of **brandy** is nice too, if you like. Ladle soup into bowls, stir, and top with garlic croutons.

*8 servings*

WINTER

# minestrone

A classic soup, deservedly popular.

1. Pick over ½ **cup red kidney beans** and soak overnight or for 6 hours in water to cover. Drain, turn into a pot, cover with **water**, and bring to a boil. Turn down heat and simmer until beans are tender.

2. Meanwhile, dice **1 small onion, 3 celery stalks with leaves**, and **3 carrots**. Turn into a soup pot with ½ **cup good quality olive oil** and fry until vegetables are golden. Add **1 teaspoon thyme** and **2 cloves garlic**, minced. When garlic wilts, add **6 to 7 cups water** and bring to a boil.

3. Cut ¼ **of a cabbage** into 1″ pieces and add to pot with **1 cup canned tomatoes** and **1 potato**, peeled and diced. Bring to a simmer and cook until cabbage and vegetables are done.

4. When beans are cooked, add them and their cooking water to soup with **1 teaspoon salt, 2 tablespoons tamari**, and **1 tablespoon pesto**, if you have it.

5. Separately cook ½ **pound ditalini pasta**. Drain and add to soup. Serve with fresh chopped **parsley** and **Parmesan cheese**, if you like.

*8 servings*

# potato celery seed soup

1. Dice ½ **bunch celery** and **3 carrots**. Save the **celery leaves** and chop. Chop **1 large onion**.

2. In a soup pot, sauté all the vegetables in ½ **stick sweet butter**. As the vegetables are browning, the bottom of the pot must be scraped vigorously. Add **3 cloves garlic**, coarsely chopped. Cook another minute, to incorporate the garlic.

3. Wash, peel, and dice **5 medium potatoes**. Add to soup pot with enough **water** to cover. Add ¾ **teaspoon celery seed, 1 tablespoon salt**, and ½ **teaspoon pepper**. Bring to a boil and simmer till potatoes are soft.

4. Add ¾ **cup heavy cream, 2 teaspoons tamari**, and a **dash of Tabasco**. Taste for seasoning. If soup is too thick, add milk or water. Warm over low heat and do not boil when reheating. Garnish with **scallion slices**.

*6 to 8 servings*

**WINTER**

# s'chee

A wonderful Russian cabbage soup that never misses meat. Time consuming to prepare, but will feed 10 people. It helps having at least 2 cooks to fry vegetables and to judge seasoning properly.

1. **Prepare vegetable broth:** preheat oven to 500°F. In a roasting pan place **1 large peeled and quartered onion, 2 carrots, 1 parsnip**, and **1 white turnip**. Drizzle with **grapeseed oil** and roast, turning often, until well browned. Remove roasted vegetables to a large soup kettle. Use boiling water to deglaze roasting pan, scraping up browned bits. Add this water to soup kettle with enough additional water to cover. Cut **celery tops from 1 bunch celery** and add. Add **2 bay leaves** and **2 well-washed leeks**. Simmer at least 1 hour. Then put broth through strainer into another large soup kettle or bowl. Press down on vegetables to get as much of their juices as possible. Discard remaining pulp.

2. **Make soup:** chop and sauté in **2 tablespoons grapeseed oil** in frying pan: **1 cup onions, ½ cup celery, ½ cup carrots**. When slightly browned, add **2 cloves garlic**, crushed. Turn off fire. Rinse **1 pound sauerkraut** in a colander. Squeeze dry and coarsely chop. Add to fry pan and sauté till kraut starts to brown, adding more oil if necessary. Turn contents of frying pan into the pot of vegetable broth.

3. Shred **1 cabbage** (about 2 pounds, or 2 quarts shredded) and sauté it in the same frying pan, again adding oil if necessary, until cabbage is wilted. Turn into soup kettle with a **28 oz. can Italian plum tomatoes**, chopped a little with a spoon, **2 tablespoons tomato paste, 3 tablespoons sugar**, and ⅓ to ½ **cup tamari**. Add water as necessary.

4. Simmer at least one hour more. Add **juice of 1½ to 2 lemons** and begin to taste. Soup will likely need more water and possibly up to **1 tablespoon salt**. It should taste sweet and sour, as well as salty. Add more lemon juice or tamari, as needed. Chop **one small bunch dill** and add. Serve topped with a dollop of **sour cream**.

*8 to 10 servings*

# french cream of mushroom soup

1. Wipe clean (do not wash) and slice **1 pound mushrooms**. Fry in soup kettle in **1 stick sweet butter** until mushrooms are well cooked, liquid is gone, and mushrooms are beginning to brown. Add **3 or 4 cloves garlic**, crushed, and stir until garlic is lightly cooked. Add **½ cup unbleached white flour** and cook, stirring, until flour is well blended.

2. Gradually add **1 quart milk**, stirring with a wooden spoon. Then add **⅓ cup dry white wine, 1 teaspoon salt**, fresh ground **pepper**, and grated **mace*** to taste. Bring to a boil and taste. Add about **1⅓ cups water, 2 tablespoons Italian parsley**, chopped, and **2 tablespoons fresh dill**, chopped.

*4 to 6 servings*

---

*Mace is more expensive than nutmeg, but has a more delicate flavor. Substitute nutmeg if necessary.

# escarole, garlic, and cannelini bean soup

A beloved soup, both for its richness of flavor and simplicity of preparation. Be sure to use the full amounts of olive oil and garlic listed – they are the keys to the superb flavor of this soup.

1. Soak **2 cups cannelini beans** (white kidney beans) overnight. When ready to cook, bring to a boil in a small pot with **5 cups water** and turn down to a simmer. Cook the beans until just done and set aside.

2. Meanwhile, wash **2 heads of escarole** and shred with a heavy knife.

3. Peel and chop coarsely **10 large cloves of garlic**.

4. Warm ¾ **cup extra virgin olive oil** in a large soup pot. Add **1 teaspoon red pepper flakes** and the garlic. Sauté gently until garlic softens but does not brown. Add the shredded escarole with enough **water** to barely cover. Bring to a simmer and cook 30 minutes.

5. While the soup is cooking, bring another pot of water to a boil and cook ½ **pound** good quality **pasta** (penne *or* ditalini). Set aside.

6. Now add the cooked cannelini to the soup pot with ¼ **cup tamari, 1 teaspoon salt**, and generous grindings of **black pepper**. Simmer a few minutes.

7. To serve: put a handful of the cooked pasta in each bowl and add the soup. Top with fresh grated **Parmesan cheese**, if desired, and add more fresh ground pepper.

*6 to 8 servings*

# parsnip and barley stew

1. Peel and slice **1 pound parsnips**. Cut **1 medium onion** into quarters and slice. Sauté in soup pot in **2 tablespoons grapeseed oil**, **¼ teaspoon ground cloves**, and **½ teaspoon dried thyme** until golden brown. Add **¼ cup flour** and stir well with wooden spoon. Add **3 cups water** and **1 medium potato**, peeled, quartered, and sliced. Cover and simmer 30 minutes.

2. Separately, cook **⅓ cup pearl barley** in **2 cups water** until done, about 45 minutes.

3. Turn barley plus cooking liquid into soup and season with freshly grated **nutmeg**, **1½ tablespoons tamari**, **1½ tablespoons lemon juice**, and **2 teaspoons salt**. Add **3 cups milk** and bring to a simmer. Top finished soup with chopped **straight leaf parsley** and freshly ground **pepper**.

*6 servings*

# curried lentil soup

Adapted from *Wings of Life* by Julie Jordan, Crossing Press, now unfortunately out of print.

1. Bring **1 cup French lentils** to a boil in a small pot with **3 cups water** and turn down to a simmer. Cook the lentils until done and set aside.

2. Chop **4 medium onions** and start to fry them over high heat in a soup pot with **4 tablespoons grapeseed oil**. Add **2 green peppers**, coarsely chopped, **3 cloves garlic**, crushed, ½ **teaspoon dry ginger**, **1 teaspoon ground turmeric**, **1 teaspoon ground coriander**, ¼ **teaspoon ground cloves**, **1 teaspoon chili powder**, and **1 teaspoon ground cumin** (we pan-roast whole cumin seeds first then crush them in a mortar and pestle). Stir the bottom of the soup pot frequently making sure the vegetables don't burn, but brown evenly.

3. When vegetables are browned, add the cooked lentils to the soup pot, adding as much **water** as necessary for the soup to be somewhat thin. (As lentils cook they continue to absorb water).

4. Turn heat on high and add **1 quart canned tomatoes**, **1 teaspoon salt**, and ¼ **cup raisins**. Let the lentil soup come to a boil, turn down to a simmer and let cook ½ hour or more to develop flavor. Taste for seasoning and add the **juice of 1 lemon** just before serving. Serve with a dollop of **yogurt** on top and a thin slice of **apple**.

*8 servings*

WINTER

# spinach salad
## with sesame-peanut dressing

1. In a food processor combine: ½ cup peanut butter (without added fat or sweeteners), 2 teaspoons agave nectar, 1 tablespoon white miso, 1 tablespoon dark (toasted) sesame oil, 1 tablespoon tomato paste, 2 tablespoons tamari, and 1 tablespoon mirin (if unavailable, use rice wine vinegar).

2. Turn processor on, gradually adding 1 cup water. Process until well mixed. Correct seasoning. Refrigerate.

3. In a 300°F toaster oven, brown 3 tablespoons sesame seeds lightly. Set aside.

4. Prepare a bed of well-washed young spinach leaves. Ladle dressing over spinach. Add slices of red onion and sprinkle with sesame seeds. Hard-boiled egg slices are an optional garnish.

*makes 1¾ cups dressing*

WINTER

# caesar salad

This is one we make at home.

1. **Prepare croutons:** cut large cubes from a good-quality **Italian bread. 1½ cups** are needed. Heat **2 tablespoons olive oil** in a frying pan and sauté croutons on all sides, stirring frequently. When brown, turn out onto paper towels.

2. **Prepare the lettuce:** the best caesar salad is made from the center leaves from **2 heads of Romaine lettuce.** Wash, slice or break and turn into a salad bowl.

3. Grate **½ cup Reggiano Parmesan.** Set aside. Put **2 garlic cloves** in a food processor. Add **1 yolk** from an organic, free range chicken egg. Turn on machine. Add **1 teaspoon mustard, 4 teaspoons lemon juice,** and drizzle in **¼ cup** of your best **olive oil.** Turn off machine. Add **1 teaspoon Kosher salt,** fresh ground **pepper,** and **⅓ cup chopped Italian parsley.** Turn machine on to blend; correct seasoning.

4. Turn dressing into salad bowl with Parmesan and croutons. Toss all together and serve right away.

*6 generous servings*

# orange escarole salad
## with sour cream vinaigrette

1. Thoroughly wash and dry **1 large head escarole**. Chill.

2. Use a small knife to peel the skin and white pith from **3 large thin-skinned oranges**, cutting pith and skin off simultaneously. Use a large sharp knife to cut oranges into slices.

3. Arrange escarole on 6 plates and place overlapping slices of oranges on each one.

4. Mix **1 cup vinaigrette** (see glossary) with **2 tablespoons sour cream**. Pour over prepared salads and top each one with **Bermuda onion slices** and a little **gomahsio** (see glossary).

*6 servings*

**WINTER**

# crimson slaw with jícama

1. Use a French chef's knife to thinly slice half of a small red cabbage. You should have 4 cups. Peel half of a small jícama* and slice into fine matchsticks, to yield 1¾ cups. Set both aside.

2. Bake ¼ cup pignoli nuts in a toaster oven set at 300°F until light brown. Cool.

3. **Mix dressing:** squeeze ¼ cup lime juice, 1 tablespoon liquid from bottled hot chilies, ½ teaspoon salt, ⅛ teaspoon chili powder, fresh grated black pepper, and ⅓ cup olive oil. Whisk together and pour over cabbage mix.

4. Combine dressing, cabbage mix, and pignolis. Serve on a bed of lettuce with sliced onions and optional quesco fresco (from a Latin market) or feta cheese.

*6 servings*

---

*Available in Latina and Asian markets

# beet, goat cheese, and watercress salad
## with walnuts

1. Rinse **1 bunch** of **medium to small beets**. Cut off ends and scrape lightly. Don't peel. Cut each beet into wedges. Turn into a pot. Add **1 cup water**, **¼ cup olive oil** and **1 tablespoon salt**. Cover and simmer until beets are tender. Let cool. (Peel beets now if you like.)

2. Make vinaigrette: combine **¼ cup tamari**, **2 tablespoons lemon juice**, **1 tablespoon balsamic vinegar**, **½ cup olive oil** and **salt** and **pepper** to taste. Pour vinaigrette over beets. Refrigerate.

3. Use a toaster oven to bake **¾ cup walnuts** at 300°F. When very slightly brown, remove, cool, chop coarsely. Finely dice **2 tablespoons shallots**. Set both aside.

4. Cut stems off **1 large bunch** of **watercress**. Arrange on individual plates. Arrange beet wedges on top and spoon vinaigrette over. Top with walnuts and shallots and slices of a **creamy goat cheese**—you will need about **3 oz.**

*4 to 6 servings*

# roquefort, grapefruit and avocado salad

1. Peel **4 large grapefruits** and separate into segments. Arrange on beds of **Boston lettuce** in pinwheel pattern alternating with slices of **avocado** (you will need 1 very large avocado).

2. Cut about **6 oz. Roquefort cheese** into 6 wedges and center each salad with the cheese.

3. Top with **onion rings** and **vinaigrette** (see glossary).

*6 servings*

GARDEN VISITOR

# potato latkes

1. Prepare **Applesauce** (see index) to serve with latkes.

2. Use grater attachment to shred **3 large potatoes**, peeled and washed, and **1 small onion** in a food processor or by hand into colander over a bowl. Set aside and let mixture drain into the bowl.

3. In a larger bowl beat **2 eggs**. Add **2 tablespoons potato starch, 1 teaspoon salt, ½ bunch straight leaf parsley**, chopped, and a little grated **pepper**.

4. Squeeze the potato-onion mixture over the colander so the bowl beneath catches all the liquid. Put the squeezed mixture into the larger bowl of mixed eggs, etc. Mix them together well.

5. Lift off the colander. In the bottom bowl will be a layer of liquid on top of some potato starch. Pour off the liquid and discard. Using a scraper, add this residual starch to the larger bowl of mixed eggs, potato, and onion. Make sure the starch is well mixed into the batter. This batter should be stored in the refrigerator in a narrow container with a light lid. The top of the batter may turn a grayish/black color—it is only potato discoloring and is not harmful. It may be lifted off and thrown away or stirred in.

6. When ready to cook, preheat a large skillet or frying pan with **grapeseed oil**. Use a fork to lift and place the batter into the hot skillet or fry pan, patting the individual latke (about 4″ wide) down with the fork. Repeat until desired amount of latkes are formed in the pan, and add oil as needed. Flip latkes when bottoms are brown and cook on other side. Press lightly with spatula. The end result should be flat, brown, lacy pancakes.

7. Serve immediately with **sour cream** and **applesauce** (see index).

*6 servings*

NOEL AND SELMA

# linguine
## with meyer lemon and arugula

A quick, easy, and delicious supper.

1. Thinly slice **1 bunch of arugula**—you should have about 1½ to 2 cups. Discard stems. Grate **skin of 1 large Meyer lemon**. Squeeze the **juice** of the lemon. Set all three aside. You will also need **1½ cups** of thick shavings of good quality **Parmesan cheese** and **1 cup crème fraîche**.

2. Cook **1 pound linguine** in **salted water** until *al dente*. Drain, saving some of the cooking water, and turn into a large bowl. Add the arugula, lemon rind, Parmesan, and crème fraîche. Grate **black pepper** over the top and toss. Add a little pasta cooking water and/or the lemon juice as you see fit.

*3 servings*

# choux paste gnocchi

These are very delicate fluffy gnocchi, made of choux paste.

1. Peel and cut up **4 large russet potatoes**. Cover with water and boil till tender. Defrost **1 small package frozen chopped spinach**. Squeeze and measure **1 cup spinach**. Purée in a food processor. Set aside.

2. Use a mixer to mash drained potatoes while they are still hot. Set aside.

3. In a pot, bring **1 cup water** to a boil with **6 tablespoons unsalted butter, 1½ teaspoons salt, ¼ teaspoon pepper**, and a **grating** of **nutmeg**. When mixture boils, quickly add **1 cup all-purpose flour** and beat vigorously with a wooden spoon. Turn off heat and beat in **2 eggs**, one at a time.

4. Add mixture to potatoes in mixer. While mixer beats slowly, add **2 more eggs**, puréed spinach, and ½ **cup** grated **Parmesan**. When all is well blended, turn into a container, cover, and refrigerate.

5. Sauté **3 to 4 chopped cloves of garlic** in **2 to 3 tablespoons olive oil** over low heat. Slice **6 to 8 fresh shiitake mushrooms** and add to frying pan. Soak **3 sundried tomatoes** in boiling water. When soft, dice. Set aside. It should take 15 minutes to thoroughly brown shiitakes. When done, combine with sundried tomatoes and the soaking liquid. Simmer until most of the liquid is gone.

6. Using two spoons, roll gnocchi into ovals and coat lightly with flour. Drop into boiling salted water. After they float to the top, simmer for 5 minutes. Drain, brush with **butter** and sprinkle with **Parmesan**. Serve with **shiitake-tomato garnish**.

*5 to 6 servings*

# kasha platter

This recipe has evolved from a Russian Jewish background to suit our vegetarian tastes. It is, we think, an excellent approximation of several side dishes never served together, since the kasha usually accompanied meat, as did the tzimmes, which usually had meat cooked with it. The cauliflower latkes was a separate "dairy" dish Fay Davidson created for family suppers. We like them served all together, with the miso gravy, our own invention. You can make a supper of the cauliflower latkes, if you like. This would be most appropriate in October when they are least expensive. Note: **miso gravy** (see index) should be made in advance.

1. **Make kasha varnitchkes:** stir **1⅓ cups whole kasha** (buckwheat groats) into a pot of boiling **water** and cook till just puffed. Taste, and don't overcook. Drain in a small-holed colander and run cold water over kasha till cool. Turn into a shallow ovenproof pan.

2. Boil **1 cup small bowtie pasta** in salted water until done. Drain and add to kasha in pan.

3. Chop **3 medium onions**. Slice **1½ cups mushrooms**.

4. Melt **½ stick sweet butter** in a fry pan and sauté **1 cup cashew pieces** for a few minutes. Add mushrooms and onions and cook until light brown. Add to kasha in pan and season with **salt, pepper,** dash **tamari,** and another **½ stick sweet butter.** Grate **1½ cups carrots** and add. Cover pan with aluminum foil and bake for 20 minutes at 350°F.

5. **Make cauliflower latkes:** steam **1 small head of cauliflower** divided into flowerets in the least amount of water possible. Mash cauliflower with the remaining liquid using a potato masher or fork. Add **3 beaten eggs, nutmeg, salt,** and **pepper** to taste,

and ½ to ¾ cup unbleached white flour. This mixture will be used to make small pancakes ("latkes") and must rest ½ hour minimum in the refrigerator before cooking. Be cautious with the flour, a little more can be added later.

6. **Make tzimmes:** peel and slice **1 bunch carrots.** Cook **2 or 3 medium yams** in boiling water. Put carrots into fry pan with **1 tablespoon honey, 1 teaspoon salt, ½ stick sweet butter, ¼ cup water,** and **5 to 6 prunes,** cut in quarters. Cover and simmer. When almost done, remove cover and brown slightly. Peel and slice cooked yams and add to carrots.

7. Both kasha and tzimmes can be reheated in a 450°F oven, uncovered, until brown. Sauté small cauliflower latkes (4" diameter pancakes) in **butter.** Pat out each latke into hot butter in fry pan with a fork. When brown, turn gently with spatula, and brown other side. Serve with **sour cream.**

8. Top kasha and tzimmes with chopped **parsley** and **miso gravy** (see index).

*6 to 8 servings*

# plasto

A rich vegetable and cornmeal pie from Thessaly (Greece) from Spiros Poulemis.

1. Wash and chop **1 pound spinach**. Set aside. Wash and chop ½ **pound escarole**. Set aside. Cut central stems from ½ **pound each collard greens** and **kale** and discard. Cut coarsely and set aside.

2. Bring a big pot of **water** to a boil and add just the collards and kale. Let boil one minute, then drain in a colander.

3. In a pot bring **1 quart milk** and ½ **pound butter** to a simmer with ½ **teaspoon salt**. Sprinkle in 2¼ **cups cornmeal**, stirring vigorously until thickened. Consistency should be like cooled cereal—neither thick and pasty nor very creamy. Add milk or cornmeal as needed. Set aside.

4. Heat **3 tablespoons olive oil** in a frying pan. Fry collards and kale until they begin to brown at the edges. Add spinach and escarole. Sauté, turning greens and adding more oil if necessary. When wilted and light brown, turn off heat and let cool.

5. Crumble **1 pound feta cheese**. Beat **5 eggs** well. Set both aside. Heat oven to 350°F.

6. Spread half the cornmeal mixture in a 12″ x 16″ pan as thinly as possible. Spread cooked greens over cornmeal. Pour eggs over the top and then the feta. Season generously with fresh ground **black pepper**. Finally, top with remaining cornmeal mixture. Drizzle top with **olive oil**. Bake 1 hour or until light brown on top.

7. Serve with **yogurt** and **greek salad** (see index).

*16 servings*

# spinach noodles
## with garlic vermouth sauce

1. **Make garlic vermouth sauce:** melt **1 stick sweet butter.** Sauté **4 crushed cloves garlic.** Add **½ teaspoon dried basil,** crumbled well in your hand. When cooked but not browned, add **½ cup unbleached white flour.** Cook gently a few minutes. Add **⅓ cup dry vermouth, juice of ½ lemon,** and **1 cup heavy cream.** Let sauce thicken a little, then add up to **1 quart milk.** Finally, season with **1 to 2 tablespoons tamari,** a dash of **Tabasco** and **1½ tablespoons pesto.**\* Taste. You may want to add **½ teaspoon salt.** Simmer ½ hour.

2. **Prepare pignoli nuts:** use a rolling pin to crush about **1 cup** of them on a counter. Then toast them, stirring often, in a 300°F oven or toaster oven till light to medium brown. Be careful, they burn easily.

3. Cook **1½ pounds of spinach ribbons** (noodles) or **artichoke ribbons** in boiling salted water. Drain and toss with a little **olive oil** and **salt.**

4. Serve noodles with sauce, fresh grated **Parmesan,** a sprinkling of **pignoli nuts** and fresh ground **pepper.**

*6 to 8 servings*

WINTER

---

\* Pesto: we grow basil in the summer, then chop the leaves in a food processor together with garlic and enough olive oil to make the machine efficient. Traditionally the nuts (pignoli, walnuts, almonds) are ground together with the basil. We prefer the nuts as a roasted topping instead. The pesto can be frozen in ice cube trays overnight, then popped out of the trays and put into a plastic bag. Use 1 or 2 cubes to flavor the sauce. Lacking pesto, add 1 tablespoon more crushed basil.

# pierogies

Polish and Eastern European filled pasta dumplings, Sometimes they are filled with cheese. This version, adapted from Elizabeth Senes, adds potatoes to her sauerkraut and dried cep (boletus, or porcini) mushrooms. We used Mary Ellen Graham's noodle dough recipe. She prefers a farmer cheese filling.

1. **Make noodle dough:*** place **3 cups all-purpose flour** in a food processor. Add **1 teaspoon salt** and **2 tablespoons butter.** Turn processor on briefly to blend. Break **1 egg** into a liquid 1 cup measure. Add **water** to make **1 cup total liquid.** Pour into processor and turn machine on. If machine is working too hard (moving on the counter, etc), turn dough into a standing mixer with a dough hook. Beat until satiny. Divide ball in half, wrap in plastic wrap and refrigerate both pieces.

2. **Make filling:** barely cover **1 cup dried boletus mushrooms** (porcini *or* ceps) with **water** in a small pot. Cover and simmer over low heat 15 minutes. Thinly slice **one large onion** and sauté in **2 tablespoons olive oil** over moderate heat. Rinse, then squeeze dry **1½ cups sauerkraut.** Add kraut to onions and continue to sauté. Add **oil as needed.** Drain mushrooms, reserving cooking liquid. Add mushrooms to frying pan and raise heat. Sauté until sauerkraut begins to brown. Boil mushroom liquid until it reduces to 3 to 4 tablespoons. Add liquid to frying pan, stir well and remove from heat. Set aside.

---

*Purchased Chinese dumpling wrappers may be used. If you omit the sour cream or use soy-based sour cream, this dinner will be vegan.

3. Peel and cut up **2 medium baking potatoes**. Boil in adequate **water** until tender. Discard water and shake pan over low heat to dry the potatoes. Use a potato masher to coarsely crush potatoes. Combine with mushrooms and kraut. Season with **salt** to taste, and generously with **fresh ground pepper**. Let cool.

4. **Make onion topping:** slice **2 large sweet onions**, preferably **Vidalia**, and sauté in **olive oil** over moderate heat for 10 to 15 minutes or until lightly caramelized. Set aside.

5. **Shape pierogies:** each refrigerated ball should yield 24 dumplings. You may use a pasta machine to gradually make a long thin sheet of dough. This may then be divided in squares, filling placed in each, edges brushed with **water**, and then folded in half to make triangles. Or the dough can be divided into 24 pieces and each rolled out into a separate round with a rolling pin to be filled, edges brushed with **water**, and folded into half rounds. A fork is perfect to press dumpling edges together. In either case, store the dumplings on **flour**-coated cookie sheets until dinnertime. Pierogies may also be frozen.

6. Cook the dumplings in lots of **salted boiling water** for 5 minutes, 5 to 6 per diner. Serve with the fried onions and **sour cream**. A salad of strong greens, such as **arugula** and **curly endive**, goes well with these pierogies.

*8 to 10 servings*

# kartofchin
### russian cheese and potato pies

You will need **russian red beans in plum sauce** and **pickled cabbage** if you want to serve Kartofchin as we do, for dinner. The cabbage needs three days to pickle. See recipes that follow.

1.  To make outer bread dough, combine in mixer: **3¼ cups unbleached all-purpose flour, 1 tablespoon dry yeast, 1½ cups milk, 2 teaspoons sugar, ½ teaspoon salt**, and a grating of **pepper**.

2.  In a small pot over low heat, barely melt **6 tablespoons butter**. Turn the warm (not hot!) butter into the mixer, and using a dough hook or a flat beater, mix the bread batter at low speed for about ten minutes, or until smooth and elastic. Add a couple of tablespoons more **flour** if bread seems sticky. Turn batter out into a floured bowl, cover with a cloth and let rise in a cool place (not a hot kitchen) for one hour.

3.  Meanwhile, wash **4 Idaho potatoes**. Cut in half crosswise, cover with water in a pot, and bring to a boil. Cook until just done. Peel while hot and turn into mixer (no need to wash it). Add **5 tablespoons butter** and **cheese**. The right cheese would be ¾ **pound bryndza**. It is very difficult to get, so we substitute **½ pound muenster** and ⅛ **pound each feta** and **cheddar**. Be sure to crumble the feta before adding it to the mixer. Add ¾ **teaspoon salt**, fresh grated **black pepper** and **1 egg**. Beat well. Let mixture stand 10 minutes to cool.

4. Turn bread dough out onto a floured board. Divide into 8 to 9 pieces. Use a rolling pin to flatten each into a 6″ circle. Shape potato cheese filling into 8 to 9 tennis ball-sized pieces. Place a ball of filling on each bread round. Pick up edges all around and gather together in pleats around the filling. Twist gathered edges like the top of a sack and then push down to flatten Kartofchin slightly.

5. Heat oven to 400°F. **Butter** a cookie sheet and place Kartofchin on it, leaving at least an inch between them. Top each with a little pat of **butter** and bake until lightly browned. You will be able to reheat them before you serve them.

6. Reheat Kartofchin and beans just before serving. Spoon beans out onto each plate. Cut individual **cabbage leaves** off the head of the **pickled cabbage**, and fold each into a flower-like shape. Serve with **kartofchin**.

*8 servings*

# russian red beans in plum sauce

A recipe from the former USSR state of Georgia.

1. The night before cooking, pick over **2 cups kidney beans**. Cover with **water** and leave overnight.

2. Drain water, cover with fresh **water** and bring to a simmer. Cook until tender.

3. In a bowl combine: **1½ teaspoons dried basil leaves**, crumbled, **¼ teaspoon cayenne pepper, 2 teaspoons salt, 1 small clove garlic**, crushed, **3 tablespoons fresh cilantro**, chopped, **2 teaspoons wine vinegar**, and **2 to 3 tablespoons damson plum jam** *or* **preserves** (we substitute a combination of Chinese plum sauce and our homemade elderberry jelly).

4. Drain most of the water from the beans (not all) and mix with seasonings in the bowl. This may be served hot or cold, and is a good accompaniment to **kartofchin** (see previous recipe).

*6 side dish servings*

# russian red pickled cabbage

1. You should prepare the pickled cabbage three to five days before you intend to serve Kartofchin.

2. Put **1 small (2 pound) green cabbage**, trimmed of its outer leaves if they are damaged, into a pot, cover with **water** and bring to a boil. Reduce heat and simmer, partially covered, 40 minutes.

3. Meanwhile, peel and dice **2 pounds beets**. Set aside. Coarsely chop **top leaves** from a **bunch of celery** and a few sprigs of **parsley**.

4. Add beets and greens to pot together with **2 cups red wine vinegar**, **1 teaspoon paprika**, and **2½ tablespoons salt**. Return to a boil.

5. Turn contents into a crock or plastic container. Cover with a heavy dinner plate and leave at room temperature several days, then refrigerate.

# potato cottage cheese dumplings
## with cabbage sauce

1. **Make cabbage sauce:** peel **1 medium onion** and chop coarsely. Sauté in a large sauce pan over moderately high heat in **1 tablespoon grapeseed oil.** Meanwhile, coarsely chop **½ head of cabbage (¾ pound)** and add to the onions when they are soft but not brown. Add more oil if necessary to cook the cabbage. Cook cabbage until somewhat browned. Add **1 quart water, 1 tablespoon salt, ½ teaspoon pepper, ¼ teaspoon caraway seed, 2 teaspoons vinegar, 1½ tablespoons agave syrup** and **1 tablespoon tamari.** Add **½ cup canned tomatoes.** Bring to a boil, adding more water if necessary to cover the cabbage. Turn down heat to a simmer. It should now cook for at least 2 hours. Cabbage sauce is easy to make but requires a good 3 hours of simmering before it develops its full flavor.

2. **Make dumplings:** wash and boil **3 small potatoes (¾ pound)** in their skins until soft. Peel and mash potatoes in a mixer while they are hot. Add to the mixer in this order: **½ stick sweet butter, 1½ teaspoons salt,** grating of fresh **nutmeg, 2 tablespoons freshly grated Parmesan cheese, 1½ cups cottage cheese, ¼ teaspoon pepper, 2 or 3 tablespoons** chopped **fresh dill,** and **1 egg.** Add **1½ cups unbleached white flour** and mix well. (Mixture should be moist but with enough flour to be slightly stiff. Do not add too much flour or dumplings will be heavy.) Refrigerate dumpling batter until ready to use.

3. Taste cabbage sauce for seasoning. If it is too sweet, add a little **lemon juice**; if too sour, more agave syrup. **Salt** and **tamari** may also be needed to develop flavor. If still not satisfactory, add a splash of **dry red wine** and let cook another hour or until it cooks into a well developed sweet and sour flavor.

4. When ready to serve, fill a large pot ⅓ full of **water** and add **1 tablespoon salt**. Bring to a boil. Dip a large spoon into the boiling water then into the dumpling mix to lift out an oval shape. Dip spoon into the pot and dumpling will slip off the spoon. Repeat. Plan about 5 to 6 dumplings per serving. Cover pot and turn heat to lowest simmer. Cook until dumplings have risen to the top and are puffed but are not beginning to fall apart. Use a slotted spoon over some absorbent paper to drain each dumpling before placing them in shallow soup bowls. Lightly **butter** dumplings. Spoon cabbage sauce around them and serve **sour cream** on the side.

*5 to 6 servings*

# four cheese macaroni

Slightly spicy, this version of the classic comfort food has ancho chile powder and jalapeño chiles added to it. Serve with a **crimson slaw with cranberries** (see following recipe).

1. Melt **6 tablespoons butter** in a saucepot. Add ⅓ **cup all-purpose flour**. Cook together, stirring, for a minute or two. Add **5 cups milk**. Whisk over high heat until mixture comes to a boil. Turn off heat.

2. Weigh: **10 oz. pepperjack cheese, 8 oz. Switzerland Swiss cheese** and **8 oz. cheddar** (mild or sharp as you prefer). Add to pot (no need to shred cheeses). Mince **1 to 2 jalapeño chilies** and add to pot. Cook, stirring, over low heat until cheeses melt. Set aside.

3. Cook **1 pound penne pasta** until barely done. Use a strainer to lift pasta into 8 individual ovenproof ramekins or one appropriately-sized oven casserole. Ladle cheese sauce over each one.

4. Mince **2 cloves garlic**. Sauté in **2 tablespoons grapeseed oil** in a small pan. Add **2 teaspoons ancho chile powder.*** When garlic is soft, add **1 cup dry breadcrumbs** and continue cooking, stirring, for a minute or two.

5. Scatter breadcrumb mixture over ramekins and top with ½ **cup Parmesan cheese**, grated.

6. Bake at 375°F for 15 to 20 minutes.

*8 servings*

---

*Or simply chili powder.

# crimson slaw with cranberries

1. Use a French chef's knife to shred ½ **head red cabbage**. Slice ½ **red onion** thinly and chop **3 scallions**. Combine vegetables with **6 oz. dried cranberries**.

2. Whisk together: ⅓ cup olive oil, 2 tablespoons red wine vinegar, 2 tablespoons sugar, ½ teaspoon black pepper, 1 teaspoon salt, ½ teaspoon ground cumin, and ¼ teaspoon dried mustard.

3. Pour dressing over cabbage and mix well. Refrigerate.

*6 servings*

WINTER

ROSE

143

# mushroom stroganoff

This easy stroganoff, from animal rights activist Esther Meckler, has exceptionally fine flavor.

1. Slice 1½ **pounds large button mushrooms.** Slice **1 large Spanish onion.** Turn into frying pan with **2 cloves crushed garlic** and **2 tablespoons grapeseed oil.** Fry over highest heat. Add **1 tablespoon** good quality **Hungarian paprika** and **1 teaspoon dried thyme.** Cook, stirring well, until mushrooms are well browned.

2. Add ½ **cup dry sherry, 1 tablespoon tomato paste, 2 bay leaves, ¼ cup tamari, 4 oz. cream cheese,** and **1 cup sour cream.** Bring to a simmer and finish seasoning with a little freshly ground black **pepper, 1 tablespoon lemon juice,** and a splash of **brandy.** If stroganoff is too thick, dilute with water.

3. Serve over cooked **egg noodles** with **poppy seeds** and chopped **straight leaf parsley.**

*4 servings*

# swiss cheese fondue

You will need a table burner and a casserole dish in which to cook fondue. The flameproof pottery casseroles specially made for fondue cooking are best.

1. **Prepare bread and vegetables:** cut **1 whole French** *or* **Italian bread** loaf into 1″ cubes, being sure each piece has crust on it. Arrange in a large bowl. Add **3 carrots**, scraped and cut into sticks, **1 bunch broccoli**, cut into flowerets with about 1″ of stem, **18 whole or halved fresh mushrooms, 2 apples** cut into wedges and cored but not peeled.

2. **Prepare fondue:** using a blender or food processor, shred **1 pound Switzerland Swiss cheese**, or even better, a mix of **Swiss** and **Gruyère**. Toss with ¼ **cup unbleached white flour**.

3. Put flameproof casserole dish on stove and add **2 cups white wine**. Spear **1 clove garlic**, peeled, on a fondue fork and bring wine and garlic to a simmer. Now add cheese handful by handful, stirring with a kitchen fork. Season to taste with **salt** and **pepper**. When cheese and wine are well blended and color and texture are smooth, add ¼ **cup Kirschwasser**. Don't substitute other liqueur if you don't have Kirsch. Discard garlic clove.

4. Bring casserole to table with bread and vegetables and give each diner a fondue fork, a plate, and a small salad. As the fondue cooks down, use fondue forks to scrape up the crust of toasted cheese on the bottom. Some of us think that part is best.

*4 servings*

# fallen chocolate soufflé cake

This delicious cake requires Valrhona chocolate and is meant to be served the day it is made.

1. Preheat oven to 375°. You will need an 8″ ungreased springform pan.

2. Melt **8 tablespoons sweet butter** with **8 oz. Vahlrona chocolate** in a covered saucepot over low heat.

3. Meanwhile, beat in a mixer at high speed for at least 5 minutes: **4 eggs**, **1 yolk**, a splash **Grand Marnier** (optional), **¼ teaspoon salt**, **1 teaspoon vanilla**, and scant **½ cup sugar**.

4. Whisk chocolate. Turn into a bowl. Pour egg mixture over chocolate. Sift **2 tablespoons flour** over it, and fold all together. Batter will not blend thoroughly; don't overdo the mixing. Pour into ungreased springform pan and place in oven. Set timer for 25 minutes. At the end of that time, look at cake. It is done when it is no longer jiggly in the middle, and may need 5 minutes more baking time. Remove from oven and cool on a rack for 15 minutes. Expect the cake to fall.

5. Serve with **whipped cream** to 6 diners.

*6 servings*

WINTER

# bûche de noël

Noel's birthday cake.

1. In a small pot, melt **7 oz. semi-sweet chocolate**—a good variety, like Valrhona, in ¼ **cup coffee** over low heat, covered. When melted, whisk in **7 tablespoons sweet butter**. Set aside.

2. Separate **6 eggs**. Beat whites until rounded peaks form, add **2 tablespoons sugar** and beat until stiff. Turn out into a large bowl. Preheat oven to 350°F.

3. Turn yolks into same mixer. Beat to ribbon stage with scant **1 cup sugar** (when you lift beater, batter falls off in ribbons). Add chocolate mixture, ⅔ **cup flour**, and **1 tablespoon Kahlùa**.

4. Butter a jelly roll pan and line with waxed paper.

5. Fold egg whites into chocolate mixture and spread in prepared pan. Bake until just done—about 10 minutes.

6. Meanwhile, sift **unsweetened cocoa** onto a dishtowel. Turn cake out onto towel. Peel off waxed paper and use cloth to roll up cake. Lift roll onto racks and let cool.

7. Beat **2½ cups heavy cream** and **3 tablespoons Kahlùa** until stiff. Refrigerate.

8. **Make chocolate ganache:** combine **1 cup semi-sweet chocolate**, **3 tablespoons unsweetened cocoa powder**, ¼ **cup grapeseed oil**, **3 tablespoons maple syrup**, and **1 teaspoon vanilla extract**. Place in a warm place (such as above the stove on a shelf). Do not stir. When chocolate melts, stir vigorously. Mixture will thicken.

148

9.  When cake is cool, unroll and spread with whipped cream. Re-roll. Cut the 2 ends off of the log diagonally so that they can be placed on the side of the log to look like a tree branch. A tray is best to hold the "Bûche de Noël." Spread with ganache, sift confectioner's sugar over, and chill.

An alternative filling is **creme praline**—make **praline** (see index). Make the **buttercream frosting** recipe from the **hazelnut torte** but use no sugar (see index). Grind praline in the food processor and sweeten the butter cream frosting to taste with it. Use this as both filling and frosting for a very elegant Bûche de Noël. Sieve **unsweetened cocoa** over the top.

*one log-shaped cake roll*

HANNAH AND GRACIE

# wiley's olive oil-
# sweet potato cake
### with penuche frosting

This delicate spice cake contains no milk or butter. It is lactose-free. From
Wiley Mullins.

1. **Make cake:** peel and grate sweet potatoes to yield
   **4 cups.** Turn into a bowl. Toss with ¾ **cup unbleached
   white flour.** Set aside.

2. In a large bowl, stir together with a dry whisk:
   **3½ cups unbleached white flour, ¾ teaspoon
   baking soda, 1 tablespoon baking powder,
   ¾ teaspoon salt, 1 teaspoon ground nutmeg,
   ¾ teaspoon cinnamon, ¼ teaspoon cloves,** and
   **½ teaspoon ground cardamom.** Set aside.

3. Separate **eggs:** beat **4 whites** with ½ **teaspoon
   cream of tartar** until stiff. Turn out into a bowl. Set
   yolks aside—you will need **2 more.** Preheat oven to
   350°F.

4. In unwashed mixer, combine **1½ cups extra virgin
   olive oil, 1½ cups sugar,** and **1 teaspoon vanilla
   extract.** Beat well. Add **1 tablespoon lemon rind**
   and **2 tablespoons lemon juice.** Also add the **6 yolks**
   and ⅔ **cup soymilk.** When mixture is well blended,
   stir in sweet potatoes and dry ingredients. Finally, fold
   in egg whites.

5. Turn batter into an ungreased tube pan. Bake 1 hour
   15 minutes or until cake tester comes out dry. Cool
   on rack. Use knife to cut between pan and cake.
   Turn out.

6. **Make penuche frosting:** lightly roast **1 cup pecans** in a 300°F toaster oven for 10 minutes. Set aside. In a small pot combine **⅔ cup dark brown sugar**, **⅓ cup coconut oil**, and **⅓ cup coconut milk**. Bring to a boil, stirring constantly for 2 to 3 minutes. Remove from heat. Add **1½ tablespoons orange zest** and **1 teaspoon vanilla extract**. Stir vigorously until cool. Sift **¾ cup confectioner's sugar** over frosting mixture and stir or beat with a whisk until smooth and thick. Coarsely chop pecans and stir into frosting. Spoon or pour over cake (penuche will not cover all of it).

*makes one 10" cake*

JENNIFER

# gâteau grand marnier

1. Preheat oven to 300°F. Grease kugelhof or any 10″ tube pan thoroughly, and dust with flour. Grate rind of **2 oranges** and set aside.

2. Whisk or sift together **3¼ cups unbleached white flour, 1 tablespoon baking powder, ¾ teaspoon baking soda, and ¾ teaspoon salt.**

3. In mixer, cream **¾ pound unsalted butter.** Add **1⅓ cups sugar** and reserved orange rind and mix well. Add **3 eggs** and beat well. Add **1½ tablespoons Grand Marnier liqueur.** Now stir in about ¼ of flour mix. Measure out **1½ cups buttermilk** and stir in about ⅓ of it. Continue alternating wet and dry ingredients, ending with dry, and finally gently stir in **¾ cup chopped walnuts.**

4. Turn batter into prepared pan and bake 1 hour 20 minutes or until cake withdraws slightly from sides. Cool thoroughly in pan on rack.

5. Meanwhile, squeeze oranges and measure juice. You will need **1 cup orange juice.** Combine with **½ cup sugar** in a pot and simmer 5 minutes. Remove from stove and add ⅓ cup **Grand Marnier.**

6. Turn cake out onto dish and pour syrup over cake and into well in center. It will be absorbed by the cake.

7. Optional: beat **2 cups heavy cream** stiff with **2 tablespoons Grand Marnier** and serve as a topping.

*one 10″ cake*

# frangelico chocolate cake

Adapted from Megan Craig's Amaretto Cake.

1. Oil and lightly flour a 10″ Bundt pan. Heat oven to 350°F. Use a dry whisk to stir together **2 cups all-purpose flour**, **½ teaspoon salt**, and **1 teaspoon baking soda**. Set aside. Melt **6 oz. semisweet chocolate** (preferably Valhrona) over very low heat in a covered pot. Set aside to cool.

2. Use an electric mixer to cream **1 cup (2 sticks) unsalted butter** together with **¾ cup organic white sugar** and **¾ cup packed light brown sugar**. When blended and fluffy, add **4 eggs**, one at a time. Now add the chocolate and stir well.

3. In a 2 cup measuring cup, combine **1 cup milk**, **2 teaspoons vanilla extract**, **1½ teaspoons almond extract**, and **¼ cup Frangelico liqueur**.

4. Add approximately ⅓ cup of the flour mix to butter and blend briefly. Now add half the milk mix and stir. Repeat, ending with flour. Don't overmix. Turn into prepared pan. Bake 45 to 50 minutes, or until cake tester comes out clean. Cool pan on rack 20 minutes. Turn out onto plate. Serve with **whipped cream**.

*one 10″ cake*

WINTER

# praline cheesecake

1. Soften **1½ pounds cream cheese**.

2. **Make praline:** put **3 cups almonds** *or* **pecans** in a 350°F oven and toast until walnut-colored. Lightly oil a cookie sheet. Combine **3 cups sugar** and **1¼ cups water** in a pot and bring to a boil without stirring. Swirl pot to melt sugar crystals. When syrup is clear, cover pot and boil several minutes. Uncover and continue boiling until syrup turns caramel brown. Immediately add roasted nuts and turn out onto greased cookie sheet. Be very careful, since pot and cookie sheet are very hot! Let praline cool 20 minutes and then grind it in food processor or blender. This amount makes much more than you will need for this cheesecake. It stores well in a covered containers.

3. Use a food processor to pulverize **½ cup graham crackers**. Add **2 tablespoons soft butter** and turn machine on. Use blended mix to pat out a bottom crust in a 10″ springform pan. Set aside. Preheat oven to 350°F.

4. Separate **6 eggs**, whites into mixer and yolks into a small bowl. Add **2** more **whites** to mixer with a **pinch** each **salt** and **cream of tartar**. Beat until stiff. Turn out into a large bowl.

5. In mixer, beat **1 cup heavy cream** stiff and turn out into another bowl.

6. Beat softened cream cheese in mixer. Add 1¼ cups sugar, 1 teaspoon vanilla extract, 2 tablespoons lemon juice, and 1 tablespoon cornstarch. While mixing, add yolks one at a time. Beat well, scrape down, and beat again.

7. Fold whipped cream into cream cheese mixture, then fold in beaten whites. Turn into prepared pan and bake 1 hour. Cake should be fully puffed and not at all brown. Now bake 1 hour at 275°F. Cake should be a light tan. Turn off oven and open door. Let cake stay like this 2 hours. Sprinkle top heavily with praline powder.

8. Chill at least 3 hours before serving.

*one 10″ cake*

PAT SHEA

# brandied bread pudding

A good use for stale homemade bread.

1. **Make bread pudding:** you will need enough stale bread to measure **5 cups** once it is cut into cubes. Rye and whole wheat are not as good for ths recipe as oatmeal or white bread. Put the cubes in a buttered pan large enough to hold the pudding (it should hold at least 12 cups of liquid). Cover with **5½ cups milk** and let rest 2 hours or more.

2. Rinse **1 cup raisins**, gently squeeze moisture out, and barely cover them with **brandy** in a small bowl. Set aside.

3. Melt **4 tablespoons sweet butter** in a small pot. In a bowl, whisk together **5 eggs**, ⅓ **cup sugar**, **1½ teaspoons vanilla extract**, and ¾ **teaspoon salt**. Stir cooled butter into egg mixture.

4. Mix raisins and brandy into eggs and pour over bread and milk. Stir well. Grate some **fresh nutmeg** over pudding. Bake at 325°F about 1 hour or until custard is set.

5. **Make brandy sauce** to serve with bread pudding: melt **8 tablespoons butter** in a small pot. Set aside. In another pot whisk **2 eggs**, ½ **cup sugar**, and ½ **cup brandy**. Cook over moderate to low heat, whisking constantly, until mixture thickens a little the way a hollandaise sauce would. This will take about 10 minutes. Add **melted butter** gradually, still whisking. Remove from heat and cool. If the brandied sauce seems too thick, thin with a little **cream**. Refrigerate.

6. Bread pudding is best served warm. Individual servings can be reheated in a toaster oven. Serve in a saucer with brandied sauce around it.

*9 to 10 servings*

Krystyna

# bourbon sweet potato pecan pie

A Southern treat.

1. Make **processor pie crust** (see index) and roll out and fit a deep glass pie dish with crust. Weight with foil and beans and pre bake at 375°F until crust is set but not brown. Remove foil and beans and let crust cool.

2. Meanwhile, bake a **sweet potato**. You will need **1½ cups**, so estimate accordingly. When sweet potato is soft, peel (measure) and turn into a food processor. Melt **3 tablespoons unsalted butter**. Add to processor and purée. Be sure mix is not too hot to cook the eggs—and so when ready, add **2 eggs, 2 egg yolks, ¼ teaspoon nutmeg, ¼ teaspoon salt, 1 teaspoon vanilla extract, 3 tablespoons brown sugar** and **3 tablespoons Kentucky bourbon**. Process, stir down and blend again. Add **⅓ cup heavy cream**. Mix.

3. Heat oven to 350°F. Sprinkle pie shell with **2 tablespoons brown sugar**. Pour in contents of processor and bake pie until set: 20 to 30 minutes.

4. Don't wash the food processor. Add **2 tablespoons butter, ⅓ cup sugar, 2 eggs, ¾ teaspoon vanilla extract, pinch salt** and **⅔ cup dark agave nectar** (or dark corn syrup). Blend well.

5. Remove pie from oven. Raise heat to 400°F. Add processor contents. Top carefully with **pecans**— approximately **2 cups**. Return pie to oven and bake until custard is set.

6. Melt a little **unsweetened chocolate** over very low heat. Drizzle streaks of chocolate over cooled pie.

*one pie*

SELMA AND CAROLANNE

# baked orange custard

1. Preheat oven to 325°F. In a mixer combine **3 eggs,
   1 cup heavy cream,** grated **rind of 2 oranges,
   1 cup fresh squeezed orange juice, 2½ tablespoons
   honey** *or* **agave syrup,** and **⅛ teaspoon salt.** Mix
   enough to blend eggs and honey, but don't overbeat.

2. Pour into 5 or 6 custard cups and place in baking pan.
   Place in oven and add enough water to the pan to
   come halfway up the sides of the custard cups.

3. Bake until knife tip comes out clean, about 40 to 45
   minutes. Cool and refrigerate. Serve with **heavy cream.**

*5 to 6 servings*

BUTTERNUT SQUASH SOUP
WITH CHESTNUT CHEESE DUMPLINGS

KARTOFCHIN

Zucchini Flan with Salad

CHOUX PASTE GNOCCHI

ZUCCHINI LATKES

PASTA WITH ARTICHOKE, ASPARAGUS SAUCE AND GREMOLATA

MOUSSAKA WITH BREAD

WILEY'S OLIVE OIL, SWEET POTATO CAKE
WITH PENUCHE FROSTING

BOURBON SWEET POTATO PECAN PIE

Butterscotch Pudding

# butterscotch pudding

This superb pudding is baked like a custard.

1. In a medium-sized pot, warm **1 cup milk** and **2 cups heavy cream** together with ¼ **cup packed dark brown sugar**. In a larger, heavy pot, combine ¾ **cup white sugar** and ¼ **cup water**. Bring to a boil and cook to form a caramel. When sugar is golden brown, remove from heat and add milk mix gradually. It will boil up suddenly and violently, which is why the caramel must be started in the larger pot. Be sure heat is off and all is combined. Set aside.

2. Separate eggs; you will need **6 yolks**. Reserve whites for other purposes. Slowly whisk hot milk into yolks, being careful to not curdle them. Add **1 teaspoon Kosher salt** and **1 teaspoon vanilla extract**. Stir well.

3. Ladle into 6 ovenproof custard cups set in a pan. Fill the pan halfway with water, being careful not to get any in the pudding dishes. Bake at 325°F for about 30 minutes, or until no longer wobbly. Let cool; chill.

4. Serve with **crème fraîche** *or* **whipped cream**.

*6 servings*

# brown rice pudding

1. In a large shallow baking pan, combine ⅓ **cup brown rice** (we use short grain), **dash salt**, grated **rind of 1 lemon, 1 teaspoon vanilla,** and **1 quart milk.***

2. Bake at 325°F for 1½ to 2 hours, stirring occasionally. The pudding will repeatedly get a brown skin which should be stirred in. About 10 minutes before it is done, stir in a **splash of brandy, 2½ tablespoons honey,** and **¼ cup raisins.**

3. Remove from oven when it still seems soft and loose. It will thicken up as it cools. Serve with **heavy cream.**

*6 to 8 servings*

*If you like a richer pudding, substitute 1 cup heavy cream and 3 cups milk for the 1 quart milk.

# lemon tart

This pie filling is a less sweet version of British lemon curd.

1. Preheat oven to 400°F. Roll out **pie crust** (see index) for 1 pie pan. Prick around bottom of crust with fork tines. Use foil and dried beans, lentils, etc. to weight down crust while it bakes. When edges start to brown (about 5 to 10 minutes), carefully remove beans and foil. Turn oven down to 375°F and continue baking until crust is golden brown (about 10 minutes more). Remove from oven and let cool.

2. Cut **1½ sticks sweet butter** into small pieces. Set aside.

3. In stainless steel pot, combine **6 whole eggs, 5 yolks, ⅓ cup honey,** and grated **rind** and **juice** of **3 lemons.** Whisk together over medium-low heat until well mixed. Add the butter and continue whisking until mixture starts to thicken. Cook and whisk about another 30 seconds until mixture is creamy and slightly thick. Do not overcook.

4. Remove from heat and whisk for another minute. Set aside to cool about 10 minutes, then pour into baked pie shell. Place pie in refrigerator until set up (about 2 hours).

5. Before serving, top pie with **honey whipped cream:** whip together until stiff **1 cup heavy cream, 1½ teaspoons honey,** and **¾ teaspoon vanilla extract.**

*one tart*

**WINTER**

# loukoumades

Traditional Greek doughnuts made with yeast. We don't deep fry often, but on some snowy winter days, we deep fry these made with choux paste. For the appropriate flavor loukoumades require Hymettus honey—the kind bees make from the wild thyme of Mt. Hymettus. It will be available in Greek grocery stores.

1. In a pot bring ¼ **pound butter** to a boil with **1 cup water**. Add **1 cup flour** and beat hard with a wooden spoon until dough forms a ball. Turn dough into a mixer.

2. Immediately add **4 eggs**, one at a time, beating hard after each addition. Add ¼ **teaspoon salt**.

3. Heat **grapeseed oil** to 375°F. A wok is a good deep fat frying pot since is uses less oil than a soup pot. You will need **2 to 3 cups oil**.

4. Prepare syrup: warm ½ **cup honey**—a blend of **Hymettus** and **a bland honey** is best—with **1½ teaspoons lemon juice**.

5. Scoop out 1-inch-sized balls to deep fry. They should have room to roll over by themselves. When puffed and brown, remove to shallow bowls. Sprinkle with **cinnamon** and serve honey syrup on the side.

*4 to 5 generous servings*

# butterball cookies

A classic winter holiday cookie. Noel's mother's favorite.

1. Preheat oven to 350°F. Bring **1 cup unsalted butter** to room temperature.

2. Whisk together **2 cups flour, ¼ cup sugar, ½ teaspoon salt**.

3. Use the flat beater of a mixer to blend together the butter, **2 teaspoon vanilla, 2 cups chopped walnuts**, and the flour mixture.

4. Roll the dough into small balls in the palm of your hand. Place on a cookie sheet and bake for 25 minutes, or until brown on the bottom. The rest of the cookie will be light. Remove from oven and cool completely. Dust generously with **powdered sugar**.

*30 cookies*

# carob almond cookies

1. Chop **1 cup almonds** in food processor or blender. Cream together **1 stick sweet butter** and **½ cup honey**. Add **2 eggs, 1 teaspoon vanilla extract, ⅓ cup carob powder, ⅔ cup whole wheat flour** and **½ teaspoon baking powder**. Add **3 tablespoons milk** and the **chopped almonds**. Drop by spoonfuls on a greased cookie sheet and bake at 350°F for 20 minutes. You will have 12 large cookies.

# lemon squares

1. Heat oven to 350°F. Melt ½ **pound unsalted butter** over low heat.

2. Use a dry whisk to stir together **1¾ cup flour, ½ cup confectioner's sugar** and **¼ teaspoon salt**. Stir in the butter, and pat out this pastry into a 9″ x 13″ pan. Bake 20 minutes.

3. Meanwhile, beat **4 eggs** together with **1⅔ cup sugar, ¼ cup flour, ¼ teaspoon salt, ½ teaspoon vanilla extract**, grated **rind of 2 lemons** and between **⅓ to ½ cup lemon juice.**

4. Pour egg-lemon mixture over pastry and bake 20 to 25 minutes longer, or until custard is set.

5. Remove pan from oven and cool on a rack for 10 minutes. Cut into squares before pastry is entirely cooled. Sift **confectioner's sugar** over the top.

*makes approximately 18 two inch square cookies*

# kourabiedes

A Greek cookie, from Alexandra Pousoula.

1. You will need mastica (gum mastic) to flavor this cookie authentically. Buy it in a Greek grocery store. A few days before you make the cookies, place **a few pieces of mastica** in **1 cup confectioner's sugar.**

2. Bring ½ **pound sweet butter** to room temperature. Finely chop ½ **cup walnuts** and ½ **cup almonds** (a food processor works well for this). Set aside.

3. Beat the butter in a mixer until whipped. Add **3 tablespoons** of the flavored **confectioner's sugar** (remove the pieces of the mastic first), **1 egg yolk, 1 tablespoon Ouzo** (*or* brandy), ½ **teaspoon vanilla extract,** ½ **teaspoon baking powder,** the nuts and **2¼ cups unbleached white flour.** Beat until mixture is well blended and forms a ball. Preheat oven to 375°F.

4. Divide dough and shape into long ropes. Cut small pieces from each rope and roll into thin pieces. Shape into crescents (you will have over 5 dozen). Place in oven and bake until light brown.

5. Sift mastic-flavored **confectioner's sugar** generously over the hot cookies while in the pan.

*makes about 5 dozen cookies*

# chocolate amazons

Adapted from *The Viennese Pastry Cookbook* by Lily Joss Reich.

1. Preheat oven to 325°F. Grease a cookie sheet with **coconut oil** or **butter**.

2. Blanch **30 almonds** and remove skins. Set aside.

3. In food processor, finely grind almonds to 1¾ cup. Using shredding blade (or box grater) grate 1½ oz. **semi-sweet chocolate**.

4. In mixer, beat **3 egg whites** until they reach soft peak stage. Add ½ **cup organic sugar** and beat a bit more until mix is shiny and sugar is dissolved.

5. Gently fold in ground nuts and chocolate; drop by spoonfuls onto greased cookie sheet and top each with a blanched **almond**.

6. Turn oven down to 300°F to bake, about 25 minutes or until cookie is firm on the surface. Remove from oven, let cool a bit then lift off pan with a spatula.

*makes 30 cookies*

# scotch shortbread

From Rachel Portnoy. Rachel spent time studying in England and came back with this recipe, quantities measured by weight. We converted to cups. Semolina flour yields good flavor and texture. It is available in Italian groceries and health food stores.

1. If available, use a mixer with a flat beater to cream together **6 oz.** (12 tablespoons) **unsalted butter** and ¼ **cup sugar.** When well blended add **1½ cups unbleached white flour** and ½ **cup semolina flour.** Add a **pinch salt** also. Blend thoroughly.

2. Heat oven to 300°F. Pat out shortbread in a heatproof glass pan. It should be quite thin, so a 12″ round pan would be best.

3. Bake for 30 to 45 minutes or until golden brown. Remove from oven and score immediately to make pie-shaped pieces.

WINTER

# cream cheese cookies

From Fay Davidson.

1. Use a mixer, pastry blender, or your fingertips to thoroughly blend **1 stick (4 oz.) sweet butter**, **3 oz. cream cheese**, and **1 cup flour**. When well integrated but not overmixed, wrap in waxed paper or foil and refrigerate.

2. Fillings for these cookies can be any jam, preserve, or chopped nuts. Try to find **fruit only-sweetened strawberry** *or* **raspberry preserves**, or cook **dried apricots** and sweeten them with **agave syrup** and purée for a filling. Or chop **walnuts** and **almonds**, flavor with **cinnamon** and mix with enough **agave syrup** to a pasty consistency. Preheat oven to 375°F.

3. Roll out small portions of the dough on a floured board. Keep remaining dough refrigerated. Cut out circles using a floured glass or large round cookie cutter and place a dab of fruit preserves on each round. Pinch edges together to make a three-cornered cookie. Press edges together to prevent cookies from opening in the oven. If you are using the nut mixture, roll out dough into a long narrow rectangle and place filling along the edge in a thick pencil line. Roll dough over two times like a jelly roll and cut off 1″ sized cookies. Save scraps of dough to re-roll. This dough gets tough with too much re-working, so try to keep re-working it at a minimum.

4. Bake cookies until light brown.

*makes 4 to 5 dozen*

# linzer tartlets

From *The Viennese Pastry Cookbook*. Traditionally half of these cookies are cut with a biscuit cutter and the other half with a doughnut cutter. After baking they are made into a jam-filled sandwich topped with confectioner's sugar. We like them plain best.

1. Finely grind **2½ cups unblanched almonds** and grate the **rind** of **1 (organic) lemon.**

2. In a medium bowl whisk together **1¼ cups flour,** **½ cup sugar, pinch** of **salt, pinch** of **cinnamon** and **pinch** of **cloves** and combine with the almond-lemon mixture.

3. Cut ½ **pound sweet butter** (cold) into small pieces and work into the flour-nut mixture by hand until the dough is smooth and all the ingredients are picked up. Divide dough in half, wrap in wax paper and refrigerate for 30 minnutes.

4. Preheat oven to 325°F.

5. Roll out first ball of dough between 2 sheets of wax or parchment paper to approximately ⅛″ thickness. Use a biscuit cutter to cut out cookies and transfer them to a cookie sheet. Reroll scraps and repeat until finished. Proceed the same way with the second half of the dough. Bake 12 to 15 minutes or until very lightly browned.

*makes approximately 20 cookies*

WINTER

# Spring

## Soups

## Salads

## Entrees

# DESSERTS

# carrot and buttermilk soup

From Sonja Bay.

1. Peel and chop **2 pounds carrots** and **1 large onion** by hand or in food processor. Sauté in soup pot in **1¼ stick sweet butter**. When vegetables start to stick to bottom of pot it will be necessary to stir and scrape often. Brown well (this is the secret to this soup), but do not burn.

2. When vegetables are quite brown, barely cover with **water**, add **¼ teaspoon ground cloves** and simmer, covered, until very tender.

3. Purée mixture in blender or food processor, adding **¼ cup flour** and **⅔ cup heavy cream**.

4. Return to pot. Add **1⅓ cups buttermilk** and **2⅔ cups milk**. If the soup seems too thick, add water. Add **fresh ground pepper, 1 teaspoon salt**, and simmer, covered, for 10 minutes.

5. Add the **juice of ½ lemon, ½ teaspoon fresh rosemary**, chopped (optional) and **1 tablespoon fresh dill**, chopped. Herbs must be fresh.

6. Taste and judge whether more salt and/or lemon is desired.

*8 servings*

**SPRING**

# knaidel soup

Matzah meal dumplings in chicken broth are traditionally served at Passover meals. They are usually made with chicken fat. We make them with butter.

1. **Prepare soup:** make a rich vegetable broth by placing **3½ quarts water** in a soup kettle. Add **1 large unpeeled onion, 2 carrots**, scraped and cut into thirds, **3 outside stalks of celery** as well as the inside leaves, **1 parsley root**, if available (if not, add 1 bunch of straight leaf parsley), **1 parsnip**, scraped and cut into thirds, **2 bay leaves**, and **½ bunch dill**. Bring to a boil and simmer for at least 1 hour, or until the vegetables are very soft and have yielded their flavor to the broth.

2. Place a colander in a bowl or large bucket and pour soup over. Use a potato masher to extract liquid from the spent vegetables and then discard them. Return soup to pot. Flavor it with ⅓ **cup tamari**. To finish soup, cut **4 peeled carrots** into matchstick pieces, and cook briefly in the broth until done. Set soup aside.

3. **Make knaidel:** in a mixer, cream **8 tablespoons softened unsalted butter**. Add **5 eggs**, one at a time, a grating of nutmeg, **1½ teaspoons salt**, and **¼ cup parsley**, chopped fine. Gradually add **matzah meal**. You will need between **1 to 1½ cups**. Mixture should seem soft and just slightly thickened. Turn into a bowl and refrigerate.

4. Before serving, bring a saucepot of **water** to a boil. Moisten your hands and roll walnut-sized knaidel balls. Drop them into the boiling water and immediately lower the temperature to a simmer. Cover pot and cook 5 to 10 minutes. Test one knaidel by eating it to see if it is cooked.

5. Reheat soup and serve each diner a bowl with 2 knaidel and chopped fresh **dill** *or* **parsley**.

*8 to 10 servings*

URBAN OAKS SEEDLING SALE

# avgolemono soup

Soup based on chicken stock is part of the cuisines of many different ethnic groups. In each of its forms it stirs memories of the people for whom it has been a staple. Most of the flavor of these soups comes from the vegetables and herbs used to season them, so we make the soups without the chicken. This version is Greek, and is delicious hot or cold.

1. Make a broth by placing **1 large unpeeled onion** in a pot. Add **3½ quarts water, 2 carrots**, scraped and cut into thirds, **3 outside stalks of celery**, plus **inside leaves, 1 parsley root**, scraped, if available (this lends wonderful flavor to the soup), or **1 bunch straight leaf parsley, 1 parsnip**, scraped and cut into thirds, and **several bay leaves**. Cover and cook for an hour or so. This will produce a broth that is like that in the old "stone soup" story. You will find that the vegetables and herbs make this soup fragrant and flavorful. When all are soft, turn into a colander placed over a large bowl or container. Use a potato masher to press down on the cooked vegetables to release as much flavored liquid as possible. Discard contents of this colander and return broth to pot.

2. To make the soup taste "chicken-y," add ¼ **cup nutritional yeast** (available in health food stores) and **½ cup tamari**. Return to a simmer.

3. Meanwhile, clean and slice **2½ cups leeks** and dice **2 cups celery**. Sauté in **2 to 3 tablespoons butter** *or* **oil** until wilted and golden. Add some broth to the pan and stir together. Then turn into a blender and purée. Add this purée to the soup pot.

4. Whisk **4 whole eggs** in a large bowl until foamy. Add ½ **cup lemon juice**, freshly squeezed. Gradually ladle hot soup into egg mixture, stirring constantly. The eggs should thicken the soup a little without curdling. Remove from heat and stir until all danger of curdling is past. Set soup aside.

5. In a separate pot, cook **1 cup orzo** (rice-shaped pasta) in **boiling water** until tender. Drain; run cold water over orzo, then add to soup. Correct seasoning. It is likely you will need ½ **to 1 teaspoon salt**, and it may be desirable to add more tamari or lemon juice to season soup properly.

6. To serve, either reheat soup carefully, stirring constantly, or serve well-chilled. In either case, chopped **fresh dill** is the essential garnish.

*10 to 12 servings*

**SPRING**

# asparagus soup

1. Break off the top three to four inches of **6 pounds asparagus** and reserve. Wash stalk bases and put into soup kettle. Add **1½ quarts water** and **1 tablespoon salt**. Bring to a boil and simmer until stalks are very soft.

2. Use a food processor or blender to purée stalks and liquid in several batches. Each batch will also have to be turned into a colander or sturdy strainer over a bowl. Press down hard on the pulp to extract the liquid and discard the stringy fiber that remains.

3. In soup pot, melt **1½ sticks unsalted butter.** Add **2 cloves garlic,** crushed, and sauté a few minutes. Add **¾ cup flour** and cook flour and butter mixture until well blended. Add **¾ cup heavy cream** and the stock from the asparagus stalks. Bring to a boil and season with grated **nutmeg, dash Tabasco,** **1 tablespoon lemon juice,** pinch **dried marjoram,** and **1 tablespoon tamari.** Taste and add **salt** and **pepper** as needed.

4. Cut reserved asparagus tips into ½″ pieces. When soup is seasoned and has simmered a few minutes, add asparagus tips and cook 2 to 3 minutes only. Serve immediately. To reheat, gently warm only as much as will be eaten at once.

*8 to 10 servings*

# artichoke mushroom soup

1. Trim **3 artichokes** and place in pot. Add **water** to come halfway up the artichokes. Cook until a sample leaf tastes tender. Remove (save cooking liquid) and let cool.

2. Remove leaves from the artichokes and discard choke. Use a serrated knife to scrape flesh off leaves and set aside. Dice the cleaned **artichoke bottoms**.

3. Boil the **artichoke water** with the **stems of ½ pound button mushrooms**. Slice the tops of the mushrooms and set aside.

4. Melt ½ **stick sweet butter** in a soup kettle. Add **1 clove garlic**, crushed, and the sliced mushrooms and sauté till well browned. Add fresh grated **nutmeg, salt**, and **pepper**. Add ⅓ **cup flour** and stir together thoroughly.

5. Add ⅔ **cup heavy cream, 2 teaspoons lemon juice, 1 tablespoon tamari**, and strained artichoke broth. Add scraped artichoke leaves and diced bottoms. Correct seasoning.

*6 to 8 servings*

**SPRING**

# creamed spinach soup

From Diane Kerner.

1. Wash **2 pounds fresh spinach**. Cook in the water that clings to the leaves in a stainless steel pot. Don't overcook. Remove from heat and purée. Set aside.

2. Meanwhile, peel and slice **2 medium onions**. Sauté in **3 tablespoons sweet butter**. Add **3 tablespoons unbleached white flour** and cook together for a couple of minutes. Add **2 cups milk** and bring to a boil whisking constantly. Remove from heat and purée.

3. Combine the puréed spinach and white sauce in pot; add **2 cups milk**, **½ teaspoon salt, fresh ground pepper**, grated **nutmeg**, and **½ tablespoon chopped fresh dill**, if available. Bring to a boil. This soup is best fresh and not overcooked. If you must reheat it, do not reheat more than once and be as brief as possible. Be sure to use a stainless steel pot. This soup is good chilled, too.

*4 to 6 servings*

# scandinavian dried fruit soup

We are all hungry for fresh fruit when winter is over but it is still too early for spring fruits. Here is a dried fruit soup for a warm day in Spring.

1. Dice **1½ cups dried apricots, 1 cup dried prunes,** and trim cores and dice **2 cups dried apples.** Turn into a stainless steel pot, and cover with **10 cups water.** Let stand 30 minutes.

2. Add **2 whole sticks cinnamon.** Slice ½ **lemon** thinly. Discard seeds. Add lemon slices with **1 teaspoon ground cardamom** and ⅓ **cup quick-cooking tapioca.** Bring to a boil and simmer, stirring occasionally, for about 10 minutes. Turn off heat.

3. Add ¼ **cup raisins** and ¼ **cup currants** to hot soup. Season with **1 scant teaspoon salt.** Cool, chill.

4. If soup is too thick at serving time, dilute with **water** *or* **apple juice.** Serve with **sour cream** if you like.

*7 to 8 servings*

**SPRING**

# fresh pea soup
# with herb dumplings

1. **Prepare dumplings first:** bring ⅔ cup water,
   ½ **stick sweet butter,** and ½ **teaspoon salt** to a boil
   in a pot. Add ⅔ **cup flour** and beat with a wooden
   spoon until mixture is smooth and thick. Remove
   from heat and add **2 large** *or* **3 small eggs,** one at
   a time, beating vigorously until each one is mixed
   into the batter. A mixer does this easiest, but it can
   be done by hand. Season dumpling batter with **fresh
   grated nutmeg** and **pepper** and **2 tablespoons
   chopped fresh herbs** such as **garlic leaves, chives,
   savory,** *or* **thyme.** Taste to be sure seasoning
   is adequate.

2. Bring a pot of **salted water** to a boil. Dip a spoon
   into the boiling water and scoop out an oval of
   dumpling batter. Place spoon in the boiling water
   until dumpling slips off. Repeat, but don't crowd
   dumplings. Cover pot and turn to lowest simmer.
   Cook about 5 minutes or until somewhat puffed.
   Drain on absorbent paper while preparing soup. You
   should get 16 small dumplings.

3. **Prepare soup:** bring 1½ **quarts water** to a boil
   and add **3 pounds freshly shelled** *or* **frozen peas,**
   reserving ½ cup peas for garnish. Barely cook; 1 to 2
   minutes of boiling is plenty. Add **2 cups cold water** to
   stop cooking.

4. Purée soup in a food processor or blender.

5. Melt **1 stick sweet butter** in a pot and add **½ cup flour**. Stir well together a few minutes to cook flour and gradually add pea purée. Finish seasoning by adding **1 cup dry white wine, 2 teaspoons salt, fresh ground pepper,** and a **dash of Tabasco**.

6. **Serve soup with dumplings:** add dumplings to soup and bring to a boil just once before serving. Overcooking will make this fresh and simple soup taste and look like a split pea soup. It should stay a fresh and minty green. Top each serving with **fresh ground pepper** and the reserved peas.

*8 servings*

YUKA AND KATE

# fay davidson's egg salad

Selma's mother made hard-boiled eggs and mashed them with onion, olive oil, salt, and pepper. No mayo necessary. Here's a slight revision: easier to digest because of coconut oil.

1. Place **3 eggs** (organic, and from free range chickens) in a pot. Cover with cold **water**. Bring to a boil. Turn off heat and let stand 20 minutes, covered. Peel under cool running water.

2. Finely mince **1 to 2 tablespoons sweet red onion**. Use an egg slicer and then a fork to mash eggs. Add fresh ground **salt** and **pepper** to taste. Add enough **coconut oil** to make the mixture soft—3 to 4 tablespoons. Finally add a dash of **balsamic vinegar**.

3. Serve on a bed of **lettuce**, or on **matzah**, during Passover, with lightly **pickled cucumbers**. Note that chilling will make the coconut oil hard, so salad will be crumbly if refrigerated.

*makes about 1½ cups*

# arugula salad with parmesan

Arugula or rocquette (rocket) is an easily grown herb in the cress family. If sown early in the spring with radishes, both will mature in about 25 to 30 days. As soon as flower buds show, it becomes too bitter to eat. Lacking a garden, you will find arugula for sale in most markets throughout the year.

1.  You will need a **small bunch of arugula** for each diner. Wash it well and combine with other greens or not, as you prefer, on each plate. Slice **radishes** over.

2.  Make a garlic dressing by combining in a screw cap jar: **1 cup olive oil**, **¼ cup wine vinegar**, **1 clove crushed garlic**, and **2 teaspoons prepared mustard**. Add **1 teaspoon salt** and **pepper** to taste. Set aside.

3.  Use a cheese plane to make **large curls of Reggiano Parmesan**. A quarter pound will yield enough cheese for a dozen salads.

4.  Just before dinner, top each salad with Parmesan curls and dressing.

*makes enough dressing for 6 to 8 servings*

# pickled carrot salad
## with sour cream dressing

1. Peel and slice **1 pound carrots**. Thinly slice **1 fennel bulb** and **2 scallions**, white parts only. Turn all vegetables into a bowl.

2. In a small pot combine **¼ cup brown rice vinegar, 3 tablespoons sugar, 2 teaspoons salt, 5 crushed peppercorns**, and **½ cup water**. Bring to a boil. Immediately pour over carrots.

3. Chop **¼ cup** firmly packed **tarragon leaves** and **¼ cup straight leaf parsley**. Combine herbs with carrots. Let vegetable mix stand at room temperature for several hours, then refrigerate.

4. Make herbed sour cream dressing: Mix together **1 cup sour cream, 1 tablespoon tamari, 2 teaspoons lemon juice**, and **1 tablespoon chopped fresh herbs**, such as **dill, burnet**, or **garlic leaves**. Add **1 teaspoon sesame seeds** and stir all together.

5. To serve, prepare a bed of **lettuce**. Top with carrot slices. Drizzle with **olive oil** and top mixture with sour cream dressing.

*6 servings*

SPRING

# new potato, carrot, and broccoli salad

## with garlic mayonnaise

This salad is made with waxy white new potatoes when they are available in the Spring. It is served with a garlic mayonnaise made with fresh herbs. If you do not have the herbs called for, use those that are accessible. For example, parsley, scallions, and ½ clove crushed garlic would work just as well.

1. **Prepare the vegetable marinade:** combine ¼ **cup red wine vinegar** with ¾ **cup oil.** We use a blend of **25% olive oil** and **75% grapeseed oil.** Add **salt** and **fresh ground pepper.** Set aside ¾ cup of this marinade for the potatoes and add **2 teaspoons good quality prepared mustard** to it. The remaining dressing is for the carrots and broccoli.

2. **Make salad:** wash and quarter but do not peel **4 pounds new potatoes.** Boil in water to cover and be sure they do not overcook. When a small sharp knife can pierce them easily, drain immediately and toss in a bowl with the dressing. Add **2 tablespoons straight leaf parsley,** chopped, and salt and pepper to taste. When cool, refrigerate.

3. Peel **2 pounds carrots** and cut into sticks. Steam until just done. Add some dressing and **chopped burnet** or **comfrey** if you have it. Refrigerate.

4. Cut **1 small head broccoli** into flowerets. Steam for a few minutes only. Add dressing and refrigerate.

5. **Prepare garlic mayonnaise:** Choose herbs such as **garlic leaves, burnet, chives,** or **parsley** and chop fine. Use an electric mixer or food processor to beat **2 egg yolks.** Add **1 tablespoon wine vinegar, ½ teaspoon salt, ½ teaspoon prepared mustard,** and **1 cup grapeseed oil,** adding the latter drop by drop while beating. When most of the oil is in, the remainder may be added in a stream. When mayonnaise has thickened, turn machine off and taste for seasoning. Mix in the chopped herbs. Refrigerate until ready to serve.

6. **Assemble salad:** make a bed of **lettuce** and place 2 large spoonfuls of potatoes in the center. Arrange broccoli and carrots around the plate. Top with thin slices of **onion** and a dollop of **mayonnaise.**

*6 to 8 servings*

# pokeweed greens

It is worth learning how to identify pokeweed. This succulent weed of waste places (it can be found in your garden, too), comes up the first few weeks in May in Connecticut. Called the poor person's asparagus, the stalks taste much like asparagus and the new leaves like spinach. Poke is delicious. Don't eat flowers or fruit which appear later in the reason. They are reputedly poisonous.

1. Use a knife to cut **pokeweed shoots** under 12″ high. Larger stalks are bitter. Poke requires minimum washing. Simmer in a little water for about 5 minutes or until tender.

2. Serve with salt and butter.

# noodle soufflé

A good dinner with salad or soup. Though this dish is reminiscent of Jewish lokchen kugel or noodle pudding it is quite different, almost like a non-sweet cheesecake with noodles, meant as a main dish.

1. Preheat oven to 325°F. Remove ½ **pound sweet butter** and ½ **pound cream cheese** from refrigerator and let come to room temperature.

2. Cook **1 pound wide egg noodles** in boiling salted water until just done. Drain. Meanwhile, set out a 3 quart Pyrex or other baking dish.

3. In mixer, cream the butter and cream cheese together with ¾ **cup plus 2 tablespoons sugar**. Mix well. Add **9 eggs**, one at a time, beating well. Add **4 cups sour cream**, ⅓ **cup lemon juice**, and **1 tablespoon salt**. Taste for sour, sweet, and salt. All flavors should be strong.

4. Turn noodles into pan; pour cream cheese batter over noodles. Stir lightly.

5. About an hour before serving, preheat oven to 325°F and bake noodle soufflé until puffed and browned. Leftover portions may be reheated, uncovered, in oven or toaster oven.

*12 servings*

SPRING

# potato kugel

Kugel means pudding. This is an easy-to-make, reheatable version of potato pancakes. Beating egg whites stiff makes this kugel lighter and crisper than the original version of this recipe. A good Passover dish.

1. **Prepare apple-apricot sauce:** in a saucepan combine ½ **cup dried apricots, 1 cup dried apple slices**, and **2 cups apple juice**. Simmer, covered, until fruit is tender. Purée thoroughly in a food processor. Return to pot with 1½ **cups water** and **4 fresh apples**, peeled, cored, and thinly sliced. Simmer over low heat, covered, until apples are cooked. If sauce seems too stiff, thin with water *or* apple juice. Set aside.

2. **Make kugel:** peel **3 large Idaho potatoes** and grate in a food processor or with a hand grater. Grate **1 medium-large onion** and combine with potatoes. Turn potato-onion mixture into a colander over a bowl and press gently to remove some liquid. Turn contents of colander into another bowl and set aside strained liquid.

3. Preheat oven to 400°F and place a metal baking pan that measures about 8″ x 15″ in oven. It is not wise to use Pyrex for this recipe. Add **2 to 3 tablespoons grapeseed oil** to pan.

4. Add the following to the potato mixture: **2 teaspoons salt**, ½ **bunch chopped straight leaf parsley**, 1½ **tablespoons potato starch**, freshly grated **pepper**, and **2 egg yolks**. Place the egg whites in a mixer.

5. Add **1 to 2 additional egg whites** to whites in mixer. Beat until stiff. Meanwhile, pour the liquid squeezed from the potatoes into a cup. Add the potato starch accumulated at the bottom of the bowl to the potato-onion mixture and stir well with a wooden spoon. You may want to add some of the reserved liquid if mixture seems too stiff and dry. The consistency should be soft enough so that egg whites can be folded into the mixture easily.

6. Add beaten whites to potatoes and use both clean hands, fingers spread apart, to "fold" whites into potatoes. This process is more like combing hair than folding. Finally, wash your hands and turn kugel into the prepared hot baking dish. Bake 45 to 60 minutes, or until kugel is puffed and crispy brown. Cut into wedges and serve with **apple-apricot sauce** and **sour cream**. Potato kugel reheats well or can be eaten cold for lunch or a snack.

*4 to 5 servings*

# parsnip pie

An English rite of Spring. The old English parsnip pies were much sweeter than this and had no peanuts and probably no ginger, either. They were more like an American pumpkin pie, i.e., a dessert. This recipe is a nice supper when served with salad. If you want to be traditional, you can put primroses on your table. Old recipes call for them on top of the pie. Adapted from *Wings of Life* by Julie Jordan, Crossing Press.

1. Peel **20 to 22 parsnips** and **2 very large onions.** Slice thinly. In 2 large frying pans, fry parsnips and onions in **grapeseed oil** with **3 to 3½ cups peanuts.** When nicely brown, turn out into bowl and sprinkle with **2½ cups golden** *or* **cocktail sherry.**

2. **Make sauce:** peel, quarter, and slice **2 very large onions** and sauté in fry pan in ⅓ **cup grapeseed oil** till light brown. Add **3 tablespoons shredded fresh ginger** (or 1 tablespoon dried ginger). Cook another minute. Add ⅓ **cup all-purpose flour.** Cook until well blended. Add **1½ cups heavy cream,** juice of **2 to 2½ lemons,** ⅔ **cup tamari, 12 oz. peanut butter, 1½ tablespoons dried ginger,** ⅓ **cup sherry, 2 tablespoons honey,** and **1 quart milk.** Taste. Sauce should taste strongly salty and gingery and be sweet-pungent.

3. Add sauce to parsnips using just enough to make a liason with the parsnips. Too much will be soggy.

4. **Prepare pie crust:** combine **9 cups all-purpose flour** and **1 tablespoon salt** in a mixer. Dice **¾ pound butter**. Add to mixer and use flat beater to blend into oatmeal-sized flakes. Fork-beat **2 yolks** (discard whites or save for another purpose) and combine with **¾ cup ice water**. Add to mixer and blend briefly. Add more ice water only if necessary. Gather dough into a ball, wrap in plastic wrap and refrigerate.

5. Preheat oven to 375°F. Roll out crust and line a 11″ x 17″ pan with it. Add sauced parsnips. Roll out top crust. Crimp edges and slash top. Bake at 375°F till browned. Leftover portions can be reheated in oven.

*about 12 servings*

SPRING

# broccoli raab, cannelini beans, tomato, and cavatelli

1. **Prepare cannelini beans:** pick over **1 cup** to remove stones and debris and soak overnight. Next morning, drain, cover with fresh water. Bring to a simmer.

2. Meanwhile, dice **2 large stalks celery** and **leaves** and add to the pot. Peel **1 large onion** and stick **2 whole cloves** into it. Add to pot with **2 bay leaves**. Cover and simmer until beans are almost tender. Add **salt** and fresh ground **pepper**.

3. **Prepare tomato sauce:** chop **3 cloves garlic** and **1 large onion**. In a saucepot sauté vegetables in **2 tablespoons olive oil** with ½ **teaspoon red pepper flakes** and **2 teaspoons dried basil**, crumbled, over low heat until softened but not browned. Add **2 cups canned plum tomatoes** and juice and use a potato masher to crush them. Cover pot and simmer for ½ hour. Meanwhile dice **2 cups fresh plum tomatoes**. Add to pot and cook 10 minutes more. Season with **salt** and fresh ground **pepper**.

4. **Prepare broccoli raab**: you will need **3 quarts**, packed. Discard stems that are over ½" thick, wash if necessary and slice thinly. Also peel and slice **3 cloves more garlic**. In a frying pan sauté half the garlic with ½ **teaspoon red pepper flakes** in **3 tablespoons olive oil**. Add half the broccoli raab and fry over high heat, stirring vigorously. Turn into a large pot. Repeat with remaining garlic and broccoli raab.

5. Add tomato sauce to pot with raab. Remove and discard bay leaves and whole onion from beans. Use a slotted spoon to add beans to sauce and raab, and add bean liquid as needed. Tomatoes, raab, and beans should be present in equal amounts. Cook all together 5 to 10 minutes. Correct seasoning. Be sure mix is adequately salted.

6. Cook **1½ pounds fresh cavatelli pasta** until barely done and serve pasta on the side of the bean and raab mix. If you like, serve with thickly grated **Romano cheese.**

*6 servings*

CATHARINE

# manicotti

You will need one box manicotti pasta. If not available, use jumbo shell pasta instead.

1. The **marinara sauce** should be made first. In a 3 quart pot fry **2 medium onions**, coarsely chopped, **3 cloves garlic**, coarsely chopped, **1 teaspoon dried oregano**, and **1 teaspoon dried basil** in ¼ cup olive oil. Let onions sauté about 10 minutes, then add a **6 oz. can tomato paste**. Cook the sauce for a few minutes and add **6 oz. of water** using the tomato paste can. A splash of **red wine** may also be added. Cook the sauce till it thickens and then add a **28 oz. can of tomatoes in purée**. Bring the sauce to a boil adding **2 teaspoons salt**, **1 teaspoon pepper**, and **3 tablespoons pesto**, if you have it (see index). Turn down to a simmer and let the sauce cook a good 3 hours to develop its full flavor.

2. The **cheese and spinach filling** should be made next. In a bowl, combine **2 pounds whole milk ricotta cheese**, **1 pound mozzarella**, diced, **¾ cup freshly grated Parmesan cheese**, **4 tablespoons Italian parsley**, chopped, **½ pound defrosted frozen spinach** (drained), **2 eggs**, **1 teaspoon salt**, **½ teaspoon pepper**, and a **grating of nutmeg**. Mix the ingredients thoroughly and taste for seasoning. Refrigerate until ready to stuff manicotti.

3. When the sauce has finished cooking, the pasta can be cooked. Fill a 6 quart pot with water and bring to a boil. Carefully drop the contents of a **1 pound box of** unbroken **manicotti** into the boiling water. Stir gently with a wooden spoon to separate any that might

be sticking together. Do not cook more than 5 to 6 minutes and drain the shells in a strainer or carefully take them out of the water with a slotted spoon. Immediately pour cold water on pasta to keep them from cooking further and splitting apart.

4. The manicotti shells should be filled immediately. Hold the manicotti carefully, and with a butter knife gently stuff each tube with the cheese spinach filling (or use a pastry bag with large tube attachment). Line them up close together in a pan and spread some of the tomato sauce on top. Refrigerate.

5. When ready to serve, bake in a 350°F oven for 20 minutes or until the manicotti are puffed and the cheese has melted. Remove from the oven, spoon more hot tomato sauce on top and sprinkle each serving, 2 manicotti per person, with freshly grated **Parmesan**. Serve immediately.

*7 servings*

SPRING

# feijoada

This elaborate Brazilian meal of rice and beans has African origins. Traditionally served with a variety of meats, we find the other customary accompaniments adequate in producing a satisfying dinner.

1. **Make feijoada:** cover **2 cups black turtle beans** with water and soak overnight. Or lacking time, bring to a boil, remove from heat and let stand, covered, for 1 hour. Prepare **fried kale** and **manioc** (see following recipes). Hard-boil **3 eggs**.

2. Drain beans, cover with fresh **water**, and simmer until tender.

3. Chop **2 medium onions**, and thinly slice **4 red peppers**. Turn into a saucepot and sauté with **3 tablespoons grapeseed oil**. Add **2 teaspoons oregano**, **4 teaspoons cumin**, and **4 cloves** crushed **garlic**.

4. When vegetables are soft and golden, add the cooked turtle beans, **2 tablespoons lemon juice**, **¼ cup red wine**, and **1 cup canned tomatoes**. Add **salt** and **pepper** to taste. Cover and simmer 30 minutes.

5. In a separate pan cook **1½ cups long grain white rice** in **2½ cups water** with **1 teaspoon salt**. Set aside.

6. **Prepare lemon pepper hot sauce:** finely chop enough **onion** to measure **¼ cup**. Continue using a good French chef's knife to chop **1 clove garlic** and **2 bottled Tabasco peppers**, mincing all very fine. Turn into a bowl and add **¼ cup freshly squeezed lemon juice**.

7. Finish beans by stirring in **3 tablespoons dark rum**. Serve beans over rice with kale and manioc on the side. Brazilians reputedly sprinkle manioc over feijoada. Use the **lemon pepper sauce** if you like spicy food. Garnish plates or platter with sliced **hard-boiled eggs**, **black olives**, and several very thin slices of unpeeled thin-skinned **oranges**.

*6 servings*

CHARLENE

# fried kale

1. Bring **3 quarts of water** to a boil in a large pot. Meanwhile, remove stems from **2 pounds kale**. Shred kale into thin strips and then wash it thoroughly in cold running water.

2. When the water has boiled, add the shredded greens to the pot, and return to the boil. Immediately drain in colander, pressing out as much excess liquid as possible.

3. In a large frying pan preheat **3 tablespoons olive oil** over medium-high heat. Add the greens and fry, stirring constantly, for about 5 minutes. (The kale will turn from bright green to a dull dark green color). Add **1 large clove minced garlic**. Fry 1 or 2 minutes more to cook the garlic, and then add **1 tablespoon tamari**. Continue frying until the soy liquid has evaporated. Taste for seasoning and add a little **salt** if necessary.

*6 side dish servings*

# toasted manioc meal

A traditional topping for Feijoada is toasted manioc, a fine, grain-like meal made from a dried root, which is also known as cassava. It is available, packaged, in Latina markets as Farinha de Mandioca. It is a nice addition, but not necessary to the dinner.

1. In a heavy frying pan over medium-low heat, dry roast **1 cup manioc meal**, stirring until pale brown. If available, add **1 tablespoon dende** *or* **palm oil** (available in Latina markets) *or* **grapeseed oil**, and stir into the meal. Turn out into a heatproof bowl.

2. Finely chop **1 small onion**. Fork-beat **1 egg** in a small bowl. Melt **2 tablespoons butter** in the same frying pan and sauté the onions until transparent and beginning to turn golden. Add the egg and stir well. Return manioc to frying pan and mix all ingredients thoroughly. Turn off heat. Add **salt** to taste. Serve at room temperature.

*5 to 6 side dish servings*

**SPRING**

# new potatoes with raclette

You will have to locate raclette cheese. It is a strong flavored hard cheese from Switzerland and should be available at a well-stocked cheese store. Raclette is traditionally done by placing a wheel of cheese next to an open fire and scraping off melting portions onto potatoes as an appetizer. Expensive machines have been merchandised to melt raclette at the table. However, the broiler in your stove works just as well, and we like raclette enough to want to make a dinner of it.

1. For each diner, scrub **4 to 5 new potatoes** (red bliss or golden), peel and cut into sticks **1 carrot**, and separate **broccoli flowerets** to provide 3 small ones for each person. Steam the vegetables until barely done. We use a tiered steamer purchased in a Chinese hardware store. Set vegetables aside.

2. Use a cheese plane to cut thin slices from a ½ **pound** piece of **raclette cheese**. Preheat broiler. Arrange the vegetables in a shallow pan, top with raclette, and broil until cheese melts and turns light brown. Serve at once, with **cornichons** or other small sweet pickles.

# spinach & mushroom crêpes
## with béarnaise sauce

Crêpes are green, mushrooms are brown, and sauce is golden.

1. It is easiest using **frozen chopped spinach** for this recipe. Defrost **4 (10 oz.) packages** of it.

2. **Make crêpe batter:** in a blender, combine **1 cup flour, ½ cup milk, ½ cup water, 2 eggs, 2 egg yolks, ½ stick butter**, melted, and **¾ teaspoon salt**. Purée thoroughly. Add about **½ pound** of the defrosted **spinach**, or enough to color the batter quite green. Purée again. Chill batter in the refrigerator for at least one hour before making crêpes.

3. **Make spinach and mushroom filling:** finely chop **3 cups mushrooms**, with their stems, and **1 medium onion**. (Both can be chopped most efficiently in a food processor). Use a large frying pan to sauté mushrooms and onions in **6 tablespoons butter** until they have dried out and are beginning to brown. Add **2 tablespoons lemon juice, 12 oz. light beer**, and **⅓ cup heavy cream**. Simmer 5 minutes. Drain remaining spinach of excess liquid (reserving it) and add to pan. Add **1½ cups grated gruyère** *or* **Swiss cheese** and stir well together. Dissolve **1½ tablespoons cornstarch** in **¼ cup spinach juice** and add to pan. Bring to a simmer, stirring constantly. Turn off heat and season mixture with **salt, pepper, nutmeg**, and a dash **Tabasco**. Add more **lemon juice** if needed. Cool. Add **2 beaten eggs**.

4. It is necessary to use a crêpe pan (preferably three of them) to make crêpes. Wipe out a heated crêpe pan with an **oiled** piece of absorbent paper and make a sample crêpe. If it is too thick, add equal amounts of **milk** and **water** to batter and mix thoroughly, so that crêpes comes out thin and delicate. This recipe should produce about 20 crêpes, so you will have extra batter for mistakes.

5. Using a butter knife, smear filling over each crêpe and roll up loosely. There will be filling enough for about 18 crêpes. Arrange in a baking dish, cover and refrigerate until ready to serve.

6. **Make béarnaise sauce:** combine in a small pot **½ cup white wine vinegar, ½ cup dry white wine, ¼ cup shallots,** chopped, **4 small cloves garlic,** unpeeled, **1 bay leaf,** a pinch each **dried thyme** and **tarragon.** Bring to a boil and simmer until liquid is reduced to ¼ cup. Strain into a measuring cup when you think it is about right, and boil down again if necessary. In a separate small pan, melt **2 sticks butter.** In a stainless steel pot place **6 egg yolks.** Whisk in the reduced and strained wine mixture. Whisk over gentle heat until foamy and slightly thickened. Turn heat to very low and add melted butter slowly until sauce thickens like a hollandaise. Season to taste with **salt** and **2 tablespoons** chopped **fresh tarragon.** Cover to keep warm. Don't try to reheat sauce.

7. Slice ½ **pound large mushrooms**. Chop **1 small onion**. Fry both in **2 tablespoons butter** over high heat until the mushrooms give up their liquid and brown nicely. **Salt** them, and add **3 tablespoons port wine**. Turn out into a bowl and cover.

8. To serve, preheat oven to 400°F and heat crêpes for 10 to 15 minutes or until light brown. Top with port-flavored mushrooms for the last few minutes of heating. Spoon béarnaise over the top and bring casserole dish to the table with the rest of the béarnaise in a sauceboat. This makes an elegant dinner. Serve with a salad.

*6 to 8 serving*

DOUBLE FLOWERED BLOODROOT

# pasta with artichoke asparagus sauce and gremolata

A good way to use up small amounts of Spring vegetables. Already cooked ones are fine, if you have been careful to save the cooking water.

1. **Make pasta sauce:** trim **2 artichokes**. Barely cover with **water** and cook until tender. Remove from broth to cool. Snap off hard bottoms from ½ **pound asparagus**. Be sure bottoms are clean before adding them to artichoke broth. Simmer to extract flavor. You will need **5 to 6 cups broth**, so judge whether you should cover the pot or leave it uncovered to reduce the liquid.

2. Slice **asparagus stalks** thinly and set aside. Scrape flesh from each artichoke leaf, trim off choke and slice base. Set aside in a separate bowl.

3. In a saucepot, stew **2 cloves minced garlic** in ⅓ cup **olive oil**. Add ⅓ **cup flour** and stir while cooking for a minute or two. Gradually add strained broth, using as much as seems appropriate, whisking the mixture together as it simmers. Season with **1 to 2 tablespoons tamari, 2 to 3 teaspoons lemon juice**, some freshly ground **pepper**, and a little **nutmeg**. Taste for seasoning. Sauce should be thin. Now add reserved asparagus, cover, and simmer 5 to 10 minutes until tender. Add reserved artichoke flesh, stir together, and set sauce aside.

4. Toast ½ **cup pignoli nuts** in the oven until golden brown. Crush with a rolling pin.

5. **Make gremolata:** chop together finely ½ **cup straight leaf parsley**, ⅓ **cup garlic leaves** (if you do not grow garlic in your garden, substitute **2 cloves of garlic**) and **grated rind of 1 lemon**.

6. **To serve:** cook pasta of your choice. **Linguine** would be a good selection. Drain pasta and return to the cooking pot. Add as much sauce as seems necessary. Heat briefly, and toss in a generous amount of gremolata.

7. Finish with toasted **pignoli nuts** and **Parmesan cheese**. Offer extra gremolata on the side.

*4 servings, with leftover sauce*

**SPRING**

# green goddess soufflé

An elegant introduction to Spring.

1.  To prepare liquid and vegetables for soufflé base, first snap off the tough lower stalks from **1 pound asparagus** and barely cover with **water**; then cook until stalks are soft. Drain, pressing down on stalks to get good flavor into the liquid. Discard the stalks. Slice the upper tender parts of the asparagus and cook very briefly in the reserved asparagus liquid until just done. Again drain liquid and set aside. You should have **2 cups asparagus pieces**. Wash **½ pound fresh spinach** and steam in the liquid that clings to the leaves. Purée in food processor or blender and strain well. Add spinach to asparagus pieces, drained liquid to asparagus liquid, and set both aside. You will need 1 cup liquid in all.

2.  Dice **2 tablespoons shallots** and **1 clove garlic** (or, preferably, **1 tablespoon garlic leaves**). Sauté in **3 tablespoons unsalted butter**. Add **¼ teaspoon dry mustard, 1 teaspoon ground coriander**, and **¼ teaspoon ground cumin**. When shallots have softened and are light brown, add **⅓ cup flour**. Cook together, stirring, until well blended. Add 1 cup of the reserved liquid and **⅓ cup dry white wine**. Whisk mixture well over low heat. It will get quite thick. Remove from heat and let cool 10 minutes, stirring occasionally.

3.  Meanwhile, separate **6 eggs**. Be very careful not to get any yolks into the whites, or soufflé will not rise well. Set whites aside. Stir the yolks into the shallot butter and flour mixture. Mix well. Add **⅓ cup grated**

**Parmesan cheese**, a little freshly grated **nutmeg**,
1 tablespoon tamari, ¾ tablespoon lemon juice,
and freshly ground **pepper**. Finally, fold in reserved
cooked vegetables, using a slotted spoon to be
sure not to add residual liquid. Taste for seasoning.
Refrigerate this soufflé base until dinner time. Also
refrigerate the reserved egg whites. Prepare **herbed
sour cream sauce** (see following recipe).

4. Let egg whites come to room temperature (about ½
   hour) before beating. You will need another **4 to 6
   egg whites** to make a light, puffy soufflé. Preheat oven
   to 400°F and butter 1 large soufflé dish, 1 straight-
   sided casserole, or 3 to 4 individual dishes. Any
   ovenproof casserole will do. You will need 1 cup of
   soufflé base and ½ cup of unbeaten egg whites to
   serve each diner. Beat egg whites in a mixer until soft
   peaks form. Fold soufflé base and whites together—
   you should not be thorough—and turn into prepared
   pans. Sprinkle tops with grated **Parmesan cheese**
   and put into preheated oven. Lower heat to 375°F and
   bake until soufflé is puffed and brown, about 25 to 35
   minutes. Since it will fall after that, serve immediately,
   with the sauce.

*3 to 4 servings*

**SPRING**

# herbed sour cream sauce

1. Stir together **1 cup sour cream, ½ tablespoon horseradish, ¼ tablespoon lemon juice**, and **1 tablespoon tamari**. Fresh herbs are what make this sauce exceptional. Cloves of garlic planted the Autumn before will yield mild-flavored garlic leaves in Spring. Chop enough **garlic leaves** to measure **2 tablespoons** and add to sauce with **1 tablespoon** chopped **straight leaf parsley, 1 tablespoon** chopped **watercress leaves**, and **½ tablespoon** chopped **dill**. Taste for seasoning. If you have no garlic leaves, do not substitute cloves of garlic. Refrigerate.

# spinach and matzah meena

A Sephardi Passover dish from Ethel Corey. Kashcaval cheese is Roumanian. It should be available at Greek stores.

1. Clean and shred **3 pounds spinach**. Dice **1 large onion**. Heat **3 tablespoons olive oil** in a frying pan, and sauté onion until golden. Add spinach in several batches, stirring each time, and cook until it wilts. Meanwhile, add **2 tablespoons fresh dill**, chopped. When all spinach is cooked, season mixture to taste with **salt**, freshly ground **pepper**, and **nutmeg**. Set aside.

2. Spread **8 whole matzahs** on trays in a single layer. Sprinkle with water to moisten, but don't let matzahs get so wet that they will fall apart when lifted.

3. Mix together **½ pound feta cheese**, crumbled, **3 cups cottage cheese**, **1 pound kashcaval**, grated, and **9 fork-beaten eggs**. Add **2 to 3 teaspoons salt**, to taste, considering the saltiness of the cheese. Add freshly ground **pepper**.

4. Pour **2 tablespoons olive oil** in a 9″ x 14″ pan. Layer matzah in pan, cutting or breaking pieces to fit. Add half of the cheese mixture and another layer of matzah. Add half the spinach mixture, more matzah, remaining cheese, etc., ending with a layer of matzah.

5. Drizzle **2 tablespoons olive oil** over the top of the spinach meena and bake in a 375°F oven for 20 to 40 minutes or until puffed and browned. Can be reheated or served cold as a snack.

*12 servings*

SPRING

# asparagus platter
## with sauce maltaise

1. You will need ¼ **pound asparagus** for each diner, so buy (or pick) **3 to 4 pounds asparagus**. Snap off the smallest amount of base possible and discard. Then, using a small sharp knife, carefully peel off the skin up to the bottom of the tip. We don't think potato peelers do this job as well as paring knives. This is a laborious job, but worth it for the tender result.

2. Simmer **2 cups white rice** in **3½ cups water** with **1½ teaspoons salt** until done, about 15 minutes. Taste rice and if it doesn't seem done and liquid is all gone, add a little more water. When rice is done, add **3 tablespoons sweet butter** and keep covered.

3. **Prepare sauce maltaise:** melt **1½ sticks sweet butter** in a small pot and set aside. In a stainless steel pot place **6 egg yolks**, **½ cup** freshly squeezed **orange juice**, and **2 tablespoons lemon juice**. Whisk over low heat until sauce thickens slightly, then add melted butter slowly while whisking. This sauce is a variation of hollandaise. Be sure sauce is tart enough. Add more **lemon juice** if needed. Remove from heat when sauce is thickened and season to taste with **salt** and freshly ground **pepper**. If you like, add some grated **orange rind**. Set sauce aside, covered.

4. Now place the asparagus in a large fry pan (or two, if they don't all fit in one) and add ½ **cup water** to each pan. Cover and steam until asparagus are barely done, no more than 5 minutes. They cook quickly when they are peeled.

5. Arrange rice on two sides of each dinner plate with asparagus in the middle. Pour the asparagus cooking liquid over the rice and serve the sauce maltaise over the asparagus, with the remainder in a sauce boat.

*6 to 8 servings*

NOEL

SPRING

# cottage cheese blintzes

This recipe from Fay Davidson makes a lot, but if you like them, you will want them for breakfast as well as for dinner.

1. **Make crêpe batter:** in blender or mixer, beat together thoroughly: **4 eggs, ½ teaspoon salt, 1 cup milk**, and **1 cup plus 2 tablespoons unbleached white flour.** (You will also need **1 cup water**, but if you are using a blender you may not have room to add it and still mix batter thoroughly. Scrape sides down and be sure batter is smooth; then add water.) Chill batter at least one hour.

2. **Make filling:** meanwhile, combine in bowl **2½ pounds farmer cheese** with **1½ pounds creamed cottage cheese, 5 eggs** (unbeaten), **⅓ cup to ½ cup sugar**, grated rind of **2 lemons** and **salt**. Mix well and taste for salt and sugar.

3. **Prepare crêpes:** you should have a crêpe pan to make the blintze crêpes; preferably you should have 3 pans to make 3 at a time. (These pans are like omelet pans in that they require seasoning: heat slowly over low heat for 15 minutes with a tablespoon of oil. Then use absorbent paper to wipe out oil. Never use the pans for anything but crêpes or omelets.) When ready to make the crêpes, heat the pans till a drop of water dances on the pan. Wipe pan lightly with a little oil on absorbent paper. Try out one crêpe by pouring batter into pan and immediately returning excess to pitcher. Crêpe should be thin. If it is not thin enough, add equal parts **milk** and **water**. It takes practice to make good crêpes. Once crêpe has started to curl away from the pan, use a spatula to loosen it and then your

fingers to turn it over to cook lightly on the other side. Don't overcook or crêpes will be brittle. Turn crêpe out and repeat. No need to add any more oil or fat of any kind. Stack crêpes as they are completed.

4. **Fill blintzes:** fill each crêpe with a large spoonful of filling. Make rectangular packages by folding 2 sides over, then 2 ends. Store on tray (covered) in refrigerator until ready to serve.

5. **Serve crêpes:** heat **2 tablespoons sweet butter** in a large fry pan until hot. Place 4 blintzes at a time in hot butter and fry till brown on one side. Carefully turn over to brown other side. Serve immediately. Allow 4 blintzes per person. Serve with **sour cream** and a bowl of fresh sliced **strawberries**.

*8 to 10 servings*

# caramel flan

Flan recipes are simple and usual. This one is exceptional, because it is made of egg yolks and is flavored with liqueur.

1.  Preheat oven to 350°F. In a small pot bring ⅓ **cup water** and ½ **cup sugar** to a boil. Cook over moderate heat until mixture turns an amber brown. Pour into a ring mold, tilting so that caramel will coat some of the sides. Be very careful handling the caramel; it can cause bad burns.

2.  In another pot bring **6 cups milk** almost to a boil. Meanwhile in a large bowl place **12 egg yolks** plus **2 whole eggs**. Whisk with ¾ **cup sugar**, scant ½ **teaspoon cinnamon, 2 tablespoons brandy**, and **2 tablespoons crème de cacao**. When well blended, gradually add hot milk, stirring carefully.

3.  Ladle mixture into prepared ring mold. Place mold in a larger pan and put into preheated oven. Add enough water to the larger pan to reach halfway up the sides of the mold. Bake for about 1 hour or until a toothpick inserted in the center comes out clean. Remove from oven and cool on a rack. Place in refrigerator. When the flan is quite cold, turn it out onto a rimmed platter, so that the thin caramel sauce is contained on the dish.

*10 to 12 servings*

SPRING

# queen of sheba cake

A European-style chocolate almond torte.

1. Remove ½ **pound unsalted butter** from the refrigerator to soften. Butter and flour a 8″ x 12″ baking tin. Set aside. Preheat oven to 350°F. Use a processor to grate finely ⅔ **cup almonds.** Set aside. Melt **8 oz. semisweet chocolate** of good quality, such as Valrhona, together with ¼ **cup rum or coffee** in a small covered pot over very low heat.

2. Separate **6 eggs,** whites into a mixer and yolks into a small bowl. Beat the whites with ¼ **teaspoon salt** until soft peaks form; add **2 tablespoons sugar** and continue beating until stiff peaks form. Stop mixer and turn whites out into a separate bowl. Whisk chocolate and remove from heat.

3. Turn softened butter into unwashed mixer. Cream (using flat beater) with **1 cup and 3 tablespoons sugar** until the mix is fluffy and pale yellow. Add reserved yolks, ground almonds, and ½ **teaspoon almond extract.** Mix well.

4. Turn cooled melted chocolate into mixer. Use rubber spatula to stir in. Sift **1 cup flour** over mix and stir in. Turn approximately one fourth of the beaten egg whites into the mix and stir well. Finally, turn the rest of the beaten whites into the bowl and fold in gently.

5. Turn into prepared pan and smooth batter with rubber spatula. Sprinkle top of cake with ¼ **cup sliced almonds.** Bake until center of cake tests clean with a toothpick, about 25 minutes. Let cool on a rack.

6. Make **chocolate whipped cream**: beat **2 cups heavy cream** until stiff, together with **2 tablespoon sugar**, **2 tablespoon unsweetened cocoa**, ½ **teaspoon almond extract**, and a **splash of Kahlùa**. Refrigerate.

7. Serve pieces of cake with chocolate whipped cream.

*12 to 15 servings*

Suzanne

# banana cake

From Fay Davidson.

1. Preheat oven to 325°F. Bring ¼ **pound sweet butter** to room temperature. Chop coarsely **1 cup walnuts** by hand, or in food processor. Measure **½ cup sour cream**.

2. Mash **3 very ripe bananas** or enough to yield 1 cup. Be sure to use a fork and plate, and not to overdo the mashing. Set aside. Butter an 8″ x 8″ pan.

3. Cream the softened butter in a mixer, using the flat beater. Add **1 teaspoon vanilla extract** and **½ cup organic sugar**. When light colored and fluffy, add **2 eggs**, one at a time. Beat each well. Add the sour cream and the walnuts. Mix just enough to blend. Turn machine off.

4. Measure **1½ cups all-purpose flour**, **¼ teaspoon salt**, **½ teaspoon baking soda**, and **1½ teaspoons baking powder**. Use a dry whisk to blend. Turn dry ingredients into the mixer and turn on briefly. Don't over mix. Turn batter into pan. Bake in preheated oven for 1 hour, or until a toothpick pushed into the middle comes out dry. Cool.

5. Serve with **whipped cream**.

*one 8″ square cake*

# coconut pie

A very easy, delicious pie, derived from "chess" pie, from the American South.

1. Make **processor pie crust** (see index) and roll out to fit a 9″ pie pan. Set aside. Preheat oven to 350°F.

2. Stir together: **1 cup sugar**, ¾ **cup unsweetened flaked coconut**, **1 tablespoon flour**, grated **zest** of **one lime**, **3 tablespoons lime juice**, **pinch of salt**, ½ **cup buttermilk**, ½ **cup organic unsweetened coconut milk**, ½ **teaspoon vanilla extract**, and **2 eggs** and **2 egg yolks**.

3. Pour mix into unbaked pie shell. Bake 50 minutes until set, but a little wobbly in the center. Cool.

4. To further accentuate the sweet-sour dichotomy of flavors, make a **rhubarb sauce:** slice **5 big stalks of rhubarb** and turn into a pot. Add ½ **cup orange juice**. Simmer over lowest heat until rhubarb is tender. Sweeten to **taste** with **organic sugar** (start with a **quarter cup**). Serve as pie topping.

*one 9″ pie*

**SPRING**

# topfenkuchen

This is an old world delicious nut torte which uses no flour or leavening, but is enriched with cheese.

1. **Butter** a 9″ or 10″ springform pan and coat bottom and sides with **breadcrumbs**. Preheat oven to 350°F. Bring ½ **pound butter** to room temperature.

2. **Separate eggs.** You will need **7 whites** in your mixer bowl. Reserve the 7 yolks in a small bowl. Add **2 more whites** to the mixer and save the yolks for other purposes. Set all aside.

3. Use a food processor to grind enough **almonds** to make **3 to 3½ cups.** Skinned almonds are preferable; however those with skins may be used. Turn almonds out into a bowl, set aside, and don't wash the processor.

4. You will need ½ **pound farmer cheese.** This is a very dry kind of pot cheese and is essential for this cake. Break it up and add it to the unwashed processor. Blend with the reserved **7 egg yolks**, grated **rind of 2 lemons, 1½ teaspoons vanilla extract, ½ teaspoon almond extract** and ½ **teaspoon salt.** Mix thoroughly. Turn off machine.

5. Beat whites at high speed with the balloon whip until they begin to thicken. Gradually add ¼ **cup sugar** and continue beating until stiff but not dry. Turn out into a large bowl.

6. Use the flat beater to cream the softened butter in the unwashed bowl. Add **1 cup sugar**. When fluffy, add the reserved ground almonds and the cheese and yolk mix. Mix well. Now add about one fourth of the stiffly beaten whiles to lighten the batter. Finally, turn off machine and fold the remaining whites into the cake. Turn all into the prepared pan.

7. Bake until cake tester comes out clean, about 1 hour.

8. Serve slices of this almond cheese torte with **whipped cream** and **raspberries** *or* **strawberries**.

*one 9 or 10″ cake*

# hazelnut torte
## with mocha buttercream frosting

This cake is very easy to make once the nuts are roasted, rubbed, and grated. With patience, the frosting is easy too. The result is rich and wonderful considering the cake has no flour, sugar, or chocolate. The biggest drawback is the price of the nuts. Of course, walnuts or almonds may be substituted. A Passover cake.

1. Roast **3 cups hazelnuts** (filberts) in a 400°F oven, stirring often. When browned, turn out onto a dishtowel or tablecloth and use cloth to rub nuts together to loosen their skins. All the skins will not come off, but separate nuts from the skins as much as possible and grate the nuts in a cheese grater or food processor, being careful not to grind them into a nut butter. Add ¼ **cup cornstarch** and process to mix.

2. Butter three 9″ cake pans or one large 11″ x 17″ pan and line with waxed paper. Preheat oven to 325°F.

3. Separate **6 eggs,** placing yolks in a stainless steel pot to make frosting later. You will need another 6 whites for the cake totaling 12, or 1½ cups. (Remaining yolks can enrich scrambled eggs or be used for Hollandaise, Sauce Isabel, etc.) Put the **1½ cups whites** into mixer with ¼ **teaspoon salt** and beat until rounded peaks form. Add **1¾ cup sugar, 1½ teaspoons vanilla extract**, and ¾ **teaspoon almond extract**. Beat until stiff but not dry. Fold in grated nuts, turn into prepared pan(s) and bake cake 1 to 1½ hours or until the sides look slightly brown and top is no longer sticky.

4. **Neoclassic mocha buttercream:** first soften **2 cups butter.** Place **6 yolks** in mixer and beat until light. Heat ½ **cup agave nectar** and ½ **cup sugar** in small pot. When at a rolling boil, very slowly pour down sides of mixer while on (or do a little at a time, turning mixer on and off). Beat in butter gradually. Add flavorings: best is **2 cups ground praline,**\* splash Kahlùa, ¾ **teaspoon salt.** Lacking praline, use **2 tablespoons** Kahlùa and the salt.

5. Frost cooled cake with this mocha buttercream. Top with a few whole **hazelnuts** if desired.

*one 9″ cake*

---

*See index for **Praline Cheesecake**.

# banana cream pie

1. Preheat oven to 375°F. Make **pie crust** (see index) to line pie pan. Prick bottom rim, line with foil and weight with dried beans. Bake until edges are light brown. Remove foil and beans and finish baking.

2. Force ½ **small jar apricot preserves** through a sieve into a small pot and bring to a boil. Simmer 5 minutes. Use a brush to coat bottom of baked pie shell with the apricot glaze. This is a waterproofing measure. Line crust with **3 sliced bananas**.

3. Scald 1¾ **cups milk**. In a bowl, beat **7 yolks** until light yellow. Add ⅓ **cup sugar** and continue beating. Add ¼ **cup unbleached white flour** and a **pinch salt**. Gradually add milk to egg mixture, stirring constantly. Return to pot and cook very slowly until mixture thickens, stirring with whisk carefully in the corners of the pot. Add 1¼ **teaspoon vanilla extract**. Let cool slightly. Pour over bananas. Refrigerate pie until it sets up.

4. Before serving, whip **2 cups heavy cream** stiff with **2 tablespoons Kirsch** and **1 tablespoon sugar**. Top pie with **whipped cream** and **banana slices**.

# coeur à la crème

You may buy crème fraîche these days, or make it yourself.

1. Optional: make **crème fraîche** by heating **1½ cups heavy cream** with **2 tablespoons buttermilk** until just warm. Turn into a screw cap jar and leave in the sun or a warm place for 8 to 12 hours or until thickened. Sometimes this won't happen until overnight. Chill.

2. Soften **8 oz. cream cheese**. Push **6 oz. pot cheese** through a strainer into a mixer. Add softened cream cheese, **½ teaspoon vanilla extract, pinch salt, 6 tablespoons confectioner's sugar** (*or* **3 tablespoons honey**) and beat well together. Turn out into bowl.

3. Whip **1½ cups heavy cream** until stiff. Fold into cheese mixture. Rinse out cheesecloth and line small ceramic heart-shaped molds, small baskets, or a large oval basket with a double layer of the cheesecloth. Add the cheese-whipped cream mixture to the mold(s) and refrigerate on a tray. Excess moisture will drip out.

4. Strain **¾ cup fruit only-sweetened raspberry preserves** into a small pot. Add **¼ cup dry sherry** and cook for about 5 minutes until blended and slightly thickened. Cool. Slice **1 pint fresh strawberries** and pour jam-sherry mix over them. Chill.

5. Turn cheese mixture from molds onto individual plates or onto a large serving dish. Spoon strawberry sauce over the "hearts of cream" and serve crème fraîche in a sauceboat.

*8 servings*

# best strawberry shortcake

1. **Make filling:** in a pot blend **3 egg yolks**, ¼ **cup sugar,**
   ¼ **cup cornstarch**, ¼ **teaspoon salt**, **2 tablespoons**
   **butter** and **2 cups half-and-half cream**. Stir over
   medium heat until thickened, stirring constantly.
   Remove from heat stirring another minute. Chill. Beat
   **2 cups heavy cream** stiff with **2 teaspoons vanilla**
   **extract**. When custard is quite cold, fold both
   together. Chill.

2. **Make biscuits:** preheat oven to 425°F. Combine in a
   mixer: **2 cups all-purpose flour**, ½ **teaspoon salt,**
   **1 tablespoon baking powder** and **2½ tablespoons**
   **sugar**. Use the flat beater to blend. Cut up ¼ **pound**
   **unsalted butter** in small cubes and add to mixer.
   Blend to oatmeal flake size. In a separate small bowl,
   use a fork to beat **1 egg**. Add ⅔ **cup half-and-half**
   **cream**. Add to flour mixture and mix briefly. Turn out
   mixture onto floured board. Pat dough down and use
   a large (2¾″ diameter) glass to cut 15 to 20 biscuits.
   Reshape scraps. If you like, brush tops with beaten
   **egg white** and sprinkle with **sugar**. Bake on top rack
   in oven. Turn biscuits over when brown on bottom.
   Watch carefully as they burn easily. Bake no more
   than 10 minutes, possibly less.

3. **Prepare strawberries:** slice **1 quart strawberries**.
   Use a potato masher to crush some of them. Add
   **sugar** to taste.

4. This luscious dessert is best served when biscuits are
   still warm from the oven. Top with custard-whipped
   cream and berries.

*8 to 10 servings*

# strawberries isabel

Named for Isabel Brach who inspired this adaptation of zabaglione. Any fruit is appropriate: oranges, mangoes, pears, or raspberries.

1. In the top of a double boiler (or in a stainless steel bowl that will fit on the rim of a pot as a double boiler does) place **5 egg yolks** and ¼ **cup honey**. The bowl or double boiler top must be stainless steel or enamel or the sauce will discolor. Put enough **water** in bottom pan to last 10 to 15 minutes without touching upper bowl.

2. Beat and/or stir constantly with whisk over low-medium heat until sauce becomes quite thick and sticks to sides of bowl (about 10 to 15 minutes).

3. Remove from heat and add a **scant ½ cup Grand Marnier liqueur**, whisking until sauce is smooth.

4. Place in refrigerator until sauce is very cold.

5. Whip **1 cup heavy cream** until stiff and fold into sauce until mixture is smooth and even. Fold, do not stir.

6. Fill each glass serving dish with **5 to 6** sliced **strawberries**. Top with the sauce.

*6 to 8 servings*

SPRING

233

# fresh strawberry sundae

1. Fill blender ⅔ full of **decapped strawberries**, about **1½ pints**. Add **good fruit juice** to come halfway up the height of the berries. Purée. Add **2 tablespoons Kirsch** (a liqueur) and purée again. Add **sugar** as needed. Turn out into a container and slice **1 cup fresh strawberries** into the sauce. Refrigerate.

2. Beat **1½ cups heavy cream** stiff with **2 tablespoons sugar** and **½ teaspoon vanilla extract**.

3. Serve bowls of **vanilla ice cream** with strawberry sauce and whipped cream over each one.

*6 to 8 servings*

# maple apricot rice pudding

1. In a large shallow baking pan, combine **⅓ cup brown rice** (we prefer short grain), **2½ tablespoons maple syrup, dash salt, ½ cup chopped or snipped dried apricots, ¼ teaspoon almond extract**, and **1 quart milk**.

2. Bake at 325°F for 1½ to 2 hours, stirring occasionally. The pudding will repeatedly get a brown skin which should be stirred in.

3. Remove from oven when pudding still seems soft and loose. It will thicken up as it cools. Serve with **heavy cream**.

*6 to 8 servings*

# strawberry whipped cream roll

1. Preheat oven to 375°F. Place **4 eggs,** in their shells, in a bowl and cover with hot tap water. This is to warm them so that when beaten they will achieve a high volume.

2. Break eggs into mixer. Add ¼ **teaspoon salt,** and **1 teaspoon baking powder** and begin beating at top speed. Slowly add ¾ **cup sugar** and **1 teaspoon vanilla extract** and beat until eggs are tripled in bulk, about 10 minutes.

3. Meanwhile, butter a jelly roll pan and line with waxed paper.

4. Remove mixer bowl from machine. Sift ¾ **cup unbleached white flour** over eggs and carefully fold flour and egg mix together. Turn into pan, smoothing top gently with spatula, and bake 10 to 15 minutes or until light brown.

5. Prepare a dish towel the size of the pan by sifting **confectioner's sugar** over it. Turn cake out onto towel and peel off waxed paper in strips. Roll up cake in towel and lift onto racks to cool.

6. Slice **2 cups strawberries.** Set aside. In mixer beat **1½ cups heavy cream, scant ¼ cup sugar,** and ½ **teaspoon vanilla extract** until stiff.

7. Unroll cooled cake. Use a rubber spatula to spread whipped cream over cake. Distribute strawberries over the whipped cream. Reroll cake and chill until serving time. Slice and serve.

*8 to 10 servings*

**SPRING**

# SUMMER

## SOUPS

## SALADS

## ENTREES

# hungarian green bean and potato soup

From Marie Gall.

1. Cut **1 quart green beans** into 1½″ lengths. Put into a pot with **2 cups water** and simmer briefly until tender. Set aside.

2. Peel and dice **6 medium potatoes** and cook in scant **water** to cover until barely done.

3. Chop **1 large onion**. Sauté very slowly in **4 tablespoons butter** and **1 tablespoon Hungarian paprika** in a soup pot. The good flavor of this soup depends on the quality of paprika used. Purchase paprika either loose ("medium sharp rose") or in cans ("Szeged") from Hungarian or Eastern European grocery stores. When onions begin to brown, add ¼ **cup flour** and continue sautéing, stirring, for 5 to 10 minutes more.

4. Pour liquids from beans and potatoes into onion roux and whisk together well. Add **2⅔ cups milk**, ¼ **cup tamari**, freshly ground **pepper**, and **3 tablespoons cider vinegar**. If you have **fresh dill** and **fresh summer savory**, chop **1 tablespoon of each** and add to soup. Add beans and potatoes and reheat. Taste to see if any **salt** or more **vinegar** is needed.

5. This refreshing summer soup tastes fine as is, but may be garnished with **sour cream** if you like.

*6 to 8 servings*

# watercress vichyssoise

1. Coarsely chop **onions** to measure **1 cup**. Slice
   **4 leeks** lengthwise and thoroughly wash. Slice thinly.
   Melt ½ **stick butter** in a pot. Add **1 clove garlic**,
   crushed, and the onions and leeks. Sauté over low
   heat until very tender.

2. Add **4 cups potatoes**, peeled and sliced,
   **1 tablespoon salt** and **2½ cups water**. Cover and
   simmer until potatoes are almost done.

3. Remove thickest stems from **1 bunch watercress**,
   chop coarsely, reserving a few sprigs. Set aside.

4. Add **1½ cups milk** and **1½ cups water** to soup and
   bring to a boil. Add cress and cook 1 minute longer.
   Purée in food processor or blender.

5. Serve hot or cold, garnished with reserved cress
   sprigs and snipped **scallions** *or* **chives**.

*6 to 8 servings*

# madzoon soup

This Armenian soup can be served hot or cold. Cold seems best to us and fresh mint a necessity.

1. Cook **1 cup oat flakes** in **4 cups water** with **2 teaspoons salt** about 5 minutes. In large bowl put **4 cups yogurt** and add the cooked oatmeal gradually so the yogurt won't curdle. Set aside.

2. Finely chop **2 small onions** and sauté in **2 tablespoons sweet butter** until slightly brown. Add this to the madzoon with **1 tablespoon fresh mint**, chopped. Refrigerate and serve cold, adding water to thin the soup if it is too thick. Garnish with a **sprig of mint** in each bowl.

*6 to 8 servings*

# chlodnik

A Russian soup, very refreshing.

1. If you grow your own tender-skinned (and, of course, unwaxed) **cucumbers**, simply dice **2** of them. We prefer the thin Japanese type, but if you use fat ones, remove and discard seeds. Waxed ones will need to be peeled as well.

2. Combine: **1½ quarts buttermilk, 1 tablespoon prepared mustard, 1 teaspoon salt, 1 teaspoon sugar,** and **2 tablespoons fresh dill**, chopped. Add cucumbers and chill.

*6 servings*

SUMMER

# chilled simple borscht

From Fay Davidson.

1. Use a knife to scrape **3 bunches medium-sized beets**. Don't wash beets, but knife may be rinsed. Trim stem and root. Put into pot with **8 cups water** and **1 tablespoon salt**. Simmer for 20 minutes.

2. Add the juice of **2 lemons** and ⅓ **cup sugar**. Cook another 5 minutes and taste for sweetness, sourness, and salt. Borscht should taste strongly of all three, and once it is chilled, will need more salt than when hot. Adjust seasoning accordingly.

3. In a large bowl, beat **4 eggs** thoroughly. Add borscht slowly to eggs, mixing well to prevent curdling. Remove beets from borscht. Refrigerate borscht.

4. While beets are still warm, make **beet and goat cheese salad** (see index), if you like.

5. Serve chilled borscht with **sour cream** and **matzah** for those who like it.

*6 servings*

# chilled leek and sorrel soup

French sorrel can be purchased in early Spring in some markets. It is a perennial plant which is also easy to grow. There is a wild sorrel which is equally good; however, the leaves are so small it would be hard to collect enough for this soup.

1. Slit **4 leeks** lengthwise and wash thoroughly, discarding dried or brown tops. Slice the leeks into small pieces and sauté in a 4 quart pot with **2 tablespoons sweet butter** for 10 minutes. Add **1 quart sorrel**, washed, and **1½ quarts water**. Let cook for a half hour.

2. Pour the leeks and sorrel through a strainer, saving the broth in a bowl. Set aside.

3. Using the same pot, melt **3 tablespoons sweet butter** and add **3 tablespoons unbleached white flour**. Cook together a few minutes. Add **2 cups heavy cream** and cook until a thick white sauce has formed.

4. Using a food processor or blender, purée the leeks and sorrel with enough reserved broth for the machine to work adequately. Add this purée to soup pot. Bring to a boil, stirring well. Add as much reserved broth as you deem necessary. Season the soup with **2 tablespoons tamari, 1 teaspoon salt**, and freshly grated **black pepper**. Soup should be somewhat thick and quite sour.

5. Chill the soup and serve with **chives** *or* **scallions**, or serve hot, garnished the same way.

*6 servings*

**SUMMER**

# chilled elderberry soup

Elderberries, like other very tart wild fruits such as choke cherries and beach plums, make an excellent chilled soup of Scandinavian inspiration.

1. Strip **elderberries** from stems and measure. Turn into a pot with half that amount of water. For example: **20 cups (5 quarts) berries** to **10 cups of water**. Bring to a simmer and cook 10 to 15 minutes.

2. Turn into a cheesecloth-lined colander placed over another pot. Drain, and twist cheesecloth to extract juice. A potato masher will help. If you squeeze too hard, a bitter green scum will come out, so just extract the purple juice. Discard pulp.

3. To the amounts above, add **1⅔ cups organic sugar**, **2 teaspoons salt** and the **juice of 3 to 4 lemons**. Measure **1 cup cold water** and add a scant **tablespoon instant agar-agar*** to dissolve in it. Add to pot and bring all to a boil, stirring with a whisk. Taste to correct seasoning. When mixture boils, remove from heat, cool, and chill.

4. A tad too much agar will make the soup jellied. It will still be delicious. Serve cold, with **sour cream** if you like, and garnished with **blue borage flowers**, if they are available.

*serves 8 for a summer first course*

---

*Telephone brand, available in Asian markets.

# curried zucchini soup

1. Wash and trim **5 medium zucchini**. Cut up coarsely
   into a pot. Add **1 large onion** and **1 seeded green
   pepper**, both coarsely chopped. Add **3 cups water**
   and **1½ teaspoons curry powder** and bring to a boil.

2. When vegetables are soft, purée in food processor
   or blender. Add **1 cup heavy cream**, **½ cup milk**,
   **2 cups plain yogurt**, **3 tablespoons tamari**,
   **¼ teaspoon ground coriander**, **½ teaspoon turmeric**,
   and a **small bunch** of **straight leaf parsley**, chopped
   by hand. Taste for seasoning. Chill. Serve cold
   garnished with matchsticks of **zucchini** and a dollop
   of **yogurt**, if desired.

*8 servings*

SUMMER

# cream of corn soup

A soup customers wait for.

1. Use fresh local August corn. Scrape kernels from cobs of **1 dozen ears of corn** using a curved-blade knife, if available. Boil **cobs** in **water** to cover about ½ hour. Set kernels aside.

2. Chop ½ **small onion**, ½ **green sweet pepper**, and **1 stalk** and **leaves of celery**. Sauté vegetables in **2 tablespoons butter**. Add **2 tablespoons unbleached white flour** and cook, stirring, two minutes. Add **1 cup half-and-half** and bring to a boil.

3. Remove cobs from their broth and discard. Add **cob liquid** to vegetables and bring to a simmer. Don't boil or soup will curdle. Add **salt**, **pepper**, and **nutmeg** to taste. Now add corn kernels. If soup seems too thick, add **milk** until consistency is right. You may add **1 teaspoon sugar** to intensify the sweet corn taste.

*6 to 8 servings*

GARLIC SCAPES

# goat cheese salad

We use Coach Farms herbed fresh goat cheese.

1. Reconstitute ½ **cup sun-dried tomatoes** by simmering in ½ **cup water** in covered pot. When cool, cut into thin slices. Put into a container with **vinaigrette** (see glossary) to cover. Spread over a **slice of whole wheat bread** with **herbed goat cheese** and put into a toaster oven.

2. Prepare a bed of **lettuce**. Cut toasted bread into thin fingers and arrange on lettuce. Add a spoonful of sun-dried tomatoes, vinaigrette, and **red onion** slices.

*10 to 12 servings*

# greek salad

1. For each diner, arrange on a bed of **lettuce** (Boston preferred) **2 to 3 slices** of **fresh tomato**, a few **Kalamata olives, 2 salonika peppers**, a few slices **celery hearts, feta cheese** cut into thin slices and some thin slices of **red onion**.

2. Drizzle on a vinaigrette of **3½ parts oil** to **1 part fresh lemon juice, salt, pepper**, and some **dried oregano**.

# beet and goat cheese salad

1. Slip the skins off **beets** which have been previously cooked for **borscht** (see index) and slice them. While they are still warm, add **1 tablespoon chopped dill** and a few **fresh sage leaves** to the beets. Also add **3 tablespoons olive oil, 2 tablespoons balsamic vinegar**, and **salt** and **pepper** to taste. Correct seasoning and chill.

2. Pile on top of **lettuce** and serve with a soft, creamy **goat cheese**.

*6 servings*

**SUMMER**

KATE AND ROSE

249

# fruit salad with creamy dressing

1.  Prepare dressing first. In a food processor or mixer, combine **2 egg yolks, 1 tablespoon lemon juice, ½ teaspoon salt**. Turn machine on and add **1 cup grapeseed oil**, drop by drop at first and, as mayonnaise thickens, in a slow dribble. When oil is entirely incorporated, let machine run another 15 seconds and turn off. Add ⅓ **cup sour cream** and **1 tablespoon honey**. Turn machine on briefly to mix again and then taste for sweet, sour, and salt. Refrigerate until ready to use.

2.  For each diner, place a **single leaf** of **Boston** *or* **Red Leaf lettuce** on a dinner plate. Cut a **wedge** of **Crenshaw melon** into bite-sized pieces on the lettuce. Cut **6 red grapes** in half lengthwise and remove seeds with a knife tip. Cut a **small wedge** of **pineapple**, remove skin and core and cut into pieces on the salad.

3.  Serve each salad with a dollop of dressing and pass extra in a bowl.

*makes about 1½ cups dressing*

# hungarian pepper
# and egg salad

From Dick Cord.

1. A basket of different peppers suits this salad best, and
   at least one fourth of them should be hot Hungarian
   peppers. Remove seeds and slice 4 cups garden
   peppers. Slice 1 large onion.

2. In a large frying pan, heat ¼ cup olive oil. Add peppers
   and onion and fry over high heat, turning mixture
   with a slotted spoon constantly. Add ½ teaspoon salt
   and continue cooking until peppers and onion are
   golden and beginning to brown.

3. Fork-beat 5 eggs in a bowl. When peppers and onions
   are well browned, turn off heat and immediately
   add eggs. Stir well until eggs are set. Taste for salt.
   Refrigerate.

4. When ready to serve, spoon peppers over a bed of
   lettuce. Serve with sliced garden tomatoes and
   whole wheat toast.

*4 to 6 servings*

**SUMMER**

# peruvian salad
## with potatoes, corn, huacatay and queso blanco

A dozen years ago, Irene Infantas gave us small huacatay plants, seed of which came from her native Peru. The annual plants grow 10-12 feet high each summer before they die and leave seeds for the next year. The pungent leaves taste somewhat like oregano, but are spicier and brighter. (Send a self-addressed stamped envelope to 85 Ferris Street, Bridgeport, CT 06605 to get some huacatay seed for yourself).

1. Peel and cut into 1″ dice **6 purple Peruvian fingerling potatoes**. Steam until tender.

2. Chop **1 to 2 jalapeño peppers** and sauté in **2 to 3 tablespoons of grapeseed oil**. When softened, combine with potatoes and dress both with a ¼ **cup vinaigrette** (see glossary).

3. Drain liquid from **one can organic corn**. Kernels should measure approximately **1⅔ cups**.

4. Dice **2 cups queso blanco** *or* **quesco fresco** (from a Latina market), chop **2 tablespoons fresh huacatay leaves** and dice **1 red onion**. Fold these ingredients into potato-corn mixture.

5. Prepare a **bed of lettuce** for each diner. Top with a large spoonful of the salad, season to taste with **salt** and **pepper** and drizzle with **vinaigrette**.

*5 to 6 servings*

# felafel

This Mideastern snack food must be made with dried beans, not canned. Often made with chickpeas, it is even better when made with half fava beans, and best if made with all fava beans. However, dried, skinned split fava beans are not easily found in one's local grocery or health food store. We get ours from Kalustyans in New York City. You can get them online at kalustyans.com.

1. **Make felafel:** rinse **2 cups chickpeas** *or* **fava beans** *or* a combination of both. Cover with **water** and leave overnight.

2. The next day, drain and rinse. Leave in a colander for at least half an hour to dry.

3. Chop **1 large onion** and a bunch of **straight leaf parsley**. Slice **3 to 4 cloves garlic**.

4. Turn chickpeas and/or beans into a food processor. Add onions, garlic, and parsley. Add also: **1½ teaspoons salt, ½ teaspoon fresh ground pepper, 1½ teaspoons baking soda, 1½ teaspoons ground cumin, 1 teaspoon ground coriander, 1 tablespoon Spanish paprika,** and **1 teaspoon chili powder** (*or* **½ teaspoon cayenne**). Process. Scrape down bowl and process again. Don't make mixture too fine. Taste and adjust seasoning as you like. Turn into a bowl and pat down with your hand firmly. Let mixture rest in refrigerator at least one hour.

5. **Prepare tahini sauce:** rinse processor. Turn into it: **½ cup tahini, ¼ cup water, 3 tablespoons lemon juice, 4 cloves garlic,** peeled, **¼ cup parsley,** chopped, and **½ teaspoon salt.** Process, scrape down, and process again to make a smooth mayonnaise-like

sauce. Turn into a serving bowl and coat with a film of olive oil.

6. **Fry felafel:** just before dinner, shape felafel into small balls. Use your hands to squeeze out extra moisture into a bowl (to discard), and then roll and pat into a ball shape (we make them a little smaller than golf ball size). Heat **grapeseed oil** in a wok. You will need enough to just cover the balls as they cook. When oil is hot enough (try one ball to see if it browns quickly but does not burn—adjust flame accordingly), deep fry 6 felafel balls per diner. Drain on absorbent paper and repeat. Alternatively, felafel may be shaped into small cakes and pan-fried, preferably in a cast iron skillet.

7. Felafel is traditionally served as a sandwich in **pita bread**, with **sliced tomatoes** and **onions** and **shredded lettuce.** Offer the **tahini sauce, cucumber yogurt sauce** (see recipe below), and **pepperoncini peppers** as well.

*6 servings*

# cucumber-yogurt sauce
### for felafel

1. Peel, quarter, and seed **1 large cucumber.** Slice thinly. Place in a bowl and sprinkle with **salt.** Leave at room temperature for at least 30 minutes.

2. Rinse cucumber slices in a colander. Squeeze slices to remove moisture and place in a bowl. Add **2 cups organic whole milk yogurt.** Mince **1 clove garlic.** Chop finely **2 tablespoons parsley.** Stir both into sauce and refrigerate.

*2¹/₂ cups*

# szechuan noodles

1. Bring a big pot of **water** to a boil and add **1¼ pounds fresh very thin Chinese egg noodles** to the pot. Cover, but stir occasionally. When the pot returns to the boil, immediately dump contents into a colander in the sink. Pour **cold water** over. Shake to drain. Turn into a very large bowl and add **1 to 2 tablespoons dark Chinese sesame oil**. Mix well.

2. Combine **½ of a 7 oz. jar Lan Chi sesame paste** and **½ cup organic peanut butter** in a food processor. Boil **1½ cups water** and brew a **tea bag** in it for 4 or 5 minutes. Discard tea bag and add tea slowly to the peanut butter mix, turning machine on and off. Add **¼ cup soy sauce** and **2 teaspoons rice wine vinegar**.

3. Mince **4 scallions** and crush **3 cloves of garlic**. Stir these vegetables together in a separate bowl with **1 tablespoon chili-paste-with-garlic** (a Chinese condiment). Add **⅓ cup tamari, 3 tablespoons rice wine vinegar**, and scant **2 teaspoons agave nectar**. Add ⅔ of the peanut butter mixture and about half of the spicy sauce to the noodles. Mix all together thoroughly and chill.

4. Serve topped with **chopped scallion, eggplant in black bean sauce** (see following recipe) and with remaining sauces on the side.

*6 servings*

256

# eggplant in black bean sauce

1. Peel and slice **1 eggplant** and cut into strips 4″ long by ½″ thick and ½″ wide. In a large frying pan, fry the strips in **3 tablespoons grapeseed oil** over high heat until tender and cooked. Turn out into a bowl.

2. Cut **3 scallions** in half lengthwise and then into strips 3″ long. Place **1 tablespoon fermented black beans** (available in Chinese markets) in a bowl, cover with cold water and let soak 5 minutes. Drain, squeeze, and chop finely with a heavy knife. Peel **3 cloves garlic**. Use same frying pan and another **2 tablespoons grapeseed oil** to sauté scallions, the crushed cloves of garlic, and the fermented black beans. Add **1 teaspoon Chinese (toasted) sesame oil** and **1 teaspoon chili-paste-with-garlic** (available in Chinese markets). Stir into cooked eggplant and add **tamari** to taste. Can be served at room temperature or hot.

# spanokopites

This recipe produces individual triangular spinach pastries instead of a large spinach "pie." From Hope Zachariades.

1. Defrost **1½ pounds frozen chopped spinach.**

2. Chop **1 medium onion** *or* **5 to 6 scallions** and sauté in **2 tablespoons olive oil** until softened. Squeeze defrosted spinach dry and add to onions. Cook until all moisture is evaporated. Remove from heat and add ⅓ to ½ **pound** crumbled **Feta cheese,** ⅓ **cup** chopped **fresh dill,** ½ **pound pot cheese** (the driest possible cottage cheese), fresh ground **pepper, nutmeg** to taste, and **1 to 2 eggs.** Start with 1 egg, mix well together, and add the second egg if mixture seems dry enough to incorporate it. A mixture that is too moist will break through the filo.

3. You will need about ½ **pound good quality phyllo pastry** (available at Greek markets; see glossary). Once the pastry is opened you must work quickly before it dries out and becomes useless. To give yourself more time, enclose it in two sheets of waxed paper and cover with a damp towel.

4. Melt ¼ **pound sweet butter** and cook over low heat until milk solids have evaporated and butter smells nutty. Use a pastry brush to butter a cookie sheet. Cut phyllo pastry in half lengthwise, using a sharp knife, and return to waxed paper enclosure. Remove one piece at a time and place lengthwise in front of you. Brush lightly with the melted butter and place 1 to 2 tablespoons of spinach filling at the narrow end nearest you. Fold phyllo over spinach in thirds,

making an even more narrow lengthwise strip. It helps to not fold evenly but to let phyllo flare slightly open at far end. **Butter** lightly along top of strip and begin folding right-angled triangles until you get to the end of the strip. It takes practice to produce neat spanokopites.

5. As you complete each piece, place on cookie sheet. The spanokopites can touch each other as they are laid in the pan. Brush each completed triangle with melted **butter**. When pan is full, it can be refrigerated or frozen.

6. Bake at 375°F until puffed and browned, about 30 minutes. Serve with a **greek salad** (see index).

*6 to 8 servings*

**SUMMER**

# zucchini flan

This savory dish is a quiche without a pie crust shell.

1. Preheat oven to 475°F. Thinly slice **6 medium to small zucchini** and **2 medium onions.**

2. Mix onions and zucchini together in 11″ x 14″ pan with **1 teaspoon dried basil, 1 teaspoon oregano**, and **salt** and **pepper** to taste. Add **1 large clove garlic**, crushed, and moisten vegetables with **grapeseed oil.** Bake in preheated oven turning often, until well browned. Remove from oven and let cool 10 minutes.

3. Slice **3 cups Swiss cheese.** Place cheese slices over onions and zucchini.

4. Beat together in a bowl **5 eggs** and **1 quart heavy cream.** Add a little **nutmeg, salt,** and **pepper.** Pour this mixture over the browned squash and cheese. Turn oven to 350°F and bake until puffed and brown. To reheat, bake at 350°F for 10 minutes or until quite hot.

*8 to 10 servings*

# zucchini latkes

From Fay Davidson.

1. Grate **2 medium zucchinis** in a food processor or by hand. Grate **1 small onion**. Turn into a colander in a sink and let drain 5 minutes.

2. Beat **2 eggs** in a bowl large enough to hold zucchini mixture. Squeeze zucchini handful by handful and discard exuded moisture. Add squeezed zucchini to eggs. Add **2½ tablespoons cornmeal**, **2½ tablespoons flour**, **½ teaspoon salt**, fresh ground **pepper**, and a pinch each **baking powder** and **sugar**. Stir all together and refrigerate until ready to serve.

3. Heat **2 tablespoons butter** and **2 tablespoons grapeseed oil** in a frying pan. Use a fork to pat out small pancakes (4″ to 5″ across) and fry until brown on one side. Turn with spatula, pressing down on the latke to flatten it.

4. Serve 3 latkes per diner with **sour cream** on the side.

*6 servings*

SUMMER

# stuffed vegetable platter

Consisting of green peppers stuffed with lentils, tomatoes stuffed
with eggplant mousse, and zucchini stuffed with rice, any one
makes a nice summer dinner. The combination is a feast.

1. **Make tomatoes with eggplant mousse:** bake **1 large
   eggplant** in a 400°F oven ½ hour or until soft (check
   with a small knife). Scoop out flesh into mixer and add
   **1 clove garlic**, crushed, ½ cup finely chopped **straight
   leaf parsley, 1 tablespoon olive oil, 3 tablespoons
   Parmesan cheese** and ⅓ to ⅔ cup **breadcrumbs.**
   Add **2 eggs** and **salt** and **pepper** to taste. Mixture
   should be soft but not sloppy. Cut off stem end of **6 firm
   local tomatoes** and scoop out flesh (reserve it). Fill
   tomatoes with eggplant mixture. Don't mound it
   too high. Dribble **olive oil** on top and sprinkle with
   **Parmesan.** Refrigerate until dinnertime.

2. **Make zucchini stuffed with rice:** choose **5 medium
   sized zucchini.** Cut in half crosswise and use an
   apple corer to make hollow tubes by first working
   from one side and then the other. Chop **1 medium
   onion.** Sauté it in **2 tablespoons olive oil** until soft.
   Remove pan from heat and add to it ½ **cup raw white
   rice, 2 tablespoons** chopped **straight leaf parsley,**
   1½ **tablespoons** chopped **fresh dill,** ¼ **cup dried
   currants,** and **2 tablespoons squash corings,**
   chopped fine. Also add **salt, pepper,** and ¼ **cup
   pignoli nuts.** Make a "broth" by mixing **1 teaspoon
   tamari** in **1 cup water** and moisten the uncooked
   rice mixture with a few tablespoons of this. Taste for
   **salt and pepper.** Use your fingers to stuff zucchini
   tubes. Place in a pan and add the "broth" to

½″ deep in the pan. Cover with foil and refrigerate until dinnertime.

3. **Make peppers stuffed with lentils:** pick over **1 cup lentils** to be sure there are no stones or debris. Cover with **water** and simmer until tender. Choose **6 small green** *or* **red bell peppers** that seem blocky enough to stand up by themselves. Remove stem and white pith and discard. Set aside. Peel and thinly slice **3 onions.** Sauté in ¾ **cup olive oil** with **1 teaspoon sweet paprika** and ¼ **teaspoon cayenne pepper** until onions are golden. Turn off heat and set aside. Add **1 cup cracked wheat** (bulgur) to the lentils. Add enough **water** to cook the wheat, and cover pan. This should take 5 to 10 minutes—taste to see. Don't add too much water, which would make the mixture porridgy. Combine lentils, bulgur, and onion-oil mix. Add **1 tablespoon salt** and fresh ground **pepper** to taste. Now add reserved tomato and zucchini pulp, chopped coarsely. Taste and correct seasoning. Stuff peppers with lentil-wheat mixture. Place in a pan and add ¼″ water. Cover loosely with foil.

4. Half an hour before serving time, bake all three stuffed vegetables in a preheated 400°F oven. The zucchini and peppers are baked covered but the tomatoes are not. Serve **yogurt** *or* **avgolemono sauce** (see following recipe) over zucchini. All 3 stuffed vegetables reheat (uncovered) very satisfactorily.

*6 servings*

**SUMMER**

# avgolemono sauce

1. In a small pot, mix together **1 tablespoon cornstarch,
1 tablespoon cold water,** and the **juice of 2 lemons.**
Add **2 eggs** and beat over moderate heat until
thickened. Thin with ⅓ to ⅔ **cup water** and season
with ½ **teaspoon tamari.** Serve over stuffed zucchini.
This sauce cannot be reheated successfully.

NOEL

264

# mid-east lentils and rice

The "Mess of Pottage" of biblical fame.

1. Pick over **2 cups French lentils** to remove stones and debris. Turn into a soup kettle with **3½ cups water** and bring to a boil. Turn heat down and simmer 15 minutes.

2. Add **1 cup long grain white rice** and **1 cup water** and simmer 15 minutes more.

3. Meanwhile, thinly slice **2 large Spanish onions**. In a frying pan, sauté the onions in **1 cup olive oil** until golden brown. Turn onions and oil into pot of lentils and rice. Add **1½ teaspoons salt**, **1 teaspoon paprika**, and **½ teaspoon cayenne**. Continue cooking until lentils and rice are well-cooked. Correct seasoning.

4. We serve this with **green bean stew**, **olive and walnut accompaniment** (see following recipes), **pita bread**, and, if you like, **yogurt** and **feta cheese**.

*6 servings*

SUMMER

# olive and walnut accompaniment

1. Coarsely chop **1 cup pitted green olives**. Chop
   **½ cup walnuts**, **½ cup straight leaf parsley**, **⅓ cup
   onion**, and **½ cup scallions**. Pit and chop **⅔ cup
   Kalamata olives**. Mix all together in a bowl.

2. Combine: **¼ cup olive oil**, **½ teaspoon paprika**,
   **⅛ teaspoon cayenne**, and **3 tablespoons lemon
   juice**. Add and stir mixture well. Refrigerate.

*makes 3½ cups*

# spiced mid-east green bean stew

The seasoning has been adjusted by Becky Gomes, whose
Lebanese grandmother made it this way.

1. Peel and slice **1 large Spanish onion**. Sauté until
   golden in **3 tablespoons olive oil** in a sauce pot.
   Add a small pinch of **ground cinnamon**, a generous
   grating of a **whole nutmeg**, and a pinch of **ground
   allspice**. Set aside.

2. Cut **¾ pound fresh string beans** in half, or in thirds.
   Add to onions. Cover and cook 5 minutes. Add **1½ cups
   chopped tomatoes**, preferably fresh, **¼ teaspoon
   salt**, and fresh grated **pepper**. Cover and simmer until
   beans are done. Serve at room temperature as a side
   dish to **lentils and rice** (see index).

*5 to 6 servings*

# justina robledo's
# puerto rican rice

1. **Make sofrito:** finely chop 1 cup onion, 1 cup green pepper, 1 jalapeño pepper, 4 cloves garlic, and ½ cup cilantro.

2. In a medium saucepan fry sofrito in ¼ cup olive oil over moderate heat until golden. Add 4 tablespoons tomato paste and continue sautéing five minutes more.

3. Add in 1 cup chopped pimento-stuffed green olives, and 1 cup plain tomato sauce. Bring to a simmer.

4. **Make rice:** meanwhile, wash 1½ cups short grain (mediano) Goya rice. Add to the sauce then stir and fry for several minutes. Gradually add up to 1 cup water, scraping the bottom of the pot. Turn heat to low, keep lid on and cool until done. Add more water if need be.

5. Add salt and pepper to taste.

*6 servings*

SUMMER

# puerto rican plantain pie

### pastelon de amarillos

from Justina Robledo and Carmen Russo

1. You will need **4 very ripe plantains**. They should be soft when pressed and have near-black skin. Use a knife to peel them, then cut each lengthwise into thirds. Fry over moderate heat in a large cast iron skillet in a mixture of **2 to 3 tablespoons grapeseed oil** and **2 tablespoons olive oil**. Turn to brown both sides. Remove plantains to a large dish and set aside. Soak **½ cup crumbled soy protein** in **warm water** to cover.

2. Make a savory filling: dice **1 large onion** and **1 large green pepper**. Slice **3 cloves of garlic**. Sauté these vegetables in the same frying pan, adding **oil** if need be, over moderate heat. When vegetables begin to brown, add **1 teaspoon crumbled oregano**, **½ cup** chopped **cilantro** and **¾ cup** diced **seitan**. Squeeze liquid from soy protein and add it. Cook and stir this mixture. When it is nicely browned and savory, it should also be moist. If you have **3 to 4 tablespoons gravy** leftover or in your freezer, add it now. Or just add the liquid from the soy protein, or even plain water. Season with **salt** and **pepper**.

3. Lightly **oil** a 9″ x 14″ glass oven dish. Place a layer of plantains in pan. **Salt** and **pepper** them. Add the filling. Top with remaining plantains. Fork-beat **4 eggs** in a bowl and drizzle over the plantains. If you like, sprinkle the top with **2 to 3 tablespoons Parmesan** (Carmen does it this way).

4. Bake in a preheated 350°F oven for 20 minutes. Don't overcook, or the eggs will be tough. For this reason this is not a dish which reheats well.

5. Serve with Justina Robledo's **puerto rican rice** (see previous recipe).

*5 to 6 servings*

CARMEN

# strozzapreti

Italian swiss chard dumplings so tasty that the priest choked on them—strozzapreti means priestchokers! You will need some good homemade tomato sauce for this.

1. **Make dumplings:** wash **1 large bunch Swiss chard**. You will need about **2 pounds** or a little less than **3 cups** once it is cooked. Cook it in the water that clings to the leaves. Drain, cool, and squeeze dry. It is easiest to use a food processor here, however a blender or even chopping by hand with a heavy knife will do. Purée the chard adding **3 eggs** (if using a machine) or beat the eggs by hand and add to finely chopped chard. Melt ⅔ **stick butter** and add with **1 cup Parmesan** and **1 to 1½ cups breadcrumbs**. Add salt and pepper to taste. Chill.

2. **Make tomato sauce:** in a large pot heat ¼ **cup olive oil**. Finely chop **2 medium onions** and sauté together with ½ **teaspoon red pepper flakes** (optional). Sauté slowly, don't let it burn. Add **2 cloves garlic**, crushed, and **1 small can tomato paste** and cook, stirring with a wooden spoon, until the paste is dry and thick. Using tomato paste can, add **1 can water** and cook again slowly, stirring often, until sauce thickens. Now add a **28 oz. can Italian plum tomatoes**. Break up the tomatoes somewhat with your wooden spoon. Add several leaves of **fresh basil**, *or* **2 teaspoons dried**. Simmer partly covered for at least one hour. Taste for **salt**. Some canned tomatoes are very salty. Add salt if necessary and **pepper** to taste. Leftover tomato sauce can be frozen.

3.  **To serve:** fill a large pot ⅓ full of **water**, add
    **1 tablespoon salt** and bring to a boil. Turn heat down
    to a simmer. Test one dumpling to see if it holds
    together in this poaching liquid. If not, stir in **more
    breadcrumbs**. The point, of course, is to keep them
    as light as possible and not have them fall apart.
    When batter is perfect, poach about 5 dumplings per
    serving using 2 spoons to shape ovals. Drain on paper
    towel before placing in a shallow soup bowl. Sprinkle
    with fresh grated **Parmesan** and serve **tomato sauce**
    on the side.

*8 to 10 servings*

SUMMER

# syrian baked stuffed eggplant
## with tempeh

The tempeh substitutes for lamb in this simple Syrian casserole, and tamari takes the place of chicken stock.

1. **Stuffing:** horizontally slice **1 cake tempeh** to make 2 thinner layers, then dice very finely. Finely chop **1 medium onion.** Sauté both in ⅓ **cup olive oil,** adding ⅔ **cup pignoli nuts,** dash **ground coriander, dash allspice,** ⅓ **teaspoon nutmeg,** ⅔ **teaspoon cinnamon, salt,** and **pepper.** Fry mixture until well browned. Turn off heat, scrape filling into a bowl and deglaze pan with a splash of **red wine,** pour into a bowl.

2. **Prepare eggplants:** preheat oven to 375°F. Peel **3 medium-sized eggplants** and slice lengthwise into ½″ thick slices. Heat frying pan or griddle very hot and sear eggplant slices on both sides, using a little **grapeseed oil.**

3. **Stuff eggplant:** in a shallow baking pan arrange slices of eggplant side-by-side, trying to find a matching slice for each one which will sit on top, sandwich-style. Spoon about 2 to 3 tablespoons stuffing between the eggplant slices. In a bowl, dilute a **28 oz. can plain tomato sauce** with **1 can water,** whisk in ¾ **teaspoon cinnamon, 1 teaspoon salt,** and freshly ground **pepper.** Pour over eggplant sandwiches and bake uncovered for 20 minutes.

4. **Meanwhile, prepare rice pilaf:** finely chop **1 small onion**. Sauté in **2 tablespoons olive oil** in frying pan with **1 oz. crushed fides** (very fine noodles available in Greek stores, sometimes called shehrieh in Arabic stores). Fry until noodles begin to brown. Add **2 cups white rice** and sauté another 5 minutes, stirring well. Stop before the noodles burn. Add **3 cups water** and **2 tablespoons tamari**. Cover and simmer until rice is tender, adding more water if necessary.

5. Serve eggplant sandwiches and pilaf with plain **yogurt**.

*8 to 10 servings*

SUMMER

# pesto mashed potatoes

Comfort food for potato lovers.

1. Peel **6 russet potatoes** and cut into 2 inch pieces.
   Peel **6 large cloves of garlic**. Turn potatoes and
   garlic into a pot and barely cover with **water**. Add
   **2 teaspoons salt** and cook about 15 minutes or until
   just done.

2. Meanwhile chop enough **fresh basil leaves** to
   measure **2 cups**. Grate ½ **cup Parmesan**. Turn
   basil and Parmesan into a food processor and add
   **1 teaspoon Kosher salt** and ½ **teaspoon crushed
   red pepper flakes**. Turn machine on and add ⅓ **cup
   olive oil**. Turn off when blended and set aside.

3. Drain water from cooked potatoes and garlic. Return
   pot to stove and shake over medium heat to dry. Use
   potato masher to coarsely crush potatoes. Now add
   the contents of the processor together with ½ **cup
   cream**. Turn off heat and cover pot to keep warm
   until serving.

4. Serve with **shredded beet latkes** (see following
   recipe).

*5 to 6 servings*

# shredded beet latkes
## (pancakes)

1. Peel and shred **1 pound beets**, either by hand or by using processor attachment. Turn into a bowl. Mince **1 teaspoon fresh rosemary** and add to beets together with **1 teaspoon salt** and **2 tablespoons flour.** Stir all together thoroughly.

2. Use a heavy large frying pan (preferably a cast iron skillet) to heat **2 tablespoons coconut oil** (*or* **2 tablespoons butter,** if the oil is unavailable).

3. Add another **1 to 2 tablespoons flour** to beets. When coconut oil is hot, use a fork to pat out small (about 4 inches in diameter) thin cakes. Fry over moderate heat until the bottoms are crispy. Turn and use spatula to press down on latkes. Sauté until crisp and brown.

4. Serve as a side dish. We like this with **pesto mashed potatoes** (see index).

*3 to 4 servings*

SUMMER

# fresh blueberry pie

1. Roll out **pie crust** (see index) to fit a pie pan. Prick at edge of bottom and sides and line with foil. Weight with beans or rice and bake at 400°F for 5 minutes. Remove foil and beans, turn oven down to 375°F and continue baking pie crust until it is done: golden brown.

2. Combine in a pot: **⅔ cup organic sugar, 3 tablespoon cornstarch, ⅛ teaspoon salt, 1 cup water, 1 cup blueberries, ¼ teaspoon cinnamon**, and the grated **rind** and **juice of ½ lemon**. Pick over enough **blueberries** to yield **3 cups** and set aside. Cook the mixture in the pot, stirring, until it comes to a simmer and thickens. Stir over heat for another 30 seconds and remove from heat. Immediately add reserved blueberries and **1 tablespoon butter**. Let cool. Turn into pie shell and chill.

3. Served with **whipped cream**: beat **2 cups heavy cream** until stiff with **1½ teaspoons vanilla extract** and **2 tablespoon sugar**.

*one pie*

# blueberry whipped cream roll

1. Place **4 eggs**, in their shells, in a bowl and cover with hot tap water. Meanwhile, preheat oven to 375°F. Butter and line a **jelly roll pan** with waxed paper.

2. Break warmed eggs into mixer. Add ¼ **teaspoon salt**, and **1 teaspoon baking powder** and begin beating at high speed. Slowly add ¾ **cup sugar** and beat until eggs are tripled in bulk, about 10 minutes. Add **1 teaspoon vanilla extract**, mix it in well, and remove bowl from machine. Sift ¾ **cup unbleached white flour** over eggs and carefully fold flour and egg mix together. Turn into pan, smoothing top gently with spatula, and bake 10 to 15 minutes or until light brown. Be careful, this cake burns easily.

3. Prepare a dish towel the size of the pan by sifting **confectioner's sugar** over it. Turn cake out onto towel and peel off waxed paper in strips. Roll up cake in towel and lift onto racks to cool.

4. Combine in a pot ½ **cup sugar**, 1½ **tablespoons cornstarch**, ½ **cup water**, ½ **cup blueberries**, ¼ **teaspoon cinnamon**, and 1½ **teaspoons lemon juice**. Simmer mixture, stirring well. As it begins to thicken, add 1½ **cups blueberries** and immediately remove from stove. Let cool.

5. Beat **1 cup heavy cream** and ½ **teaspoon vanilla extract** until stiff. Unroll cooled cake and spread with whipped cream. Top with cooled blueberry mixture. Reroll cake and store in refrigerator until time to serve.

*8 to 10 servings*

# fruit cheese tart

1. Roll out **pie crust** (see index) to fit pie pan and chill in refrigerator. Soften **6 oz. cream cheese**.

2. In a pot combine **3 cups peeled sliced peaches**, ½ **cup blueberries**, ⅓ **cup sugar**, **1 tablespoon flour**, ⅛ **teaspoon cinnamon**, and grated **rind of** ½ **lemon**. Stir together well, cover and simmer about 5 minutes or until fruit is tender. Uncover pot to cool fruit. Preheat oven to 375°F.

3. Separate **3 eggs**, whites into mixer and yolks into a bowl or food processor. Beat whites until stiff but not dry. If you have a food processor, yolks and remaining ingredients can be mixed in it. If not, turn whites out into another bowl and beat yolks in mixer, combining them with **2 tablespoon lemon juice**, the **softened cream cheese**, **1 tablespoon flour**, ¼ **cup sugar**, **1 teaspoon grated lemon rind**, ½ **teaspoon salt**, and lastly, add ½ **cup heavy cream**. Scrape mixer bowl or food processor sides and beat again. Fold egg whites and cheese-yolk mixture together carefully but thoroughly.

4. Turn cooked fruit into chilled pie shell. Top with cheese mixture and place in oven. Bake for 30 to 40 minutes or until cheese topping is light brown. Serve tart at room temperature.

*one tart*

# almond berry tart

1. Make **processor pie crust** (see index). Roll out and fit into a 10″ quiche pan with removable bottom. Weight with foil and beans and bake in a 350°F oven until just set but not brown. Remove foil and beans (save for future pie baking) and set prebaked crust aside.

2. Soften **2½ tablespoons unsalted butter**. Put **¾ cup almonds** into a food processor and pulverize with **3 tablespoons sugar**. Add **butter**, **½ teaspoon vanilla**, **¼ teaspoon almond extract**, and **3 egg yolks**. Process.

3. Spread almond butter mix over pie crust. Top with **berries**: raspberries will require **2 cups** to bake in the pie at 350°F for 20 minutes. Cool pie and top with **2 more cups of fresh raspberries**, uncooked. For **cranberries**, top pie with **12 oz. fruit**, sprinkle with **⅓ cup sugar** and bake until berries pop, about 30 minutes. Cool.

4. Serve either pie with **crème fraîche** *or* **whipped cream**.

*one 10″ fruit tart*

# blueberry peach sundae

1.  Peel and slice enough fresh **peaches** to yield **3 cups**. Place in a pot with **½ cup blueberries**, **⅓ cup sugar** and a dash **cinnamon**. Add **⅓ cup** good **fruit juice**, cover the pot and simmer 5 minutes or until fruit is tender. Cool and chill.

2.  Serve blueberry peach sauce over **vanilla ice cream** and top with whipped cream (**1 cup heavy cream** beaten stiff with **1 tablespoon sugar** and **½ teaspoon vanilla extract**).

*6 servings*

# blueberry peach flummery

A New England version of Russian kissl.

1.  In a blender, in 2 or 3 batches, purée **5 unpeeled peaches**, **1 cup blueberries**, **2¼ tablespoons lemon** *or* **lime juice**, **¼ teaspoon salt**, **¼ cup honey**, **6 tablespoons cornstarch** *or* **arrowroot**, and **¾ cup fruit juice** (without sugar or additives). Turn each batch into a pot. Rinse blender with **¾ cup water** and add to pot with **2 cups fruit juice**.

2.  Bring to rolling boil, stirring well. Let cool about 10 minutes. Turn into custard cups or glass serving dishes and chill.

3.  Serve with **heavy cream** and **slivered almonds**.

*12 servings*

SUMMER

# blueberry peach pie

1. Prepare enough **pie crust** for a two crust pie
   (see index).

2. Preheat oven to 450°F. Pick over **3 cups blueberries**
   and combine with **2 tablespoons cornstarch**, a
   **dash of salt, ½ teaspoon fresh grated nutmeg,**
   **⅔ cup sugar**, and **1 tablespoon flour**. Toss together.

3. Peel and slice **4 small peaches** and squeeze
   **1 teaspoon lemon juice** over them.

4. Roll out pie crust and fit into pie pan. Add blueberry
   mixture evenly. Top with peach mixture. Dot with
   **1½ tablespoons butter**. Roll out top crust and place
   over the fruit. Trim pastry, crimp edges and slash top.

5. Bake 450°F for 10 minutes and at 350°F for about
   30 minutes more. Best served warm, with **vanilla ice
   cream**.

# clafouti

A French country style pudding with fruit. It must be served warm.
From Rachel Portnoy.

1. Break **1 egg** into a food processor and add **1 yolk**
   (reserve white for other purposes or discard it). Add
   **⅓ cup sugar** and process until mix is fluffy. Heat oven
   to 375°F.

2. Add **¼ cup all-purpose flour** and blend briefly.

3. Add **¾ cup crème fraiche** (if you have no source to
   buy it, it can be made by leaving 1 cup heavy cream
   and 1 tablespoon buttermilk at room temperature
   overnight.) Flavor with **1½ tablespoons Grand.
   Marnier liquor** and **½ teaspoon vanilla extract**.

4. You will need **10 to 12 oz. of fresh fruit**: pitted
   **cherries, raspberries**, sliced **strawberries**, sliced
   **pears**. Place fruit in an ovenproof dish which you can
   bring to the table. Pour pudding mix over. Bake until
   puffed and slightly brown. Serve with a little **heavy
   cream** on the side.

*6 servings*

# peach cobbler

1.  Chop ½ **cup walnuts**, using a food processor or a knife. Set aside.

2.  Preheat oven to 400°F. In mixer, use a flat beater to combine **3 cups unbleached all-purpose white flour**, ¾ **teaspoon baking powder**, and ¾ **teaspoon salt**. While mixing, add ½ **pound sweet butter** cut into small pieces. Do not worry about over-beating. Remove ⅔ cup of this mixture for streusel and set it aside. Turn the rest into a 9″ x 12″ baking pan. Press down lightly.

3.  Peel about **5 peaches** and cut into slices. Press peach slices into the dry mix. Pour ⅔ **cup maple syrup** over slices and sprinkle lightly with **cinnamon**. Bake 10 minutes.

4.  Add walnuts to mixer together with reserved streusel mix, **2 tablespoons date sugar** and ½ **teaspoon cinnamon**. Mix together. Set this streusel aside.

5.  Meanwhile, in mixing bowl combine **3 cups sour cream**, **3 egg yolks**, and ¼ **cup maple syrup**. Whisk thoroughly. If too thick for pouring, add up to ¼ **cup buttermilk** or an appropriate juice. Pour sour cream mixture over the peaches. Spread evenly. Sprinkle streusel over cobber and continue baking about ½ hour more. Cobbler is done when top is golden brown and there is a minimum of movement of when pan is jiggled.

6.  Serve with **heavy cream**.

*8 to 10 servings*

# plum upside down cake

1. Preheat oven to 375°F. Remove ½ **cup sweet butter** from refrigerator to soften.

2. Place a 9″ round cake pan on a burner on the stove. Melt **2 tablespoons sweet butter** in pan and tilt to butter the sides as well as the bottom. Sprinkle ½ **cup brown sugar** evenly over the butter.

3. Slice **3 to 4 ripe Italian (prune) plums** (unpeeled) to cover bottom of prepared pan. The half moon shapes of the plum slices lend themselves to creative spiral patterning.

4. In a medium bowl use a dry whisk to blend together **1½ cups flour, 1½ teaspoons baking powder,** and ½ **teaspoon salt.**

5. In another bowl use your clean hands to cream together softened butter while gradually adding **1 cup sugar.** When sugar no longer feels grainy to the touch, wash your hands and use a wooden spoon to beat **2 eggs** plus **one egg white** into the mixture, one at a time. Beat well with wooden spoon until well mixed.

6. Measure out ⅓ **cup milk.** Add ¾ **teaspoon vanilla extract.** Alternatively add flour mixture and milk to batter, beginning and ending with flour. Stir only enough to blend; do not overmix. Turn batter into plum-prepared pan. Bang pan once on counter to eliminate large air bubbles.

SUMMER

7. Bake at 375°F until sides of cake have shrunk slightly from sides of pan and cake is golden brown, about 45 minutes. Cool 5 minutes on a rack. Run knife around rim and turn cake out onto a plate. If you like, make **whipped cream**: beat **2 cups heavy cream** with **2 tablespoons Japanese Plum Wine** until cream is stiff. Serve on top of plum cake.

*10 servings*

# shrikhand

A very simple delicious Indian dessert, from the state of Gujarat.

1. Turn **1 quart** of **whole milk plain yogurt**, preferably from an Indian market, into a cheesecloth-lined colander. Tie up the four corners of the cheesecloth so that the bag of yogurt will be lifted above a bowl. You can use the faucet of your sink or a chopstick to support the bag over a tall container. Let drain at least 3 hours.

2. Use a small pot to stew ½ **teaspoon saffron pistils** in **1 to 2 tablespoons milk**. Once it simmers, turn off the heat. Crush cardamom pods, remove seeds and use a mortar and pestle to crush seeds. You will need ½ **teaspoon** freshly ground **cardamom seed**. Chop ⅓ **cup pistachios**.

3. When yogurt has drained sufficiently, turn it into a bowl. Add saffron milk, cardamom and pistachios (keep some nuts to the side for garnish). Stir all together with up to ¼ **cup sugar**. Taste to decide how sweet you want it to be.

4. Put spoonfuls of shrikhand in small bowls. You should have enough for 6 to 7 diners. Top with reserved pistachios and serve with **fresh raspberries**.

*6 to 7 servings*

# hot fudge sauce

For ice cream sundaes.

1. Melt **10 oz. unsweetened chocolate** together with **6 tablespoons unsalted butter** in a covered pot over very low heat. We prefer unsweetened Scharffen Berger chocolate.

2. Bring ¼ **cup water** to a boil. When chocolate is melted, whisk it and add the hot water. It will immediately "seize," or become stiff. Remove from heat.

3. Add **1 cup sugar**, ½ **cup agave nectar**, ¼ **teaspoon salt**, and ¾ **cup heavy cream**. Use whisk to stir all together and return to a simmer, stirring well.

4. Use over best-quality, locally-made **vanilla ice cream**, with a **whipped cream** topping. Or turn into a container and refrigerate until needed. Reheat, stirring, over a low flame.

*makes about one pint of hot fudge*

# toffee cheese cream

This surprising recipe is of British origin. It is a rich treat over fruit.

1. Cover **1 can condensed milk** with water in a pot and bring to a boil. Simmer, covered with water, 3 hours. Let cool, then chill.

2. Soften **½ pound cream cheese** and **½ pound Mascarpone cheese** by leaving at room temperature for an hour.

3. Open can. Scrape contents into a food processor. Add **¼ cup heavy cream** to thin the caramelized milk. Turn on machine briefly. Turn off; add both cheeses and process until smooth.

4. Beat **2 cups heavy cream** together with **¼ cup sugar, 1½ tablespoons brandy** and **1½ tablespoons Kahlùa**. Beat to soft whipped stage.

5. Fold contents of processor and whipped cream together. Chill. Serve over fresh **peaches** *or* **pears**.

*about 1 quart*

SUMMER

# lime tart

1. Preheat oven to 400°F. Roll out **pie crust** (see index) and fit crust into a pie pan. Prick at intersection of rim and bottom with fork. Line crust with aluminum foil and weight with dried beans or lentils. Bake for 5 to 10 minutes, or until edges are light brown. Carefully remove foil and beans and bake until crust is nicely browned, about 10 minutes more. Remove from oven and cool.

2. In a stainless steel pot, combine **6 eggs, 5 egg yolks,** ⅓ **cup honey**, grated rind and juice of **4 limes**. Place over medium to low flame and stir with whisk. When mixture warms, add **1½ sticks sweet butter**, cut into pieces. Continue stirring until mixture starts to thicken. Cook, whisking constantly, another 30 seconds until mixture is creamy and slightly thick. Do not overcook. Remove from heat and continue whisking another minute. Let cool 10 minutes and them pour into the baked pie shell. Place in refrigerator until set up, about 2 hours.

3. Before serving, top pie with **honey whipped cream**: beat together until stiff **1 cup heavy cream, 1½ teaspoons honey** and ½ **teaspoon vanilla extract**. A grating of **lime rind** over the whipped cream is a finishing touch.

KARTOFCHIN

# Breads, Breakfast & Miscellany

# bread baking

Making your own bread differs from other cooking in that it depends less on accuracy of measured ingredients and time elapsed between steps than it does on learning the "feel" of the dough and sensing how temperature and humidity are affecting it. So bread baking is more subjective and intuitive than calculated. It is very satisfying in that it is hard to produce an inedible loaf. Once you have some practice, there's no reason you can't make excellent bread, and no excuse for over-sweetened and over-yeasted loaves that pass for "good" homemade.

Having a mixer with a dough hook is a necessity for us. Kneading by hand takes time and one is tempted to add more flour than necessary to make the dough stop being sticky sooner than is possible. You can knead by hand if you don't mind the mess and will give the kneading enough time before more flour goes in.

We rise bread twice: once after kneading and once in the pans. We don't make a "sponge" or proof the yeast since both procedures seem a waste of time. The first rising is long, 1½ to 2 hours. This requires a cool place in the kitchen and if that is not possible, then a cool place elsewhere in the house. Rising that is too rapid produces a yeasty-tasting bread with underdeveloped flavor. The second rising should be brief, ½ hour to 45 minutes. The remaining yeast growth takes place in the oven.

Potato cooking water (and mashed potatoes themselves) seems to do something wonderful to bread. Some old-fashioned sourdough starters begin with potatoes, which purportedly attract very particular wild yeasts. We save potato-cooking water in the refrigerator for sourdough pancakes and for bread making.

Bread freezes very well. Place cooled bread in a plastic bag and freeze. To reheat, remove from bag and heat in a 350°F oven for half an hour.

BREAD

# cottage cheese dill bread

From Menga Thurm.

1. Gently warm **2½ pounds cottage cheese** in a pot over low heat, stirring occasionally.

2. Dissolve **4 tablespoons yeast** in **1 cup warm water** (potato water if available) in a mixer or large bowl, and add ⅓ **cup honey, 2½ tablespoons caraway seed, 2 bunches fresh dill**, chopped, **1 stick sweet butter**, cut into pieces, **1 onion**, peeled and chopped fine, **1½ tablespoons salt, 1 teaspoon baking soda**, the warmed cottage cheese, and **4 large unbeaten eggs**. Turn mixer on or begin to beat, adding about **10 cups unbleached white flour**. Beat thoroughly. This dough should be made drier than other breads, so you may need up to **8 cups more flour**. There should be no dampness or stickiness when you pinch it. When well beaten and silky smooth, turn out into bowl and let double for 2 hours, covered with a dish towel or tablecloth.

3. Punch down, **butter** or use **lecithin oil** (see glossary) to grease 3 to 4 large bread pans and divide dough. This bread rises more than most, so shape dough into smaller loaves than you would ordinarily. Let rise in pans 30 to 40 minutes. Preheat oven to 350°F. If you like, brush loaves with beaten **egg white** while they are baking and sprinkle with **coarse salt**. Bake until brown and hollow-sounding when rapped.

*makes 2 to 3 loaves*

# chile cheese cornbread

A cross between spoon bread and quiche.

1. Preheat oven to 425°F. Melt **2½ tablespoons butter** in an 8″ cast iron skillet. Let cool. In a bowl, stir together **1 cup fine yellow cornmeal, 3 tablespoons flour, 2 teaspoons baking soda**, and **1 teaspoon salt**.

2. Whisk together **1 egg** and **1¼ cups milk**. Add cooled butter. Stir quickly into dry ingredients and turn back into cast iron skillet. Place in oven for 5 minutes.

3. Use same bowl to whisk **1 egg**. Add **1 cup heavy cream**. Grate ⅓ **cup Switzerland Swiss cheese** and ⅓ **cup Muenster cheese** and add to bowl. Add **1 cup** drained **organic canned corn,** ½ **teaspoon salt, grated pepper**, and 1 chopped **roasted jalapeño chile**. Stir all together thoroughly.

4. Open oven door and spoon cheese custard over cornbread. Try not to disturb the cornbread. Turn heat down to 375°F and bake until browned, 15 to 20 minutes.

*8 servings*

BREAD

# cardamom bread

A Scandinavian winter treat—a little fussy and time consuming to make, but worth the trouble. Freshly ground cardamom is essential.

1. In your mixer, combine ⅓ **cup warm water** and **1½ tablespoons dry yeast**. When bubbly, add **2 tablespoons sugar, 3 egg whites** (reserve yolks) and **2 cups bread (high gluten) flour**. Use flat paddle beater to blend for 4 to 5 minutes. Turn off machine. Remove flat beater. Let dough stand from 30 minutes to 2 hours.

2. Put dough hook in machine. Add: another ½ **cup sugar**, the reserved **3 egg yolks**, ¼ **cup crushed ice** and **1 tablespoon salt**. Turn machine on and add **3 cups more flour**. Knead on low speed for about 5 minutes or until very elastic, though sticky. Meanwhile, **crush whole cardamom pods** and use a spice mill or mortar and pestle to crush (grind) **1½ teaspoons cardamom**. Add to mixer together with ⅓ **cup currants**, ¾ **cup half-and-half** and ½ **cup sour cream**. Mix well and let stand 10 minutes.

3. Meanwhile, melt **5 tablespoons unsalted butter**. Add to mixer with **1 more cup flour**. Mix well. Mixture will be very soft and stringy. Cover and refrigerate at least 45 minutes, or overnight.

4. Turn dough out onto counter. Deflate; cover with bowl and let rest 10 minutes. Divide into 6 parts and make 2 braided loaves. Place on a large **oiled** cookie sheet. Brush with a beaten **egg**. Sprinkle with **cinnamon sugar** and **sliced almonds**. Loaves must rise for 2 hours. After 1½ hours, heat oven 400°F, and brush again with the beaten egg.

5. Place loaves in the oven. Immediately turn heat down to 350°F. A pan of boiling water on the floor of the oven is a good idea. Bake for 1 hour.

*2 large holiday loaves*

# croissants

In 1998 Rachel Portnoy spent a summer producing these pastries for a bakery (Patisserie Gerard di Tomasi) in Cannes, France. Here is her recipe for this classic 3 day process. When we made these, we changed ingredient amounts from grams to ounces or cups. Both measurements are listed here.

1. In a mixer, whisk together **1 cup plus 2 tablespoons (250 ml) warm water, 1⅓ cups (187.5 gm) all-purpose flour** and **50 gm fresh yeast** (we used **2 tablespoons dry yeast**). Stir together 1¼ cups **(200 gm) all-purpose flour** and ½ cup **(50 gm) bread flour**. Pour into mixer. Don't stir. When the top cracks (about 10 minutes), add: 1⅞ cups **(417 ml) milk**, ¼ cup **(30 ml) water**, 7¼ cups **(938 gm) bread flour, 2 tablespoons (31 gm) salt** and ½ cup **(100 gm) sugar**. Use dough hook to blend and add ¼ **pound plus 2 tablespoons (137.5 gm)** softened unsalted **butter**. Blend all with dough hook until mass comes together and makes a nice pallet of dough. Wrap well, refrigerate and let rise overnight.

2. Dough now must be divided in two parts. The whole piece should weigh almost 6½ pounds (29 kg). You will need **2¼ pounds plus 2 tablespoons (1050 kg)** of somewhat soft **butter**. Divide butter in half and beat each half between two layers of plastic wrap, using a rolling pin, to ½″ thickness. Roll half of the dough until it is slightly larger than the butter. Place butter on dough (removing plastic first) and use the palm of your hand to smooth it evenly over the dough but not quite to the edges, leaving a 1″ border.

3. Fold in thirds like a letter, making sure corners are as square as possible. Roll dough out long for the first turn to ½″ thickness. Fold in thirds again. Make sure mid-seams are square. Wrap well and refrigerate for 1 hour. Repeat for other half of dough and butter. Repeat this rolling and folding with a 1 hour rest period 2 more times. Refrigerate overnight.

4. Roll out dough again. Cut it in thirds to make it easier to work with, and roll each piece to ⅛″ thick. Trim edges. Make a cardboard template 7″ long and 4 to 5″ wide. Cut rectangles of dough the size of the template then divide each into 2 triangles. Gently stretch tip of triangle before rolling up, starting with the 5″ base. Keep palms at top corners rolling dough toward you, stretching outward slightly. Place croissants 2″ apart on greased trays (or on parchment paper). Let rise at room temperature for approximately 4 hours. Preheat oven to 400°F. Brush croissants with beaten **egg** and bake for about 18 minutes.

*4 to 6 dozen*

BREAD

# cheese babka

A coffeecake.

1. In mixer or bowl, dissolve **1 tablespoon yeast** in **1 cup tepid water** with **1 tablespoon sugar**. After 5 minutes, add **2 teaspoons salt, 1½ sticks sweet butter**, cut into bits, **⅓ cup sugar, 2 eggs**, and **2 egg yolks** and mix well. Begin adding **3 cups unbleached white flour** and knead until dough is silky smooth. Up to **3 more cups flour** may be added if dough is too loose, but be sure it remains soft. Turn into a bowl to rise about 1½ hours in a cool place.

2. Meanwhile, prepare filling. Plump **2 tablespoons yellow raisins** in **1 tablespoon brandy** *or* **cognac**. Cream together **1 cup dry cottage cheese** *or* **pot cheese** with **¼ cup sugar, 1 tablespoon flour, 1 egg yolk, ½ teaspoon grated lemon rind, ½ teaspoon vanilla extract** and **1 tablespoon sour cream**. When well mixed, add raisins and brandy and stir.

3. Deflate dough on a floured board and shape into a rough rectangle. Brush with melted **butter** and spread filling over. Roll up like a jelly roll and fit into a large buttered loaf pan or coil into a buttered angel food or other large circular pan. Don't use a pan that is too small. Bread should come to no more than ¾ up the sides of the pan. Let rise 45 minutes.

4. Preheat oven to 350°F. Bake babka until well browned, about 45 minutes to 1 hour.

   *Optional:* after bread has risen in the oven, it may be brushed with beaten **egg white** and sprinkled with streusel—use your fingers to rub together ⅓ **cup butter**, ½ **cup sugar**, and ½ **cup flour**.

*makes 2 to 3 loaves*

ALISON

BREAD

# poppy seed cakes

These are made from a yeast dough. However, other recipes for poppy seed cakes use cake batter or cookie dough and hold strong emotional connotations ranging from grandmother-lore in Eastern Europe to celebration of Jewish rebellion against oppression in the form of triangular-shaped cookies called "Humentaschen," made for Purim. We chose to make poppy seed cakes in memory of ancient Jewish women's celebration of the new moon, when lit candles were floated on water and round- or crescent-shaped cakes filled with seeds or nuts were eaten.

1. **Start filling:** cover **1½ cups poppy seeds** with boiling water and soak 1 to 2 hours.

2. **Make dough:** soften **1 stick sweet butter**. In a small pot, warm **½ cup milk** with **¼ cup honey** until honey dissolves and milk is lukewarm. Turn into mixer or bowl and add **3 tablespoons yeast**. Beat in **3 cups unbleached white flour**, 1 cup at a time. Add **2 unbeaten eggs** and the softened butter, cut into pieces. Beat or knead dough thoroughly. Add **1 cup more flour** and beat until dough is quite dry and well-mixed. Shape into a ball and place in a bowl covered with cold water. In 15 minutes to half an hour, the dough will have risen above the water. Pat it dry, return to mixer or place on floured board and knead again for 5 to 10 minutes. Place in a **buttered** bowl, cover, and let rise in a cool place 1 to 2 hours.

3. **Finish filling:** drain poppy seeds well in a fine mesh strainer. Place in a blender with **1 cup milk** and **2 tablespoons flour** and blend for a few minutes to grind poppy seeds as fine as possible. Turn into a small pot, add **⅓ cup honey**, and cook, stirring, until

smooth and thick. Add ⅓ **cup chopped almonds,**
**1 cup raisins,** coarsely chopped, and **2 teaspoons**
grated **lemon rind.** Fork-beat **1 egg** and add to filling,
mixing well.

4. **Shape and bake dough:** preheat oven to 375°F.
   Divide dough in half. Melt ½ **stick sweet butter.** Roll
   one piece at a time on a floured board to ¼″ thickness
   and in as square a shape as possible. Brush each
   half with half the melted butter and spread thinly
   with half the poppy seed filling. To form "moons,"
   roll up jelly roll fashion, slice in ½″ to ¾″ rounds and
   place on a buttered baking sheet. To form crescents,
   divide dough into 9 to 12 squares and cut each square
   diagonally into triangles. Roll each triangle from a
   wide end to the point and curve to form crescent.
   Place on buttered baking sheet.

5. Place rolls in oven. When they have puffed and
   browned a little, brush with **1 egg yolk** beaten with
   **2 tablespoons cream.** Bake till medium brown. Rolls
   may be frozen and reheated in an oven or toaster
   oven. Serve with butter, if you like.

*makes 35 to 40 crescents*

# cornbread

1. **Butter** an 8″ x 8″ x 2″ Pyrex baking dish. Preheat oven to 400°F. Melt ½ **stick sweet butter** together with **3 tablespoons molasses**.

2. Whisk together **1¼ cups unbleached white flour, 1 tablespoon baking powder, 1 teaspoon baking soda, 1 teaspoon salt, 1 cup cornmeal,** and **2 tablespoons sugar**.

3. In a small bowl, beat well **2 eggs**. Stir in **1¼ cups buttermilk** and the melted butter.

4. Combine wet and dry mixtures until just blended. Do not overmix. Turn into pan and bake until lightly browned (about 20 to 25 minutes).

*8 servings*

# southern cornbread

A recipe from Alabama via Julia McClure. An almost identical version from Louisiana came from Kaia James. Both tell us this all-cornmeal cornbread is served with black-eyed peas and rice and greens.

1.  Preheat oven to 450°F. You will need a 10″ cast-iron skillet, preferably one which is divided into pie-shaped sections.

2.  Whisk together **2 cups water-ground cornmeal, 1½ teaspoons baking powder, 1 teaspoon salt,** and **1 teaspoon baking soda.** Use a fork to whip **2 eggs** in a small bowl. Add **2½ cups buttermilk** to the egg mix together with **3 tablespoons melted butter.** Set aside.

3.  Heat skillet on stovetop until hot enough to spatter a drop of water. Add **2 tablespoons butter** to the pan. Now quickly combine cornmeal and egg-buttermilk mix. Immediately turn into hot pan and then into the very hot oven. Cornbread will rise very quickly. Bake until golden brown, 25 to 30 minutes.

*8 servings*

BREAD

# scones

These are the best. Rich and not too sweet. Perfect.

1.  In a small bowl blend **1 egg** with **1 tablespoon water**. Set aside. Preheat oven to 375°F.

2.  In a mixer or bowl combine **2¾ cups white flour, ⅓ cup sugar, 2 teaspoons baking powder**, and **½ teaspoon salt**.

3.  Cut **12 tablespoons** cold **unsalted butter** into small cubes. With your fingers or the flat beater of a standing mixer, blend the butter into the flour mixture. Don't overdo. The butter pieces should look like large oatmeal flakes. Next, add in **1 cup dried currants** *or* **cranberries** or other dried fruit and **1 tablespoon orange** *or* **lemon zest**. Stir in **1 cup heavy cream**. Mix until just blended. The mixture will be dry and flaky.

4.  Turn out onto floured board and gently knead the dough until it comes together. Pat into a circle or rectangle and cut into wedges or diamond shapes. Place scones on cookie sheets, brush with egg mixture and sprinkle with **sugar**.

5.  Bake until golden brown, about 15 minutes. It may be necessary to flip the scones over toward the end of the baking in order to brown them evenly.

*2 dozen*

# apple muffins

1. Preheat oven to 425°F. Use **lecithin oil** (see glossary) to grease muffins tins or line them with papers.

2. Melt ½ **stick sweet butter.**

3. Use a whisk to stir together **2 cups unbleached white flour, 2 teaspoons baking powder, ½ teaspoon baking soda, ½ teaspoon salt, scant ⅔ cup sugar, ¼ teaspoon nutmeg, ½ cup chopped walnuts** and **½ teaspoon cinnamon.**

4. Beat **2 eggs** well; stir in **1 cup sour cream**, the melted butter, and **½ cup apple cider** *or* **juice.**

5. Peel, core, and dice **1½ cups apples.** Do not peel, but core and slice an additional **apple** into 14 segments.

6. Combine wet and dry mixtures and the diced apples. Do not overmix. Spoon batter into prepared muffin tins. Gently press one of the apple slices (skin side up) into the center of each muffin. Bake at 425°F until lightly browned, about 20 to 25 minutes. These can be frozen and then reheated in a 350°F oven or toaster oven.

*12 to 14 muffins*

# cranberry walnut muffins

1. Preheat oven to 425°F. Use **lecithin oil** (see glossary) to grease muffin tins.

2. Melt ½ **stick sweet butter.**

3. Chop **1¼ cups cranberries** fine by hand or in food processor (they can be frozen whole and chopped, still frozen, in food processor).

4. Use a whisk to stir together **2½ cups unbleached white flour, ¾ cup sugar, ½ tablespoon baking powder, ½ teaspoon baking soda,** and **½ teaspoon salt.**

5. Beat **1 egg.** Grate the **rind of 1½ oranges** into the beaten egg. Squeeze enough juice to make **1¼ cup orange juice** (you may use up to ¼ **cup water** to make up the whole amount if necessary).

6. Combine melted butter, eggs, and orange juice. Mix this liquid mixture together with the dry ingredients and the chopped cranberries and **½ cup chopped walnuts.** Don't overmix.

7. Spoon mix into muffin tins and bake in preheated oven until lightly brown (about 20 to 25 minutes).

*about 15 muffins*

# refrigerator bran muffins

This batter should be made up ahead and stored in a closed
container in the refrigerator where it will keep for 2 to 3 weeks. The
recipe makes about 40 to 44 good-sized muffins. You bake only the
number you want on a given day.

1. Pour **2 cups boiling water** on **2 cups bran flakes.***
   Let stand until cool.

2. In large bowl, stir together **2½ cups honey** and **1 cup
   grapeseed oil**. Beat in **4 eggs, 1 quart buttermilk** and
   the cooled bran. A whisk works well for this mixing.

3. Sift or whisk together **2½ cups unbleached all-purpose
   flour, 2½ cups whole wheat flour, 5 teaspoons
   baking soda**, and **1½ teaspoons salt**.

4. Combine wet and dry mixtures.

5. Fold in **4 cups more bran** and **12 oz (3 cups loosely
   packed) raisins**.

6. Store batter covered in the refrigerator. Do not stir.

7. When ready to bake, preheat oven to 425°F and
   **butter** muffin tins or line them with papers, or use
   **lecithin oil** (see glossary).

8. Gently spoon batter into prepared tins. Don't stir! Fill
   the tins quite full since most of the rising has occurred
   in the refrigerator. Bake in 425°F oven. Lower the heat
   to 400°F after the muffins have risen. Bake till brown
   on top (about 20 to 25 minutes altogether).

*40 to 44 muffins*

---

*Use bran flakes from a health food store.

# blueberry muffins

1. Preheat oven to 400°F. melt **1 stick sweet butter.**

2. Pick over **2½ cups blueberries,** removing stems, leaves, etc., and purée ½ cup of them in a food processor or blender (if using a blender, you may want to add some of the milk from step 5 to make the berries wet enough to purée efficiently). In a small bowl, dust the remaining 2 cups with a little **flour** to separate them.

3. Line muffin tins with papers, or use **lecithin oil** (see glossary) to grease them.

4. Stir together, using a whisk: **⅔ cup sugar, 2 cups white unbleached flour, 2 teaspoons baking powder, ½ teaspoon salt, ⅓ teaspoon cinnamon, and a grating of fresh nutmeg.**

5. Beat **2 eggs.** Stir in **½ cup milk,** the melted butter and the puréed berries.

6. Quickly mix together the liquid and dry ingredients along with the whole berries. Don't overmix.

7. Spoon into prepared muffin tins and bake at 400°F until lightly brown on top, (about 20 to 25 minutes). These muffins can be frozen and reheated in a 350°F oven.

*12 muffins*

# peach plum pecan muffins

1. Preheat oven to 400°F. Melt **4 tablespoons butter.** Cut **3 plums** into slices, separating fruit from the pits. Set aside. Chop **pecans** to yield ⅞ **cup.** Peel **2 to 3 peaches.** You will need ¾ cup diced and ¾ cup puréed. You can use a food processor to purée peaches, then measure. Set both kinds of peaches aside. **Butter** a muffin tin, or use **lecithin oil** (see glossary).

2. In a bowl whisk together ¾ **cup whole wheat flour, 1¾ cups unbleached white flour, ½ teaspoon baking soda, 1 tablespoon baking powder, ½ teaspoon salt, ½ teaspoon cinnamon, and ⅔ cup sugar.**

3. In a processor (or mixer) beat **2 eggs.** Add **1 cup buttermilk,** then pour in melted butter and puréed peaches. Turn this wet mixture into bowl with dry ingredients, adding diced peaches and pecans. Fold gently together spoon into muffin tin. Top each muffin with plum slices. Bake about 25 minutes or until puffed and brown.

*makes 12 muffins*

# omelets

Having an omelet pan doesn't guarantee you will be good at making omelets; not having one requires your being especially skilled before your omelets slide out mottled brown and gold on the outside and moist and tender within. Heavy aluminum or other metal designed especially for omelet making, preferably with a wooden handle, is best. Season an omelet plan as you do a crepe pan by slowly heating a tablespoon of oil in it for 15 to 20 minutes and then wiping it clean with absorbent paper. Don't ever wash it. Any burnt-on material can be removed with oil and salt.

**Two** or **three eggs** make a nice omelet. Do try to obtain eggs from free-range chickens. You will be amazed at their superior flavor. Fork-beat them in a small bowl with a **dash** of **Tabasco** and **1 tablespoon beer**, which add flavor and lightness. Very little beating is necessary, just enough to mix the eggs. Have your filling ready. Heat **1 tablespoon butter** in the omelet pan until it begins to turn brown. Turn heat moderately high, add egg mixture and shake the pan vigorously until the omelet sets up. Or you can use the fork, flat side down, to stir the mixture as it sets, or a combination of stirring and shaking may please you best. In any case, the egg mixture should end up opposite the omelet pan handle. Turn heat down, **salt** the omelet and add filling. Now holding the handle in your right if you are righty, in your left if you are lefty, keep your palm under the handle, thumb on top with a pan at a right angle to your arm. Hold the plate in your other hand and roll the omelet out onto the plate by gradually turning the pan upside down against the plate. It does take a little practice, but not too much!

The most popular omelet here is **cheese and sprouts**. We use thin slices of **Port Salut cheese** and **alfalfa sprouts**. A dash of **tamari** before rolling finishes it. Spanish **Manchego sheep cheese**, cut with a cheese plane, makes a good filling, topped with **roasted red peppers.**

**Creamed spinach** (see index) is also popular and so are **mushrooms in Port wine**: fry sliced mushrooms and onions (**1 small onion** to **1 pound button mushrooms** *or* **oyster mushrooms**) in **butter** until liquid has evaporated and mushrooms begin to brown. Turn off fire and add a **splash** of **port wine** and **dash** of **salt**.

Omelets are an excellent way to use up leftovers. Leftover **applesauce** in Autumn may be laced with **brandy** for an omelet filling and **cranberry applesauce** (see index) is good as is. Leftover cooked peeled **asparagus** stalks from the asparagus platter can be cut up for a Spring omelet filling. If there is leftover cooking liquid, it can be thickened with a roux (**1 tablespoon butter, 1 tablespoon flour** cooked together before **1 cup asparagus liquid** is added), and a little **Swiss** *or* **Raclette cheese** melted in this sauce. Warm the asparagus in the sauce and top the omelet with it as well. Washed shredded **sorrel leaves** cooked in their own liquid with a **splash** of **heavy cream** is another Spring omelet specialty.

Leftover **ratatouille niçoise** (see index) makes a wonderful late summer omelet. For a **zucchini and pesto** omelet, simmer ½ **cup pesto** (see index) and a **28 oz. can tomatoes** together for 5 minutes. Slice **1 medium zucchini** and a **small onion** and fry in **1 tablespoon olive oil** with ½ **teaspoon oregano** over high heat. Use the zucchini as the omelet filling, add some grated **Parmesan cheese** and a little of the pesto sauce. Turn the omelet out and top with more sauce.

**Omelet grandmère** is made up of several ingredients Grandma had on hand. Stale **homemade bread** is cut in cubes and toasted in the oven. The last **herbs** of the garden year or the first ones of Spring are chopped fine and mixed with the eggs. We prefer **burnet** and **garlic leaves**, but almost any herbs will do. You will need leftover gravy (see index for **miso gravy**) and **sour cream**. Fill the herb omelet with the croutons, moisten with a little heated gravy, and turn out onto the plate. Top with more gravy and a dollop of sour cream.

Homegrown **mung bean sprouts** make an excellent omelet. Fry them in a little **oil** with chopped **scallions**. When they are barely cooked and still crisp, add a **dash tamari** and a little **toasted sesame oil**, if you have it. Use as an omelet filling alone or with **cheese**, as you like.

If you can find good quality **rose hip jam**, it makes a nice omelet filling. Top the omelet with **sour cream**. Finally, for an elegant orange omelet, thinly slice and cut **oranges**. Heat in orange marmalade in a small pot. Fill omelet and add a **splash** of **Grand Marnier liqueur** to remaining juices in the pot. After the omelet is rolled onto the plate, heat the sauce and tilt the pot to flame it. Pour over the omelet and serve for a fancy breakfast.

# mexican omelet

Beautiful and delicious.

1. You will need **leftover bean soup**, preferably **black bean** (see index). Heat it with **cornmeal**, adding it gradually to thicken the mixture. A half hour of cooking will make the bean mixture quite thick. Approximately **2 tablespoons cornmeal** to **1 cup** of **soup** should yield a filling appropriately thickened.

2. You will need **salsa**, purchased, or see index. You will also need **avocado, sour cream, onion slices**, and **jalapeño pepper strips** from a jar or can.

3. Make omelets in the standard way (see recipe if need be). Fill with bean mixture. Roll onto plate.

4. Spoon on 2 crosswise stripes of salsa. Center a middle stripe of sour cream. Top with avocado. Finally, balance an onion slice at right angles to the avocado, and finish with a jalapeño chile slice.

# home fried potatoes

As good as many foods are reheated for omelets,
potatoes have to be fresh cooked to make good
**homefries** or filling for a **spanish omelet**. Idahos
are best. Cook scrubbed **potatoes** in their skins until
tender. Peel or not as you like and cut up into small
slices. Add chopped **onion** and chopped **green
pepper**, **salt** and fresh ground **pepper** and moisten
with **grapeseed oil**. Fry potatoes in your largest
well-heated cast iron skillet or on a griddle, turning
occasionally and sprinkling with **paprika**. When
browned and crisp, turn out to serve with **fried eggs**
and Johnson's Table Sauce (available at health food
stores) or use the potatoes as an omelet filling with
slivers of **Swiss cheese**. Top with **spanish sauce**.

# spanish sauce

Chop **1 small onion** fine and sauté in **olive oil** with
**2** crushed **cloves garlic, 2 teaspoons oregano,
1 teaspoon basil (dried)**. After a few minutes, add
**15 oz.** canned **plain tomato sauce**. Rinse out can
with ¼ **cup red wine** and add **1 tablespoon** finely
chopped **hot peppers**. taste for **salt**, and simmer
10 minutes.

# matzah brie

A breakfast dish from Fay Davidson.

1. Break up **6 large squares** of **matzah** in a large bowl and cover with water.

2. Beat **6 eggs** thoroughly and add **2 teaspoons salt**. Stir well.

3. When matzah is uniformly soft, turn into a colander, then squeeze out the water, one handful of matzah at a time. Put each dry handful into egg mixture. When all the matzah is in the egg mix, stir together with a fork.

4. Melt **butter** in a large frying pan and when quite hot, pat out small thin cakes in the hot fat using the fork. When browned and crispy, turn each cake over and brown the other side. The matzah brie can be turned over several times until properly crisp and brown. Serve immediately, telling diners to add **salt** to taste. Repeat, making more cakes. Matzah brie requires a lot of butter, but you can use part **oil**. For this quantity you will probably need ½ **to** ¾ **pound** of **butter**. Some people (not us) like it served with **jam** *or* **sour cream**.

Note: obviously, the cook doesn't eat until all the matzah brie is cooked. You can trade off cooking or keep matzah brie hot in the oven (it won't be as good) or only make it for yourself! One matzah and 1 egg serves 1 person.

*6 servings*

# poached eggs in spinach nests
## with hollandaise sauce

1. Thaw **2 (10 oz.) packages** of frozen chopped **spinach** several hours or overnight. Drain and gently squeeze liquid from spinach. Melt **3 tablespoons butter** in a pot. Add **3 tablespoons flour** and stir together for a few minutes. Add **½ cup heavy cream** and bring to a simmer. Add the drained spinach and cook over low heat, stirring occasionally. Add **1 teaspoon salt, fresh ground pepper**, and **fresh grated nutmeg**. Don't overcook; cover and set aside.

2. **Prepare hollandaise sauce:** melt **1 stick unsalted butter**. Set aside. In a stainless steel pot, use a whisk to blend **2 egg yolks, 2 teaspoons lemon juice**, and **2 teaspoons water**. Whisk over low heat until mixture foams and thickens slightly. Add melted butter very slowly, whisking and cooking over lowest heat until mixture becomes the consistency of thick cream. Remove from heat, whisking for another minute. Add **salt** to taste and **a drop** of **Tabasco**. Cover. Sauce will keep warm enough for an hour.

3. In a shallow sauce pan, bring enough **water** to a boil to adequately cover the eggs you will be poaching. Don't try to poach more than 4 eggs at a time. You may add **1 teaspoon white vinegar** to the water to help egg whites coagulate, but the best way to get good poached eggs is to find a source for free range, organic **eggs**. Bring water to a boil, drop in eggs, turn heat down to a simmer and cover. If you are making **toast**, the eggs and toast will usually take the same

318

amount of time to get done. Without toast, allow three minutes to poach the eggs.

4. Make a spinach "nest" by heaping spinach in the middle of a plate and using a small spoon to make a central depression in it. Use a slotted spoon to remove eggs from simmering water, drain on absorbent paper, and slip into "nest." We serve 2 eggs in each nest. Toast goes around the sides and the hollandaise sauce over the top.

*6 servings*

CATHARINE

# oyster mushroom quiche

1. Preheat oven to 400°F. Prepare **pie crust** (see index) and line a 10″ quiche pan with it. Prick intersection of rim and bottom with a fork and line pie crust with foil and weight with dried beans, corn, or lentils. Bake 5-10 minutes, or until edges of the crust are a very light brown. Remove foil and beans and turn oven down to 375°F. Remove pie crust from the oven.

2. Meanwhile, wipe clean (do not wash) and slice **1 pound mushrooms**. You may use **button mushrooms**; these days we use **oyster mushrooms**. Finely chop **3 tablespoons onions** and sauté onions for about a minute in a large frying pan in **2 tablespoons butter**. Add mushrooms; turn heat up high until liquid evaporates and they begin to brown. Stir occasionally. Add **1 teaspoon salt** and ¼ **cup tawny port**. Set aside.

3. Beat **3 eggs** together in a mixer or a bowl. Add a **grating of nutmeg, 1½ cups heavy cream**, and some **fresh ground pepper**.

4. Add mushrooms to pie crust. Sprinkle ½ **cup grated Swiss cheese** over them and return pie to oven. Carefully add custard to the quiche. Bake until puffed and browned, ½ hour to 45 minutes. Individual pieces of quiche may be wrapped, frozen, and later reheated in a toaster oven.

*one 10″ quiche—8 servings*

# baked apple pancake

Adapted many years ago from a New York Times recipe, this breakfast treat is a relative of popovers and Yorkshire Pudding.

1. Preheat oven to 425°F. Peel and thinly slice **1 small crisp apple.** You must have a 10″ to 12″ cast iron skillet. Melt **4 tablespoons sweet butter** in the skillet.

2. Whisk together: **2 eggs, ½ cup flour, ⅔ cup half-and-half, pinch nutmeg,** and **½ teaspoon salt.** Don't over beat; leave batter lumpy.

3. Pour batter into hot skillet. Scatter apple slices over the top and immediately place in preheated oven. Lower temperature to 400° and bake 20 minutes.

4. Open oven and sift **1 to 2 tablespoons confectioner's sugar** over pancake. Bake 5 minutes more. Remove from oven and sprinkle the **juice of ½ lemon** over the pancake. Cut into big wedges and serve.

*breakfast for 2 to 3*

# granola

From *A Woman's Place*, Athol, NY, no longer in existence. This recipe is a delicious antique from 1970's feminism.

Note: vegans may delete the powdered milk and use soy milk powder, and then substitute agave nectar *or* maple syrup for the honey. A mix of soy milk and coconut milk will serve for breakfasts.

1.  Preheat oven to 375°F. In a large shallow pan, combine ⅓ **cup sesame seeds**, ⅓ **cup sunflower seeds**, **3 tablespoons flax seed**, ⅓ **cup wheat germ**, ⅓ **cup bran**, ½ **cup powdered milk**, ⅓ **cup dried coconut**, ½ **cup mixed nuts** (such as cashew pieces or chopped Brazil nuts), **2 cups oats**, ⅓ **cup soy powder**, ½ **teaspoon** ground **cardamom** and a **dash salt**. Roast, stirring occasionally, for 30 to 40 minutes.

2.  Meanwhile, mix together ⅓ **cup honey**, ⅓ **cup grapeseed oil**, ½ **ts. vanilla extract**. Pour over mixture in oven; stir well and bake another 30 minutes. When done and still quite warm, add ½ **cup raisins**. Other dried fruits can be added as well. Store in covered container. Serve with **milk** *or* **yogurt** as breakfast food or keep as a snack.

*makes about 6 cups*

# coquida

A Puerto Rican party punch.

1. Use a hammer and screwdriver to punch holes in the "eyes" of a large **coconut** that sounds as if it has a lot of liquid in it when you shake it. Drain the liquid into a bowl. Break up the coconut with the hammer, pry off shell and peel inner skin off with potato peeler.

2. Warm **2 cups heavy cream** and put in a blender with coconut pieces and reserved coconut liquid. Blend.

3. In mixer, beat **6 organic, free range eggs** for 20 minutes. While eggs are beating, add **1 teaspoon cinnamon, 1 teaspoon nutmeg**, and **1 tablespoon vanilla extract**.

4. Strain coconut cream into the eggs, pressing down on the strainer to squeeze out all the liquid. Also add **1½ cups half-and-half**. You may also add a can of **concentrated coconut cream** (available in Puerto Rican markets), for intensified coconut flavor. Beat another 15 minutes.

5. Add a fifth bottle of **añejo rum** and chill for several hours before serving.

*makes approximately 2 quarts coquida*

# broiled stuffed mushrooms

1.  Use a fork to mash together ¼ pound cream cheese, 1½ teaspoons lemon juice, 2 teaspoons red miso, and 1½ teaspoons tamari. If mixture is too stiff, add a little water. Mince 1 scallion and add to mixture.

2.  Use a dessert spoon to scoop stems from 1 dozen large button mushrooms. Use fork to stuff mushrooms with cheese mixture. Sprinkle with paprika.

3.  When ready to serve, broil only until tops are brown.

4.  Serve with ice water-crisped, thinly sliced fennel and Italian oil-cured olives.

*makes appetizers for 6*

# VEGETARIAN RECIPES
## EASILY MADE VEGAN

Tomato, Cabbage and Rice Soup—omit sour cream

Lima Bean Squash Soup—omit sour cream

Beet and Cabbage Soup—omit sour cream

Butternut Squash Soup with Chestnut Dumplings—omit
dumplings and garnish with chopped chestnuts

Solianka—omit sour cream

Cranberry Kissel—omit heavy cream

Minestrone—omit Parmesan

S'chee Soup—use oil to fry, omit sour cream

Escarole Garlic and Cannelini Bean Soup—omit
Parmesan

Curried Lentil Soup—omit yogurt

Spinach Salad with Sesame Peanut Dressing—omit
hardboiled egg

Crimson Slaw with Jicama—omit queso fresco

Scandinavian Dried Fruit Soup—omit sour cream

New Potato, Carrot and Broccoli Salad with Garlic
Mayonnaise—omit mayonnaise or substitute almond
mayonnaise made with herbs

Broccoli Raab, Cannelini Beans, Tomato and Cavatelli—
omit romano cheese

Feijoada—omit hardboiled egg garnish, cook manioc in
palm oil without eggs or butter

Chilled Simple Borscht—omit sour cream

Chilled Elderberry Soup—omit sour cream

Szechwan Noodles—use egg-free noodles

Stuffed Vegetable Platter—omit yogurt and avgolemeno
sauce

Felafel—omit cucumber yogurt sauce

Middle East Lentils and Rice—omit yogurt

Syrian Eggplant—omit yogurt

Granola—omit yogurt

Pierogis—use asian dumplings wrappers instead of
noodle dough, omit sour cream garnish

Black Bean Chili—omit corn dumplings and serve with
spicy corn bread (see index)

# BOOKS OF GREAT MERIT

We are encouraged that the year 2005 saw the publication of three books which affirm us as a feminist vegetarian restaurant/bookstore. If you like our cooking and our politics, find copies of these three superb books:

*The China Study*, by T. Colin Campbell is a powerful documentation of the health benefits of a vegetarian (and even better, vegan) diet. What we thought all along.

*Women's Lives Men's Laws* is a collection of Catherine MacKinnon's recent fiercely feminist views. She renews our hopes and fire.

*Not for Sale* is a collection of essays about pornography and prostitution. Best are the articles which reveal the interconnectedness of globalization, armed aggression, poverty, pornography and prostitution—the sum of which is the essence of patriarchy. We make every effort to live in opposition to this evil conglomerate.

Our gratitude to the authors respectively; Colin Campbell, Catherine MacKinnon and editors Rebecca Whisnant and Christine Stark, and the publishers; Benbella Books, Harvard University Press and Spinifex Publishers in Australia.

# CHIEF COOK & BOTTLE WASHER

It seems an old-fashioned concept. Today, whoever hears of the boss, the owner of a restaurant, washing the dishes or mopping the floor? In small immigrant businesses, this still happens, but it's not something visible in upscale establishments. Unheard of, really.

As feminists we believe that each person should be in charge of the maintenance tasks required of her daily life as much as possible. For an able-bodied person to expect another to clean up after her/him seems disrespectful and condescending. To take care of our own physical needs fulfills a most basic human responsibility, rounding out the picture of what a human being, a creature on this earth, is.

At Bloodroot we all wash dishes at one time or another. Dirty dishes are a part of life, like weeds in the garden or dust in the corners. The Talmud says, "There is no work that dishonors a person." Exactly. And we think it is important to do every job well—whether sometimes tedious but necessary, or sometimes wonderfully creative. We take pride in all aspects of our work.

# MY TRUE CONFESSION

## A PERENNIAL PASSION

Have you ever been in love? Ecstatically, painfully in love? If you have, like me, then you know what a problem it is. Everything else in life pales. Friends, work, small pleasures like a good book or a fine meal...all unimportant in the physical rush and the fascination with the beloved, far more wonderful than anyone else in the world could know. All waking hours are consumed with reveling over one's good fortune in possessing the very best of lovers.

Of course, after a while there are small annoyances, either to be overlooked, or in the case of unattractive quirks, corrected!

Later comes the first quarrel, or perhaps an infidelity, and after a while (a few months?) the realization that the beloved is less than perfect. Oh well. It is disappointing of course, but whether or not the relationship stabilizes or ends, there is blessed relief.

The good book is again interesting; the meal once more delicious, and how fortunate to remember good friends and work one loves.

So perhaps you understand why I am grateful for November. Garden passion has ebbed for another year. Even though the first seed catalogue appears right after Thanksgiving, I resist breaking the seal of the envelope. All through January and February I smile and agree (so hypocritically) with those who yearn for Spring, while I am grateful it is a long way off.

Of course by early February, I had better check out what few seeds I will indulge in this year. It doesn't seem dangerous to turn on the cellar fluorescent lights to start some impatiens and tomato seeds, even though all that repotting will be a bother.

Then come those first few warm days in April, and the astounding beauty of May. And I am off again, totally swept away. I have no more control over the ecstasy, which verges on pain... than the cat does coming into heat. Look at how lovely the trees are, leafing out! See how the wild ladyslipper has multiplied, how elegant the big white bleeding heart is, and how graceful is *Clematis montana rubens*. I gloat that surely my garden is the loveliest of all...

I work in the garden to beyond exhaustion, and am ambivalently resentful and relieved each rainy day. I am convinced the weeds and adelgids will be controlled this year. And all those new gorgeous annuals demanding a place! Small annoyances, the aggressive *Ranunculus* I once admired, I'll weed out. I hope to enjoy cool wet weather for the lettuces, and then warm and hot for the tomatoes and just enough rain for each, right? But before the end of June the lettuces are slug-eaten and by the end of July the squirrels are picking each ripening tomato. The woodchucks re-appear. August proves too wet and the winter squash rots. The deer have destroyed the hostas, and the weeds...well, just don't look. Reality sets in. I have to clean the greenhouse and repot the orchids before frost, and of course rake all those leaves.

So many disappointments, but some great satisfactions, too. It really was a good year after all. There were enough tomatoes to freeze sauce, and enough blueberries for jam, and many of the orchids are showing flower spikes to bloom in Winter.

But the passion, the ecstasy, the indescribable joy of Spring is past. Calm sets in. What a relief. Soon it will be November...

# SHOPPING TRIPS

Sometimes diners claim they don't know where to find ingredients listed in our recipes. Luckily for us, in Bridgeport we have access to the riches to be found in Latina, Mid-Eastern, Thai, Greek, Italian, Indian and Asian markets. Health food stores are in neighboring communities. Visiting ethnic markets is a great opportunity to experience smells and tastes of diverse cultures.

We try to indicate where to find ingredients as they occur in each recipe. Perhaps however, you will want to plan a shopping trip to a market to stock up on particular ingredients. Following is a very brief guide to what may be purchased in specific markets, listing foods we use at Bloodroot.

Farmers markets will have the best produce, but be sure to ask if it is organic. Community supported agriculture makes a wonderful alliance between the farmer and those who want to eat the best, freshest food.

A good health food store is a must for vegetarians and vegans. There you should be able to find miso, kombu, seitan, tempeh, tofu, tamari or shoyu (quality soy sauce), dried shiitake mushrooms, organically grown grains, beans and lentils, kudzu, agar-agar, quality catsup, organic sugar and Sucanat, quinoa, barley malt, carob, date sugar, nutritional yeast, brown basmati rice, wild rice, pepitas, arame, soy milk, coconut oil and coconut milk.

In Latina groceries you can find fresh jalapeño chiles as well as various dried peppers; ancho, pasilla, mulatto and guajillo, dried corn, fresh cilantro, fresh epazote, calabaza squash, plantains, fresh coconuts, good quality inexpensive long-grain rice (in 10-pound bags), queso blanco (white cheese), corn tortillas or the masa harina to make them, ready-made corn or wheat tortillas, annatto (achiote), tamarind, jicama, and pigeon peas, as well as excellent mangoes, papayas and watermelons. Not to mention yucca, yautia, batata and many other tropical root vegetables.

A Greek or Middle Eastern market should have bulgar in three sizes and calamata olives; Greek stores will have gigande beans, feta, phyllo pastry leaves, mastica to flavor kouribiedes, green lentils, fides (very fine noodles), Hymettus honey, and salonika peppers. Arabic stores have pita bread, Labanee (thickened yogurt), Shoosh (pomegranate concentrate), orzo, and meloukhiya.

Italian groceries carry wrinkled olives, large green olives, water buffalo mozzarella, quality olive oil, good canned tomatoes, quality pasta (look for DeCecco or Rusticella), fresh cavatelli and other pastas, capers, Arborio rice, porcini (dried boletus mushrooms), pignoli nuts, sun-dried tomatoes, arugula and broccoli raab in season, balsamic vinegar, quality Parmesan cheese, and semolina flour.

Asian markets should have chili-paste-with-garlic in small jars, rice noodles, rice wine vinegar, toasted sesame oil, dried shiitake mushrooms, tree ears (another dried mushroom), fermented black beans, baby eggplants, soy paste (look for Kim Lan brand in Chinese markets), cilantro, mung bean sprouts, rice papers, bean curd skins, mirin (in Japanese stores), Chinese rice wine (in Chinese stores), and in Thai stores: Maesri brand canned Thai red curry paste, lemongrass, Thai basil, green papayas and "Telephone" brand instant agar-agar.

In Indian stores there will be chutneys, dahls (lentils and peas) in variety, kolongi (which are the same as czerniska seed), fresh hot peppers, cilantro, basmati rice, whole mustard seed, poha (pounded rice), fresh ginger, besan (chickpea flour), and cardamom. Quality cumin, coriander, and turmeric can be found in Indian stores, and other spices as well.

# glossary

**Achiote (annatto)**—Rusty red dried seed which colors cooking oil bright yellow-orange. It is necessary for making a "sofrito," seasoning for Puerto Rican and other Latina dishes.

**Agar-agar**—A thickener also known as kanten. Available in long strips, flakes, or as a powder ("Telephone" brand in Thai markets). It is a seaweed, used as standard growing medium for biological research and for orchid seedlings. The flake or strip form should be softened in cold water without stirring, and then brought slowly to a simmer. The instant powdered form can be boiled with liquid ingredients. Once it dissolves, cool and chill. The texture of agar-agar is somewhat like gelatin (an animal product). Also see **kudzu**.

**Agave nectar**—A liquid syrup-sweetener which can be used in the same proportion as maple syrup. We prefer it because it has no flavor and is not associated with the genetically modified corn industry as brands such as Karo are. It comes in both light and dark forms.

**Avocado Leaves**—Will season a black bean purée in an Oaxaca, Mexico manner. Buy dried ones in a Mexican market to be sure to get the right variety of leaves. Rinse and toast in a dry skillet. Sauté with onions and garlic. Purée with beans in a food processor. Add bean cooking water to make a thin purée with wonderful flavor.

**Banana leaves**—These leaves are available frozen in Latina and Thai markets. They impart a subtle flavor to tamales when used as wrappers, instead of corn husks.

**Bragg Liquid Aminos**—A non-fermented soy protein used as a flavoring agent. Available in health food stores.

**Chickpea flour (besan)**—Available in Indian markets and some health food stores. Besan makes pancakes, dumplings, and is an excellent thickener. We use it to make vegan crêpes.

**Chilies**—Hot peppers come in many forms. Ancho, mulatto, and pasilla are dried. They are sweet and only a little spicy. We like to soak these chilies in hot water after removing the seeds, then we use them and their liquid as gravy bases. Guajillo and ancho chilies make a lovely sauce. Guajillos are Mexican favorites. Poblanos are fresh, undried ancho chilies. They are often stuffed and fried or baked. When we need some heat, we use jalapeños. Hatch chilies are available fresh in the Southwest or canned from New Mexico. They have their own unique flavor. Hungarian paprika, as opposed to Spanish paprika, is essential for Eastern European dishes such as stroganoff.

**Chocolate**—Chocolate is good for you, argues Rowan Jacobsen in his book *Chocolate Unwrapped* (Invisible Cities Press, 2003). It is the fillers and sugars which are not. Chocolate has very little caffeine in it and is very high in antioxidants, containing twice as much as red wine and seven times as much as green tea. So enjoy it. However, chocolate grown in parts of Africa, especially the Ivory Coast, are products of child slavery and rainforest destruction. Do research where your favorite chocolates come from, and try to buy fair trade and organic certified chocolate if possible. We prefer Scharffen Berger, Valrhona and El Ray.

**Coconut milk and coconut oil**—See Lagusta's introduction to the vegan volume. We use Thai Kitchen premium organic coconut milk and Omega coconut oil.

**Coffee**—Use coffee in moderation, and not at all if using homeopathic remedies. Of course the only coffee appropriate is organic and fair trade certified. We use Equal Exchange in our restaurant, and we sell whole beans of Zapatista brand (303-744-7346)—delicious Mexican coffee, putting human values before profit values.

**Curry spices**—Curry powder is widely available. But try making your own **garam masala** by roasting ⅓ **cup cinnamon, coriander seed**, ¾ **cup cardamom pods**, and ¼ **cup peppercorns** at 200'F 20 minutes. Discard the husks of the cardamom (patience!) and grind all together in a coffee mill. Store in a tightly closed jar. When cooking Indian "style," add **whole cumin seed** to whatever is being sautéed, much **less ground coriander seed**, and **even less ground turmeric** to, say, potatoes and eggplant. This is a delicious and widely adaptable combination.

**Czernishka**—The seeds of *Nigella sativa* ("love-in-a-mist") used by Poles and Russians to top rye breads, and sometimes in sauerkraut. Mistakenly called black caraway, it belongs to another plant family altogether. It is available in Indian markets as *kolongi*.

**Daikon**—Very large white radishes used in Japanese cuisine. They are crisp and sweet.

**Eggs**—Chickens that are allowed to run free and are well taken care of produce the most delicious eggs. Some good farmers provide them with social security so that they may live out their days after they stop laying. Factory farmed eggs are products of cruelty.

**Epazote** (*Chenopodium ambrosioides*)—is a weed in our garden. Fresh leaves are a very desirable addition when cooking beans. They impart a clean, pungent flavor. Epazote is usually available in Mexican markets.

**Fats and oils**—We do not use: corn oil, soy oil, peanut oil, or canola oil. We prefer grapeseed oil for general cooking and frying since it has a high smoke point and delicate flavor. We combine it with quality olive oil for our salad dressing. When sautéing over low heat, we use olive oil in dishes where its flavor will be beneficial. We use toasted sesame oil and pumpkin seed oil for their interesting, intense flavors. We carry organic sweet butter, and often use coconut oil instead of butter for desserts and baked goods.

**Flax seed "eggs"**—We found this recipe in the *Candle Café Cookbook*: soak ¼ **cup flax seeds** in ¾ **cup hot tap water** in a blender for 15 minutes. Turn machine on and blend until quite thick and most seeds are crushed. It will look like grey caviar. Store these "eggs" covered in the refrigerator. They will keep 2 to 3 weeks. Use a rounded tablespoon to replace 1 egg in cornbreads or cakes.

**Gomahsio**—Pan-toasted sesame seeds mixed with noniodized salt in a 7:1 ratio, then ground in a spice mill. Sprinkle gomahsio on salads.

# gomahsio

1. Rinse **2 cups unhulled sesame seeds** briefly.

2. Pan-roast ¼ **cup sea salt** for a few minutes over low heat. Add drained sesame seeds.

3. Continue pan-roasting, stirring often for 20 minutes or until seeds have absorbed the salt and have dried out.

4. Pulse briefly in a processor, or use as is: Turn into a large open-holed shaker to use on salads.

*makes about 2 cups*

**Jasmine rice blend**—Jasmine rice mixed with split baby garbanzo beans and daikon radish seeds. Order from Indian Harvest at 1-800-346-7032.

**Jícama** (*Pachyrrhizus erosus*)—is a fat root. Peeled and sliced or julienned, it is a crisp, slightly sweet salad addition. Traditionally in Mexico it is sliced, sprinkled with salt, chili powder, and lime juice.

**Kudzu**—a notorious vine of the South, where it suffocates other vegetation. We use a dried ground Japanese product which thickens much like cornstarch or potato starch. Similarly, it must be softened in cold water. Since when dry it comes in clumps, we estimate amounts. We use it in conjunction with agar-agar to make fruit mousses. It is reputed to have more nutritional value than corn or potato starch.

**Lecithin**—A natural extract of the fatty part of the soybean. It contains vitamins and minerals and emulsifies fats (keeps them dispersed). This recipe makes an excellent mixture for greasing bread, muffin or cake pans. No flouring is necessary. Use a funnel to pour **1 part lecithin** to **3 parts grapeseed oil** into a plastic squeeze bottle. Shake well so that oil and lecithin are thoroughly mixed together. Use sparingly—a little goes a long way.

**Manioc meal** (*Manihot esculenta*)—A grainy flour-like meal made from cassava root. When toasted, it is called *farofa*, and is a staple of Brazilian cuisine. Tapioca is another form of it, and another name for the fresh root is *yucca*. It originated in South America and is used all over the world in its tapioca form.

**Masa harina**—Dried corn treated with slaked lime. Necessary to make corn tortillas and tamales, as well as for dumplings. Masa dough is sometimes available in Mexican markets. The dry masa harina should be available in the flour section of any supermarket in a Latina community.

**Miso**—Miso is fermented soy bean paste. We use red or brown misos to flavor gravies as well as to make soup. White (really yellow) miso is delicately sweet, and flavors scrambled tofu. It makes a good soup also.

**Mushrooms**—There are many wild mushrooms, previously available only to mushrooms hunters that are now under cultivation. Probably our favorite is shiitake (*lentinus edodes*), followed by maitake (hen of the woods, *polyporus frondosus*), chicken of the woods (*polyporus sulfurous*), and oyster (*pleurotus ostreatus*). Portobello and cremini are variations of the button mushroom (*agaricus*) and are less interesting. Dried mushrooms are very valuable for vegetarian cooks. Best are shiitakes and porcini (*ceps* or *boletes*). The latter are very strongly flavored, so use them sparingly.

**Organic**—We do our best to purchase fruits and vegetables which are organic and locally grown. We think it is critical to use organic lemons and limes. Since we use the zest often from these fruits, we don't want to eat or smell the pesticides used on non-organic citrus. Obviously, lettuce must be organic, and potatoes.

**GLOSSARY**

**Organic/biodynamic gardening**—Attempts to heal land from declines brought about by intensive farming. It also uses natural rhythms such as moon phases to guide planting and harvesting. Biodynamic wines are often exceptional. We particularly like Cooper Mountain Pinot Gris and Pinot Noir (from Beaverton, OR, 503-649-0027).

**Pesto**—Finely chopped fresh basil, garlic, and olive oil. Traditionally includes nuts such as pignoli or walnuts. Use a food processor to make in the summer and freeze it in ice cube trays, then turn into a plastic bag to store in the freezer. We add the toasted, chopped nuts and sometimes Parmesan at serving time.

**Phyllo**—Tissue paper-thin pastry sheets originating in Greek and Middle Eastern cuisines. Usually brushed with melted butter, sheets can be brushed with melted coconut oil or grapeseed oil. It must be dealt with quickly or it dries out and becomes too brittle to shape. Keeping it between two sheets of waxed paper and covered with a dampened dishtowel will help retain flexibility.

**Pomegranate**—An Autumn fruit, the seeds of which are a delicious addition to salads and autumn soups. Pomegranate syrup makes delightful drinks.

**Pumpkin seed oil**—Dark green pumpkin seed oil is popular in Austrian cuisine. Pumpkin seed oil is high in Omega 3 fatty acids (which are essential for all major bodily functions, and especially useful for optimal brain function and healthy skin), as well as zinc, phosphorus, vitamin A, and calcium. Because it is unrefined, it should not be cooked. It is available in health food stores.

**Quinoa**—Quinoa (pronounced "keen-wa") is one of the few grains we eat—along with wild rice and a few others—that is native to the Americas. Quinoa cooks very quickly, is high in several nutrients and has a light nutty flavor. It has the highest protein of any grain (16%) and, unlike other grains, is a complete protein. It contains more calcium than milk and is high in lysine, an amino acid that is scarce in the vegetable

340

kingdom. It is also rich in many other vital nutrients, including iron, phosphorus, B-vitamins, and vitamin E. Native to the Andes, it was once so important to the Incas that they called it their "mother grain." Quinoa is coated with a bitter substance called *saponin*, so it is vital to rinse it well in order to remove any trace of bitterness. With water or stock covering it by 1", quinoa will cook in 15 minutes over low heat.

**Seaweeds**—Kombu is kelp, necessary as the base of Japanese dipping sauces (dashi). It is also useful in dried bean soups, thickening them slightly. We get ours from Ironbound Island Seaweed (207-963-7016) and add to cannelini bean soup. Wakame also flavors soups, especially hearty winter ones. Nori is used to wrap sushi. And hiziki and arame make interesting salads. The seaweed we use most often is agar-agar. An excellent book (out of print) is *Cooking with Sea Vegetables*, by Sharon Ann Rhoads, Autumn Press.

**Seitan**—Wheat gluten, available in health food stores. The starch is washed out of wheat so that only the gluten (protein) remains. Stewed in soy sauce with kombu and ginger, it has a texture something like meat, and is therefore useful for vegetarians who sometimes want an approximation of that texture.

**Sunchokes or Jerusalem Artichokes** (*Helianthus tuberosus*)— A Native American perennial sunflower, less showy than garden varieties. It grows invasively and requires a plot of its own. Dig the tubers after the first frost, wash and refrigerate. Cut in thin slices, they are crisp additions to salads, or they may be roasted for a treat.

**Shiso**—A Japanese herb which self-sows readily. It is in the mint family. A red form called *perilla* is used as a decorative annual. The green-leafed varieties have superior flavor as an ingredient in tempura, or shredded, as a tofu or soba topping with tamari and shredded baby ginger.

**Sourdough**—Sourdough starter produces pancakes, biscuits, and breads of wonderful lightness and "clean" flavor. The starter is made up of wild strains of yeast which must be fed fresh water and flour every two to three weeks, so once you have starter, you must use it with some regularity. Always turn it all out, add as much flour and water (potato cooking water, if available) as seems necessary to make a thin batter, and stir well. The batter will be lumpy. Leave overnight. Be sure to remember to return some starter to the refrigerator before adding ingredients such as milk or eggs to the batter. We have had some very close calls. In each instance some of our original starter had been given to a friend who was able to replenish our supply.

You can obtain starter in one of three ways. Getting some from a friend is best, since it will be oldest and therefore will have the best developed flavor. Ours is over 35 years old. Some gourmet or health food stores sell sourdough starter as a dry powder. Or you can try to grow your own: wash, peel, and shred **2 large potatoes**. Add ⅓ **cup sugar** and **flour** and **water** to make a thin mixture. Or, cook the potatoes, mash, and add honey *or* agave syrup, flour and water. Either way, leave this mixture uncovered in a warm place in the kitchen for 5 to 7 days, stirring every day. When it smells fermented and like alcohol, it is ready to use. If it smells rotten, however, discard it and start over. Rye flour will make rye starter.

Once you have the starter, you will note that it has a changeable personality. Weather, humidity, and time of year affect its liveliness. Many times we thought we were preparing a batter which was either too thick or too thin only to have the yeasts grow in the opposite fashion from our expectations. Good luck!

**Sweeteners**—We have no artificial sweeteners in our restaurant. We use organic sugar, organic honey, and agave nectar. We have stevia packets and use maple syrup, molasses and occasionally barley malt syrup (see the recipe for **pumpernickel bread**) in our baking. Date sugar and Sucanat (both available in health food stores) are delicate sweeteners.

**Tamari**—We use this traditional wheat-free version of soy sauce to protect any customers who have a severe wheat allergy.

**Tamarind**—A fruit with pulpy seeds. Used as a souring agent in the way lemon is used. It has its own dark wonderful flavor.

**Tea**—Our favorite teas are blended by a company called Serendipitea (1-888-832-5433). They are all loose and therefore must be pot brewed. Our favorite herbal teas are made by an Austrian company, Sonnentor (www.sonnentor.com). They sell a number of "moon" teas: rising, full, new, etc. All are organic, delicious blends.

**Thickeners**—We do love agar-agar and kudzu. However, we also use cornstarch out of habit, and potato starch in Eastern European recipes.

**Tomatillos**—Originally used by the Aztecs, called *miltomatl*. It is *Physalis ixocarpa*, relatives are Chinese Lanterns, cape gooseberries, and ground cherries. It self-sows readily in our garden, and is available in Mexican markets. Tomatillos sliced thin are tart additions to salads, and grilled, make a fine salsa.

**Vinaigrette**—The quality of your salad dressing depends on the quality of your oils and vinegar. Note that the oil-vinegar relationship is 4½ to 1.

# vinaigrette

Combine in a jar: ⅓ **cup good quality wine vinegar** (you may blend part balsamic vinegar, if you like) *or* ¼ **cup** fresh-squeezed **lemon juice**, ½ **teaspoon salt**, and 1½ **cups oil**. We mix **grapeseed oil** with the best **extra virgin olive oil**. Add fresh ground **pepper**, and, if you like, 1 **teaspoon prepared mustard**. Shake well.

*almost 2 cups*

**Wasabi**—Often thought of as Japanese horseradish, it comes from another plant family altogether. It grows well only at the edges of cold running streams. It is more fragrant and less sharp than Western horseradish. Buy it powdered, mix with a little tepid water and let stand 10 minutes before serving.

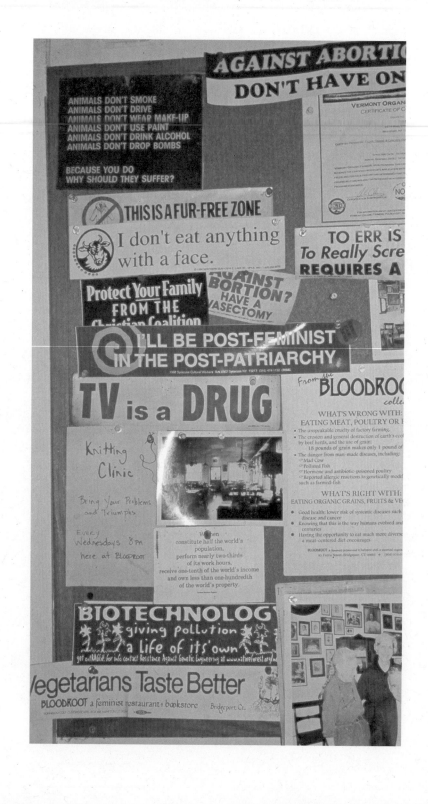

# INDEX

Green color indicates recipe will be found in *The Best of Bloodroot, Volume Two, Vegan Recipes.*

Green color indicates recipe will be found in *The Best of Bloodroot, Volume Two, Vegan Recipes.*

INDEX

Green color indicates recipe will be found in *The Best of Bloodroot, Volume Two, Vegan Recipes.*

Green color indicates recipe will be found in *The Best of Bloodroot, Volume Two, Vegan Recipes.*

Green color indicates recipe will be found in *The Best of Bloodroot, Volume Two, Vegan Recipes.*

INDEX

Green color indicates recipe will be found in *The Best of Bloodroot, Volume Two, Vegan Recipes.*

Green color indicates recipe will be found in *The Best of Bloodroot, Volume Two, Vegan Recipes.*

Green color indicates recipe will be found in *The Best of Bloodroot, Volume.Two, Vegan Recipes.*

Green color indicates recipe will be found in *The Best of Bloodroot, Volume Two, Vegan Recipes.*

INDEX

Green color indicates recipe will be found in *The Best of Bloodroot, Volume Two, Vegan Recipes.*

Green color indicates recipe will be found in *The Best of Bloodroot, Volume Two, Vegan Recipes.*

**Index created by Kelly Harran and Carolanne Curry.**

Green color indicates recipe will be found in *The Best of Bloodroot, Volume Two, Vegan Recipes.*

## ABOUT THE TYPE

This book was composed using
ITC Cheltenham, Metro, and Mrs. Eaves.

Typography by Farrington & Favia, Inc.
New York, New York